J. de Alencar

Iracéma

The Honey-Lips

J. de Alencar

Iracéma
The Honey-Lips

ISBN/EAN: 9783337151119

Printed in Europe, USA, Canada, Australia, Japan

Cover: Foto ©ninafisch / pixelio.de

More available books at **www.hansebooks.com**

IRAÇÉMA

THE HONEY-LIPS

A LEGEND OF BRAZIL

BY

J. DE ALENCAR

TRANSLATED, WITH THE AUTHOR'S PERMISSION,

BY

ISABEL BURTON

LONDON
BICKERS & SON, 1 LEICESTER SQUARE
1886

Ballantyne Press
BALLANTYNE, HANSON AND CO.
EDINBURGH AND LONDON

PREFACE.

I CANNOT allow my readers to remain ignorant of the name of Senhor J. de Alencar, the author of this and several other works; for he deserves to be as well known in England as in Brazil, and it must be the result of the usual modesty of a really clever man that he is not so.

He is their first prose and romance writer. His style, written in the best Portuguese of the present day—one to be learnt and copied—is in thorough good taste and feeling. It contains poetic and delicate touches, and beauty in similes, yet it is real and true to life.

I cannot thank him sufficiently for having allowed so incompetent a translator as myself to be the first to introduce him to the British public. I have endeavoured to be as literal as possible, but I cannot pretend to do him justice, for our harsh Northern tongue only tells coarsely a tale full of grace and music in the Portuguese language; but I have done my best, and if he permits me to translate all his works, I hope to do better as I go on, especially if he will again—as he has already done—give me instructions in Tupy, the language of the aborigines.

ISABEL BURTON.

Santos São Paulo, Brazil.

HISTORICAL ARGUMENT.

This legend of the aborigines is laid in Ceará, a northern province of Brazil, at that time unknown and unconquered.

In 1603, Pero Coelho, a gentleman of Parahyba, another northerly province, then already belonging to the Portuguese, arrived at the mouth of the river Jaguaribe in Ceará, with a command of 80 colonists and 800 Indians. He there founded the first settlement in Ceará, and called it Nova Lisboa.

This Pero Coelho was abandoned by his comrades when a certain João Soromenho was sent to him with reinforcements, and was authorised to pay the expenses of the expedition by making captives or slaves. He did not respect even the Indians of the Jaguaribe river, who were friendly to the Portuguese.

This proved the downfall of the growing settlement. The natives resented such tyranny. Pero Coelho, with his wife and young children, was compelled to fly by land to his own province.

In the first expedition was Martim Soares Moreno, a youth from Rio Grande do Norte, another northerly province belonging to the Portuguese. He entered into bonds of friendship with Jacaúna and his brother Poty, who were chiefs of the Indians of the seaboard. In 1608, by order of Dom Diogo Menezes, he returned to establish a colony, and in 1611 he founded the fortified place of Nossa Senhora do Amparo, or "Our Lady of Protection."

Jacaúna, who lived on the borders of Acáracú—"River of the Heron's nest"—settled near it with his tribe, to protect it from the Indians of the interior, and from the French, who then infested the coast.

Poty eventually became a Christian, and was baptized Antonio Phelipe Camarão. He highly distinguished himself when the Dutch invaded the coast, and his services were richly rewarded by the Portuguese Government.

Martim Soares Moreno became a Field-Marshal, and was one of those brave Portuguese leaders who delivered Brazil from the Hollander invasion. Ceará should honour his memory as that of a good and valiant man, and—the first settlement by Coelho at the mouth of the Jaguaribe having proved a failure—hold him to be her true founder.

My readers will better understand this tale by my explaining that the Pytiguáras were an aboriginal tribe who occupied the shores between Parnahyba and the Jaguaribe, or Rio Grande.

Their chiefs were Jacaúna and Poty (afterwards Camarão, "the Prawn"), two brothers, who were firm allies to the Portuguese. They were at war with the Tabajáras, another tribe occupying the mountains of

Ibyapaba, and the interior as far as the province of Piauhy.

The Chiefs of these inland people were also two. The first was Irapúam, which, translated into Portuguese, means Mel Redondo, or "Round Honey," a wild and vicious bee of that name. This famous bloodthirsty chief ruled in Ceará, but Gráo Deabo—Big Devil—was Lord of the Tabajáras in Piauhy. Both were bitter enemies of the Portuguese, and allied themselves with the French of Maranhão—another northerly province—who had penetrated into and taken possession of the lands as far as the mountain range of Ibyapaba.

IRAÇÉMA.

CHAPTER I.

WILD green seas of my Native Land, where sings the Jandáia-bird [1] in the fronds of the Carnaúba-palm ! [2]

Green seas which sparkle like liquid emerald in the rays of the orient sun, as ye stretch along the snowy beaches shaded by the cocoa-tree !

Be still, ye green seas ! and gently smooth the impetuous wave, that yon venturesome barque may softly glide over thy waters.

Where goes that hardy Jangada-raft,[3] which rapidly flies from the Ceará coast, with her broad sail spread to the fresh breeze of land ?

Where goes it, like the white halcyon seeking his native rock in the ocean solitudes ?

Three beings breathe upon that fragile plank, which scuds so swiftly out—far into the open sea.

A warrior youth, whose pale skin betokens that the blood of the Indians does not colour his veins ; a

---

[1] *Jandáia* is a small yellow, red, and green talking parroquet.
[2] *Carnaúba*, a well-known Brazilian palm of large size, with many thorny branches all the way up the trunk, instead of being plain and smooth. Each branch-tip is like a fan-palm. When young, it has a large fruit, full of oil, which is given to pigs and cattle. When grown up, its fan-leaves, dried, thatch the houses, and make hats and mats ; its thorny branches are used for stakes ; it also has a delicious small black fruit, and from other parts they extract wax for making the Carnaúba candles.
[3] *Jangada*, a raft.

child, and a mastiff, who both first saw the light in the cradle of the forest, and who sport like brothers, the sons of the same savage soil.

The intermittent breathings from the shore waft an echo which, rising high above the ripple of the waves, sounds forth—

"Iraçéma!" * * *

The young warrior, leaning against the mast, raises his eyes, which are fixed upon the fleeting outline of the shadowy shore. From time to time his sight becomes dim, and a tear falls upon the Giráo-bench,[1] where frolic the two innocents, the companions of his misfortune.

At such moments his soul flies to his lips in a bitter smile.

What left he in that land of exile?

A tale which they told me on the beautiful plains that saw my birth, during the hush of night, whilst the moon, sailing through the heavens, silvered the prairies; whilst the breezes murmured amid the palm groves.

The wind freshens.

The surf rolls in higher billows. The barque leaps upon the waves—disappears on the horizon. Wide yawns the waste of waters. The storm broods, condor-like, with dusky wings over the abyss.

God keep thee safe, stout barque, amidst the boiling billows! God steer thee to some friendly bight! May softer breezes waft thee, and for thee may the calm jasper seas be like plains of milk!

But whilst thou sailest thus at the mercy of the winds, graceful barque, waft back to that white beach some of the yearning[2] that accompanies thee, but which may not leave the land to which it returns.

---

[1] *Giráo*, a sort of rude bench for sitting upon in the Jangada raft.
[2] Yearning, in the original *saudade*—an untranslatable Portuguese word for which we have no equivalent; it means a soft sad regret for some person, place, or happy time missed and past—in fac', the Latin *desiderium*.

CHAPTER II.

Far, very far from that Serra which purples the horizon, was born Iraçéma.

Iraçéma, the virgin with the honey lips,[1] whose hair, hanging below her palm-like[2] waist, was jetty as the Graúna[3] bird's wing.

The comb of the Játy-bee[4] was less sweet than her smile, and her breath excelled the perfume exhaled by the vanilla[5] of the woods.

Fleeter than the wild roe, the dark virgin wandered freely through the plains and forests of Ipú,[6] where her warlike tribe, a part of the great Tabajára[7] nation, lay wigwamed. Her subtle, naked foot scarcely pressed to earth the thin green garment with which the early rains clothe the ground.

One day, when the sun was in mid-day height, she was reposing in a forest-clearing. The shade of the Oitycíca,[8] more refreshing than the dew of night, bathed her form. The arms of the wild acacia dropped their blossoms upon her wet hair. The birds hidden in the foliage sang for her their sweetest songs.

Iraçéma left the bath. Pearl drops of water stood upon her, like the sweet Mangába,[9] which blushes in

---

[1] *Iraçéma* literally means "Lips of Honey."
[2] The Indians, speaking of a tall straight graceful figure, generally use the palm-tree as a simile.
[3] *Graúna* is a bird known by its shining black plumage and sweet song.
[4] *Játy* is a little bee which makes delicious honey.
[5] The vanilla tree, *Baunilha.*
[6] *Ipú,* a district in Ceará, in which there were spots of wonderfully fertile land.
[7] *Tabajára* literally means "Lord of the Villages."
[8] *Oitycíca,* a leafy tree whose shade exhales a delicious freshness.
[9] *Mangába,* the fruit of the Mangábeira, the milk of which tree resembles indiarubber.

the refreshing dawn-dew. Whilst reposing she refits her arrows with the plumes of the Gará,[1] whilst she joins in the joyous song of the forest Sabiá,[2] perched in the nearest bough.

A beautiful Ará,[3] her companion and friend, plays near her. Now the bird climbs the branches and calls the virgin by her name; then he slips down and shakes the little satchel[4] of coloured straw in which the wild maid carries her perfumes, her white threads of the Crautá,[5] her needles of Jussára-thorn,[6] with which she works the grass-cloth, and her dyes that serve to tinge the cotton.

A suspicious noise breaks the soft harmony of the siesta. Iraçéma raises the eyes which no sun can dazzle, and her sight is troubled.

Standing before her, absorbed in gazing upon her, is a strange warrior, if indeed it *is* a warrior, and not some evil spirit of the forest.[7] His face is white as the sands that border the sea, his eyes are sadly blue as the deep. He bears unknown weapons, and is clad in unknown cloths.

Rapid as her eye-glance was the action of Iraçéma. An arrow shot from the bow, and red drops ran down the face of the unknown.

---

[1] *Gará* or *Guará*, the ibis of Brazil, a bird of the marshes, with beautiful red colour.

[2] *Sabiá*, a well-known bird about the size of our thrush, which sings beautifully, and can be taught like a bullfinch. It is the nightingale, the bulbul of South America.

[3] *Ará*, parroquet.

[4] *Urú.* I have called it satchel, but it is a little coffer or basket, in which the savages keep their treasures, and which accompanies them as does a lady's dressing-case in Europe.

[5] *Crautá*, a bromelia or wild pine-apple, from which are drawn fibres finer than thread.

[6] *Jussára*, a palm with large thorns, which are used here even in these days to divide the threads in making lace.

[7] *Máo espirito da floresta.* The natives called those evil spirits *Caa-pora*, "an invisible misfortune." Those who lived in the forest were most feared.

At the first impulse his nimble hand sought his sword-cross; but presently he smiled.

The young warrior had been brought up in the religion of his mother, wherein Woman is a symbol of tenderness and love. He suffered more in his soul than from his wound.

What expression was in his eye and whole face—who knows? But it made the virgin cast away her bow and Uiraçába,[1] and run to the warrior, pained at the pain she had caused. The hand so swift to strike more rapidly and gently staunched the dripping stream.

Then Iraçéma brake the murderous arrow. She offered the shaft to the unknown, and she kept the barbed point.

The warrior spoke:—

"Dost thou break with me the arrow of peace?"[2]

"Who taught the white warrior the tongue of Iraçéma's brethren? How came he to these forests, which never saw other warrior like to him?"

"Daughter of the forests, I come from afar: I come from the land which thy brothers once possessed, and wherein mine now dwell."

"Welcome be the stranger to the Prairie of the Tabajáras, Lords of the Villages, and to the wigwam of Araken, father of Iraçéma."

CHAPTER III.

The stranger followed the virgin through the glades. When the last sun-rays fell upon the crest of the

---

[1] *Uiraçába* (aljava), quiver for arrows.

[2] *Guebrar a frecha.* To break an arrow with an Indian was a bond of alliance which could not be broken. It was owing to this circumstance, and to Martim Soares Moreno throwing away his European costume, and dressing and painting like the Red Men, entering also into their customs and language, that he acquired such an influence over them.

mountains, and the turtle-dove cooed forth her first lament from the forest depths, they sighted upon the plain beneath them the great Taba;[1] farther on, hanging as it were from a rock, under the shade of the lofty Joaseiro,[2] the wigwam of the Pagé.[3]

The ancient man was seated at the doorway upon a mat of Carnaúba, smoking and meditating on the sacred rites of Tupan.[4] The gentle breath of the breeze fluttered his hair — long, thin, and white as flocks of wool. So statue-like was he, that life only appeared in his hollow, sunken eyes and deep wrinkles.

The Pagé descried, nevertheless, from afar the two forms, advancing, he thought, towards a solitary tree, whose dense foliage was casting a long shadow adown the valley before him.

When the travellers entered the deep gloom of the wood, his eye, made, like the tiger's, for darkness, recognised Iraçéma, and saw that she was followed by a young warrior of a strange race and a far-off land.

The Tabajára[5] tribes beyond Ibyapába were full of a new race of warriors, pale as the flowers of the storm,[6] and coming from the remotest shores to the banks of the Mearim.[7] The old man thought that it was one of these warriors who trod his native ground.

Calmly he awaited.

---

[1] *Taba*, a village settlement.
[2] *Joaseiro*, a tree which produces the *joaz* fruit, the jujube.
[3] *Pagé*, priest, Druid, magician, soothsayer, or fetish-man.
[4] *Tupan*, the Great Spirit—Thunder, and, since their conversion, the Consecrated Host of the Tupy Indians.
[5] *Ibyapaba*, the Serra or mountain range which bounds the province of Ceará, and separates it from Piauhy.
[6] In the original, *alvos como flores de borrasca*. They speak of white clouds announcing a storm, and this is, literally, "white as the flowers of the storm."
[7] *Mearim*, a river which rises in Maranhão, and empties itself into the ocean.

The virgin advancing, pointed to the stranger and said :—

"He came, father."

"He came well. Tupan sent this guest to the wigwam of Araken."

And thus saying the Pagé passed the calumet[1] to the stranger, and they both entered the wigwam.

The youth took the principal hammock, which was suspended in the centre of the habitation. Iraçéma lighted the fire of hospitality, and brought out food to satisfy hunger and thirst. She produced the spoils of the chase, farinha-water, wild-fruits, honeycombs, wine of the Cajú[2] and the pine-apple.

The virgin then went to the nearest spring of fresh water, and returned with the full Igaçába,[3] to wash the stranger's hands and face. When the warrior had eaten, the venerable Pagé extinguished the Caximbo and spoke for the first time.

"Thou camest?"[4]

"I came," replied the unknown.

"Thou camest well. The stranger is master in the wigwam of Araken. The Tabájaras have a thousand warriors to defend him, and women without number to serve him. Let him speak, and all will obey him."

"Pagé! I thank thee for thy hospitality. As soon as the sun shall be born, I leave thy wigwam and thy

[1] Calumet, original *caximbo*, the pipe of hospitality.

[2] *Cajú*, the cashew of India—a tree with a fruit like an apple: it is singular because, unlike other fruit, its nut is outside at the top, as if a schoolboy had stuck it in for fun. This must not be confounded with the *Cajá*, which is another Brazilian fruit like a yellow plum.

[3] *Igaçába*, a large earthen pot or jar for wine or any other liquor.

[4] *Vieste* (?) *Vim*. The salutation of hospitality was—

Tupy.	*Brazilian.*	*English.*
Ere wubê.	Tu vieste.	Thou camest.
Pa-aiotu.	Vim, sim.	I came, yes.
Auge-be.	Bemdito.	Be blessed.

prairies, where I strayed, but I would not leave them without telling thee who the warrior is whom thou hast made thy friend."

"It is Tupan whom the Pagé serves. He sent him a guest, and he will take him away again. Araken has as yet done nothing for him. He does not ask whence he comes nor whither he goes. If he would sleep, may the happy dreams descend upon him; if he would speak, Araken listens."

The stranger said:—

"I am of the white warriors who raised a Taba on the banks of the Jaguaribe,[1] near the sea, where dwell the Pytiguáras,[2] who hate thy blood. My name is Martim,[3] which in thy tongue means Son of a Warrior. My race is that of the Great People who first saw the lands of thy country.[4] Even now my brethren, routed and beaten back, return by sea to the margins of the Parahyba,[5] whence they came, and my chief,[6] abandoned by all, crosses the vast regions of the Apody.[7] Of so many I alone remain, because I was amongst the Pytiguáras of the Acaraú,[8] in the wigwam of the valiant Poty, brother of Jacaúna, who planted with me the Friendship-tree. Three suns have set since we went forth on the hunting path. I lost sight of

---

[1] *Jaguaribe*, the largest river of the province of Ceará: from *jaguar*, small tiger, and *ibe*, plenty.

[2] *Pytiguáras*, the great Indian nation who inhabited the littoral of the province from Parahyba to Rio Grande do Norte, whose chiefs were Poty and Jacaúna, brothers, and firm friends of Martim Soares Moreno, and of all the Portuguese. They were at war with the Tabajáras and the French.

[3] Descendant of Mars.

[4] The Portuguese.

[5] *Parahyba*, a province south-east of Ceará on the Atlantic.

[6] *Pero Coelho* and his party.

[7] The *Sertão desconhecido* or unknown regions of Rio Grande do Norte, the most north-easterly province of Brazil on the Atlantic.

[8] *Acaraú*, or "Stream of the Herons," also called *Acáracú*, "Stream of the Herons' Nests," a river of Ceará.

my friends, and thus I strayed to the prairies of the Tabajáras."

"It was some bad spirit of the forest that blinded the pale-face warrior in the darkness of the woods," replied the old man.

The Cauâm [1] chirped at the other end of the valley. Night had set in.

CHAPTER IV.

THE Pagé shook the Maraca-rattle [2] and left the cabin, but the stranger remained not alone.

Iraçéma returned with the maidens summoned to serve the guest of Araken and the warriors who came to obey him.

"May happiness rock the White Warrior's hammock during the night, and may the sun bring light to his eyes and joy to his soul."

Thus saying, Iraçéma's lip trembled, and the tear stood in her eye.

"Thou leavest me then?" asked Martim.

"The most beautiful virgins [3] of the great Taba remain with the warrior."

"The daughter of Araken was mistaken in bringing them here for the guest of the Pagé."

"Iraçéma may not wait upon the stranger. It is she who guards the secret of the Juréma [4] and the

---

[1] *Cauâm*, a bird of evil omen, which feeds on serpents, and chirps its own name.

[2] *Maracá*, an instrument used in the religious and war-like ceremonies of the Indians; a kind of loud rattle.

[3] *As mais bellas mulheres*. Any Indian's idea of complete hospitality.

[4] *Juréma*, a kind of acacia with thick foliage. It has a bitter fruit and acrid smell, and, mixed with the pulp of its own leaves and other ingredients, it made a kind of hasheesh, which is said to have produced vivid and happy dreams. The making of this dram was kept secret by the Pagés.

mystery of dreams. Her hand prepares for the Pagé the drink of Tupan."

The Christian warrior crossed the wigwam and disappeared in the darkness.

The great village lay in the bottom of the valley, which was illuminated by bonfires. Loud rattled the Maracá. The savages were dancing and beating time to their slow surging of the savage song. The inspired Pagé headed the sacred rejoicing, and taught to the believers the secrets of Tupan. The principal chief of the Tabajára nation, Irapúam,[1] had descended from the highest point of the Ibyapaba Serra, to lead the inland tribes against the Pytiguára foe. The warriors of the valley celebrate the arrival of the chief and the coming fight.

The Christian youth saw from afar the glare of the feast-fire, and walked on, gazing at the deep-blue, cloudless sky. The "Dead Star"[2] glittered upon the dome of the forest, and guided his firm step towards the fresh banks of the Acaraú.

When he crossed the valley, as if about to enter the forest, the figure of Iraçéma arose before him. The virgin had followed the stranger like the soft and subtle breeze which passes through the tangled wood without stirring a leaf.

"Wherefore," she murmured, "has the stranger left the Wigwam of Hospitality without taking with him the Gift of Return?[3] Who harmed the pale-faced warrior in the land of the Tabajáras?"

---

[1] *Irapúam* was the celebrated Tabajára chief in Ceará. The word means *Mel-Redondo* in Portuguese, in English Round-Honey. He was so called after a wild and vicious bee of that name, whose honeycomb is round. Irapúam was a bloodthirsty chief, and his tribe were bitter enemies of the Pytigúaras, and their allies the Portuguese. They supported the French of Maranhão.

[2] *Estrella morta*, dead star. They so called the Polar star on account of its immobility, and it was their guide by night.

[3] *O presente da volta*, a hospitable Indian custom.

The Christian felt the justice of her complaint and his own ingratitude.

"Daughter of Araken! No one hurt thy guest. It was a longing to see his friends which made him leave the prairies of the Tabajáras. He did not take the Return Gift, but he carries in his heart the memory of Iraçéma."

"If the memory of Iraçéma dwelt in the heart of the stranger, it would not suffer him to depart. The wind blows not away the sand of the desert when the sand has drank deep of the water of rain."

And the virgin sighed.

"The pale-faced warrior should wait till Cauby returns from hunting. The brother of Iraçéma has quick ears. He can hear the Boicininga [1] amidst all the noises of the forest. He has the eyes of the Oitibó,[2] which sees best in the dark. Cauby will guide him to the banks of the river of the herons."

"How long will it be before the brother of Iraçéma returns to the wigwam of Araken?"

"The rising sun will bring the warrior Cauby to the plains of the Ipú."

"Thy guest will wait, daughter of Araken; but if the returning sun bring not the brother of Iraçéma, it will take the pale-faced warrior to the Taba of the Pytiguáras."

And Martim returned to the cabin of the Pagé. The white hammock, perfumed by Iraçéma with Beijoim,[3] gave the guest a calm and sweet sleep. The Christian was lullabied to sleep by the murmurs of the forest and the low tender song of the Indian maid.

---

[1] *Boicininga*, rattlesnake.
[2] *Oitibó*, a night-bird of the owl family.
[3] *Benzoin*, in the original *Beijoim* or *Beijuim*, an odoriferous drug.

CHAPTER V.

The Prairie-cock raises his scarlet crest from out his home. His clear trill announces the approach of day.

Darkness still covers the earth, but already the savage people roll up the hammocks in the great Taba, and walk towards the bath. The old Pagé, who had watched all night, talking to the stars, and conjuring the bad spirits of the darkness,[1] entered furtively into the wigwam.

Lo! thundered forth the Boré,[2] filling the valley with its booming sound.

The active warriors seize their weapons and rush to the prairies; when all were collected in the large and circular Ocára,[3] the chief Irapúam sounded the war-cry.

"Tupan gave to the great Tabajára nation all these grounds. We guard the Serras which supply with water the rivers and the fresh Ipús,[4] where grows the maníva,[5] and the cotton. We have abandoned to the barbarous Potyuára,[6] Eaters of Prawns, the naked sands of the sea, with the table-lands wanting wood and water. Now these fishers of the beach, always conquered, give sea-way to the white race, the Warriors

---

[1] *Os máos espiritos da treva:* the savages call these spirits *Curupira*, wicked imps.

[2] *Boré* or *Muré* means a pipe of bamboo, which gives out a hollow, roaring sound.

[3] *Ocára*, a circular space in the centre of a village, upon which all the wigwams open.

[4] *Ipú*, a small fertile oasis in the prairies.

[5] *Maníva* is the root of mandioca, which is like our parsnip, but larger. The Indians dry and grind it, make bread of it, or eat it as farinha (flour).

[6] *Potyuára* means a "*Comedor de Camarão*," or "Eater of the Prawn." This was a spiteful soubriquet given to the Pytiguáras by their enemies, because they lived on the shores and chiefly ate fish.

of Fire,[1] the enemies of Tupan. Already the Emboabas[2] have stood upon the Jaguaribe river. Soon they will be in the prairies of the Tabajáras, and with them the Potyuáras. Shall we—Lords of the Villages —do like the dove, who hides in her nest while the serpent curls himself along the branches?"

The excited chief brandishes his tomahawk,[3] and hurls it into the middle of the circle. Bending down his forehead, he hid his eyes, ruddy with rage. " Irapúam has spoken," at length he said.

The youngest of the warriors advances.

" The Sparrow-hawk hovers in the air. When the Nhambú[4] rises, he falls from the clouds and tears out his victim's heart. The young Tabajára warrior, son of the Serra, is like the sparrow-hawk."

The Poçema[5] of war thunders and re-echoes. The young warrior lifted up the tomahawk, and in his turn brandished it. Whirled rapidly and menacingly in the air, the chief's weapon passed from hand to hand.

The venerable Andíra, brother of the Pagé, let it fall, and stamped upon the ground with his foot, still firm and active.

The Tabajáras are struck by this unusual action. A vote of peace from such a tried and impetuous warrior! The old hero, who grew to bloodshed as he grew in years—the ferocious Andíra—is it he who lets fall the tomahawk, herald of the coming struggle?

Uncertain and silent, all gave ear.

" Andíra, the old Andíra, has drank more blood in

---

[1] *Guerreiros de fogo*, "warriors of fire," the Portuguese.

[2] *Emboabos*, a name given to the Portuguese, and afterwards to all strangers, on account of their trousers. Its literal meaning is a fowl with feathers down its legs, and alludes to the European practice of wearing nether garments.

[3] *Tacapé*, tomahawk.

[4] *Nhambú*, the Brazilian partridge.

[5] *Poçema*, the great noise made by the savages on solemn occasions—war or triumph. It consisted of clapping their hands and beating palms, accompanied by war-cries or shouts.

war than all these warriors who now gladden the light of his eyes have drank Cauim [1] at the feasts of Tupan. He has seen more combats in his life than moons which have stripped his brow. How many Potyuára skulls has his implacable hand scalped before Time plucked off his first hair! And old Andíra never feared that the enemy would tread his native ground; he rejoiced at their coming, and, as the breath of winter revives the dried tree, he felt youth return to his decrepid body when he scented the war from afar. The Tabajáras are prudent. They will lay aside the Tomahawk to play the Memby [2] at the feast. Let Irapúam celebrate the coming of the Emboábas, and give them all time to swarm upon our plains. Then Andíra promises him the banquet of victory."

Irapúam could no longer restrain his fury.

"The Old Bat [3] can remain hidden amongst the wine-jars, because he fears the light of day, because he drinks the blood only of the sleeping victim. Irapúam carries the war at the point of his tomahawk. The terror which he inspires flies forward with the hoarse boom of the Boré. The Potyuára already trembles as he hears it roaring in the Serra, roaring louder than the rebounding of the sea."

CHAPTER VI.

MARTIM strolls pace by pace amongst the tall Joazeiros which encircle the wigwam of the Pagé.

[1] *Cauim*, wine of the Cajú.
[2] *Memby*, horn or trumpet.
[3] *Andíra* means "Velho Morcego," or "Old Bat;" hence the taunt of Irapúam.

It was the hour in which the sweet Aracaty[1] comes up from the sea and spreads over the arid plains its delicious freshness. The plant breathes, and a gentle shiver upraises the green tresses of the forest.

The Christian looks upon the setting sun. The shadow gliding down the mountains and covering the valley enters into his soul. He thinks of his native place and the beloved ones he has left behind. He wonders if he shall some day see them again. Nature all round bewails the death of day. Murmurs the tremulous, tearful wave; moans the breeze in the foliage; even silence is sorrowful.

Iraçéma stood before the young warrior.

"Is it the presence of Iraçéma that disturbs the peace of the stranger's brow?"

Martim looked softly in the virgin's face.

"No, daughter of Araken! thy presence gladdens me like the morning light. It was the memory of my native land that brought a saudade to my anxious soul."

"A bride awaits him there?"

The stranger averted his eyes. Iraçéma's head sank upon her shoulder, like the tender palm of the Carnaúba when the rain overhangs the plains.

"She is not sweeter than Iraçéma, the maiden of the honied lips, nor more beautiful!" murmured the guest.

"The forest flower is beautiful when it has a branch to shelter it, a trunk round which to entwine itself. Iraçéma does not live in the soul of a warrior. She never felt the freshness of his smile."

Silent were both; their eyes fell to the ground. They heard nought save the beating of their hearts.

[1] *Aracaty*, the savages of the interior so call the sea-breezes, which blow regularly towards the evening over the valley of the Jaguaribe, and refresh the interior after the scorching heat of summer days. Aracaty is the quarter whence comes the monsoon, and in some Brazilian places the evening sea-breeze still retains that name.

The virgin was the first to speak.

"Gladness shall soon return to the heart of the pale-faced warrior, because Iraçéma wishes that before nightfall he may see the bride who expects him."

Martim smiled at the young girl's artless wish.

"Come!" said the virgin.

They crossed the forest and descended into the valley. The wood was thick on the hill-skirts; a dense dome of dark-green foliage protected the sylvan shrine dedicated to the mysteries of barbarous rites.

This was the sacred wood of the Juréma. Around stood the rugged trunks of the Tupan tree; from the boughs, hidden by thick greenery, hung the sacrificial vases; ashes of the extinct fire, which had been used for the feast of the last new moon, still strewed the ground.

Before entering this place of mystery, the virgin, who was leading the warrior by the hand, hesitated, and applied her subtle ear to the sighings of the breeze. Each slight noise of the forest had a meaning for the wild daughter of the desert. However, there was nothing suspicious in the deep respiration of the forest.

Iraçéma signed to the stranger to wait and be silent, whilst she disappeared in the thickest of the wood. The sun still hung over the mountain ridge, and night began to shroud the solitary spot.

When the virgin returned, she brought in a leaf some drops of an unknown green liquor, poured from an Igaçába, which she had taken out of the ground. She presented the rude bowl to the warrior.

"Drink!"

Martim felt a sleep like death take possession of his eyes; but soon his soul seemed full of light, and strength exhilarated his heart. He lived over again days better and happier than any that he had ever known. He enjoyed the reality of his brightest hopes.

Behold! he returns to his native land. He kisses his aged mother. He sees the pure angel of his boyish love, more beautiful and more tender than before.

Then why, hardly returned to his native home, does the young warrior again abandon his father's roof and seek the desert?

Now he crosses the forests; now he arrives at the plains of the Ipú. He seeks in the forest the daughter of the Pagé. He follows the slight trail of the coy virgin, incessantly sighing forth her sweet name to the breeze:—

"Iraçéma! Iraçéma!" . . .

Now he finds her, and winds his arm round her sweet form.

The young girl, yielding to the warm pressure, hides her face upon the warrior's bosom, and trembles there like a timid partridge when its tender mate ruffles with the beak its delicate plume.

The warrior more than once sighed forth her name, and sobbed as though to summon another loving lip. Iraçéma felt her soul escaping to merge itself in a fiery kiss.

And his brow bent low, and already the flower of her smile hung down as though calling to be culled.

Suddenly the virgin trembled. Quickly disengaging herself from the arm that encircled her, she seized her bow.

CHAPTER VII.

Iraçéma threaded the trees silent as a shade; her sparkling eyes pierced through the foliage like starbeams. She listened to the profound silence of the night and inhaled the balm-blowing breeze.

She stopped. A shadow glided amongst the

boughs and the leaves were crackled by a light step, unless indeed the report was the buzzing of some insect. Slowly the soft sound waxed louder, and with it the shadow became darker.

It was a warrior.

With one bound the virgin confronted him, trembling with fear, and still more with wrath.

"Iraçéma!" exclaimed the brave, recoiling.

"The Anhánga[1] hath doubtless disturbed the sleep of Irapúam, that he has lost himself in the Juréma wood, where no warrior enters save by the will of Araken."

"It was not the Anhánga, but the thought of Iraçéma that disturbed the sleep of the bravest of the Tabajára braves. Irapúam hath descended from his eyrie to follow up the plain the white crane of the river. He came, and Iraçéma fled from his gaze. The voices of the Taba related in the hearing of the Chief that a stranger had sat under the roof-tree of Araken."

The virgin trembled. The warrior fixed upon her his burning eyes.

The heart here in Irapúam's breast became a tiger's heart. It panted with rage. He came scenting the quarry.

"The stranger is in this wood, and Iraçéma accompanied him. Irapúam will drink all his blood: when that of the white warrior shall fill the veins of the Tabajára Chief, perhaps the daughter of Araken may love him."

The maiden's black pupils flashed in the dark, and a smile of contempt dropped from her lips, bitter as the gouts of caustic milk which the Euphorbia sheds.

"Never will Iraçéma give herself to the basest of the Tabajára braves. The spirit of Tupan alone fills

---

[1] *Anhánga*, the spirit of evil. A ghost is also thus called, the word being composed of *anho*, alone, and *anga*, a soul or spirit. Thus it means a spirit simply, a phantom.

her breast. Vile is the vampire that hides from the light and drinks the blood of the sleeping victim."

"Daughter of Araken! provoke not the Ounce. The name of Irapúam flies farther than the Goaná [1] of the lake when he scents the rain beyond the mountains. Let the white warrior appear, and let Iraçéma open her arms to the victor."

"The white warrior is the guest of Araken. Peace brought him to the plains of Ipú, and peace guards him here. Whoso offends the stranger shall offend the Pagé."

The Tabajára chief roared lion-like in his rage.

"The fury of Irapúam now hears only the vengeance-cry. The stranger shall die."

"The daughter of Araken is stronger than the Chief of warriors," said Iraçéma, seizing the war-trumpet.[2] "She holds here the voice of the Tupan-god, who calls on his people."

"But she will *not* call," said the Chief scoffingly.

"No, because Irapúam shall be punished by the hand of Iraçéma. His first step will be the step of death."

The virgin with one bound retreated as much as she had advanced and drew her bow. The chief still grasped the handle of his formidable tomahawk, but he felt for the first time that it was heavy for his strong arm. The blow that was about to strike Iraçéma had already wounded his own heart. He then knew how easily the strongest brave is, out of his very strength, vanquished by love.

"The shadow of Iraçéma will not always hide the stranger from the vengeance of Irapúam. Vile is the warrior who allows himself to be protected by a woman."

Thus saying, the Chief vanished amongst the trees.

The virgin, always on the watch, returned to the

---

[1] *Goaná*, a large species of wild duck.
[2] In the original *Inubia*, a war-trumpet of large size.

sleeping Christian, and guarded him for the rest of the night. The emotions so lately undergone agitated her soul, and ripened all those sweet affections of her heart which the stranger's eyes had quickened to life.

She longed to protect him from all peril, to shelter him as though she were an impenetrable asylum. Then, deeds following her thoughts, she passed her arms round the sleeping warrior's neck and she pillowed his head upon her bosom.

But when the joy of seeing the stranger saved from the perils of the night had passed away, the thought of new dangers about to arise caused her the liveliest disquiet.

"The love of Iraçéma is like the wind of the desert-sands; it kills the flower of the forest," sighed the virgin.

And slowly she withdrew.

CHAPTER VIII.

THE white gleam of dawn awoke the day and opened the eyes of the white warrior. The morning light dissolved the visions of the night and drew from his mind the remembrance of his dream. There remained but a vague sensation, as the perfume of the cactus clings to the forest clump, even after the sharp wind from the mountains has laid it bare in the early morn.

He did not know where he was.

Leaving the sacred grove, he met Iraçéma. The virgin was leaning against a rough trunk in the holt. Her eyes were on the ground; the colour had fled her cheeks, and her heart trembled upon her lip, like drops of dew on the bamboo[1] frond.

---

[1] *Bambú*, the well-known Indian cane.

No smile, no freshness, had the Indian maid; no buds, no flowers, has the acacia scorched by the sun; no azure, no stars, has the night when loud jars the wind.

"The forest bloom has opened to the sun-ray; the birds have already sang," said the warrior. "Why does only Iraçéma hang her head and remain silent?"

The daughter of the Pagé trembled. Thus trembles the green palm when its bole is shaken; thus the rain-tears are showered from its frond; thus its fans quietly murmur.

"Cauby the brave is coming to the Taba of his brothers. The stranger can depart with the now rising sun."

"Iraçéma then would see the stranger go from the prairies of the Tabajára; then will gladness return to her heart?"

"The Juruty-dove [1] abandons the nest wherein she was born when the tree decays. No more shall joy visit the breast of Iraçénia. She will remain like the bare trunk, without branches, without shade."

Martim supported the trembling form of the maiden; she rested wearily upon the warrior's bosom, like the young tendril of the Baúnilha which twines tenderly round the sturdy branch of the Angico-acacia.[2]

The youth murmured—

"Thy guest remains, maid with the black eyes! he stays to bring back upon thy cheek the flower of happiness, and to sip like the bee the honey of thy lips."

Iraçéma disengaged herself from the youth's arms and looked at him with sadness.

"White warrior! Iraçéma is the daughter of the Pagé, and keeps the secret of the Juréma draught. The brave that shall possess the Virgin of Tupan will die.

---

[1] *Juruty*, a species of Brazilian dove.
[2] *Angico*, a large cedar much prized by joiners and carpenters.

"And Iraçéma?"

"If thou shouldst die!"...

This word was a sigh of agony. The youth's head fell upon his breast, but soon he raised his form.

"The warriors of my race carry death with them, daughter of the Tabajáras! They do not fear it for themselves; they do not spare it to their foes. But never, unless in combat, do they leave open the Camocim[1] of the maiden in the wigwam of their host. Truth hath spoken by the mouth of Iraçéma. The stranger should leave the Tabajára camp."

"He should," said the maiden, like an echo.

Then her voice sighed forth—

"The honey of Iraçéma's lips is like the honeycomb which the bee makes in the trunk of the Guabiroba:[2] poisonous is its sweetness. The maiden with the blue eyes and sunny hair[3] keeps for her brave in the Taba of the pale-faces the honey of the lily."

Martim withdrew quickly and returned but slowly. A word trembled on his lips.

"The guest will go, that peace may return to Iraçéma's bosom."

"And he bears with him the light of Iraçéma's eyes and the flower of her soul."

A strange noise re-echoed through the forest. The youth's glance sped in its direction.

"It is Cauby the brave's cry of joy," said the maid. "Iraçéma's brother announces his safe return to the prairies of the Tabajára."

"Daughter of Araken, conduct thy guest to the wigwam. It is time to depart."

[1] *Camocim*, also called *Camotim*, the urn or chest which served as coffin to the aborigines. The word *c' am 'otim* means "hole to bury the dead," f. om *co*, hole, *ambyra*, dead, and *anhotim*, to bury.

[2] In the original *Guabiroba* or *Andiroba*, a tree which gives a pungent, bitter oil.

[3] Portuguese, *cabellos do sol*, hair like the sun; in Tupy, *guaraciába;* so they called the yellow hair of Europeans.

They paced side by side, like two fawns who at the sunset hour return through the wood to their nighting-place, whence the scent of suspicion is borne by the breeze. When they reached the Joazeiros, they saw Cauby crossing beyond them, his broad shoulders bending under the weight of his chase. Iraçéma went to meet him.

The stranger entered the wigwam alone.

CHAPTER IX.

The morning sleep weighed down the eyelids of the Pagé like the fair-weather mists hang at daybreak over the deep caverns in the mountain-side. Martim hesitated, but the sound of his step reached the old man's ear and startled his decrepit frame.

"Araken sleeps!" murmured the warrior, slackening his pace.

The venerable Pagé remained motionless.

"The Pagé slumbers because Tupan hath turned his face to the Earth, and the Light hath frightened away the evil spirits of Darkness. But sleep sits lightly on the eyes of Araken, like the smoke of the Sapé-grass [1] on the top of the Serra. If the stranger came to see the Pagé, speak; his ears are open."

"The guest came to tell Araken that he is about to go forth."

"The stranger is Lord in the wigwam of Araken; all the roads are open to him. May Tupan guide him to the Taba of his race."

Cauby and Iraçéma came up.

"Cauby has returned," said the Tabajára brave. "He brings to Araken the best of his game."

---

[1] *Sapé*, leaves for thatch; coarse grass which grows on worn-out lands.

"The warrior Cauby is a mighty huntsman of the mountains and the forests. The eyes of his father are proud to dwell upon him."

The old man opened his eyes, but they soon closed again.

"Daughter of Araken! choose for thy guest the Return Gift, and prepare the Moquem[1] for the journey. If the stranger need a guide, Cauby, the Lord of the Path,[2] will accompany him."

And sleep once more closed his eyes.

While Cauby hung up the quarry over the smoke, Iraçéma took her own white hammock of cotton fringed with feathers, and folded it into the Urú of plaited straw.

Martim awaited her at the doorway of the wigwam, and the maiden came to him and said—

"Warrior that takest away the sleep from Iraçéma's eyes, take also her hammock. When he sleeps in it, may dreams of Iraçéma speak with his heart."

"Thy hammock, maiden of the Tabajáras, shall be my companion in the wilds. Let the cold wind of night blow fiercely, it will protect the stranger with its warmth and breathe the sweet perfume of Iraçema's bosom."

Cauby went forth to see his wigwam, which he had not visited since his return. Iraçéma departed to prepare provisions for the voyage. There remained in the cabin only the Pagé, who was sleeping aloud, and the youth with his sorrows.

The sun was setting when Iraçéma's brother returned from the great wigwam.

---

[1] *Moquem*, in the original, from *mocaem*. The Brazilian Indians roasted their game before a bright fire to prevent its putrefying when they took it on a journey, and in their tents they hung it over the smoke.

[2] *Senhor do caminho*, "Lord of the Path," is what the aborigines called their guide.

"The day ends sadly,"[1] quoth Cauby. "The nightshade is already falling. It is time to depart."

The virgin laid her hand gently on the hammock of Araken.

"He goes," murmured her trembling lips.

The Pagé stood upright in the midst of the wigwam and lit his Calumet. He and the youth exchanged the pipe of farewell.

"Well-go[2] the Guest, even as he was welcome to the wigwam of Araken."

The old man walked to the door and puffed forth a cloud of smoke upon the wind. When it had dispersed in thin air he said—

"May the Jurupary[3] hide himself, and allow the guest of the Pagé to pass unmolested."

Araken returned to his hammock and slept again.

The youth took his arms, which seemed to be heavier than when he had first hung them to the stakes round the wigwam, and prepared to depart.

First went Cauby; at some little distance followed the stranger, and directly after him Iraçéma.

They descended the hill and entered the dark forest. Already the Sabiá of the wold, sweetest songster of eventide, deep hidden in the thick myrtle-brake,[4] warbled the prelude of her plaintive song.

The virgin sighed forth—

"The evening is the Sorrow of the Sun. The days of Iraçéma will be long evenings without a morn, until the Shadow of the Great Night shall fall upon her."

---

[1] *O dia vae ficar triste.* The Tupys called evening *Caruca*, a word composed of "Che carac acy," "I am sad." They drew their image of grief from the twilight and the approaching gloom.

[2] In Portuguese they can say, "Well-gone be the guest as his welcoming;" but we have no single English word as a pendant to welcome.

[3] *Jurupary*, a demon, which word literally means "crooked mouth" (*juru*, a mouth, and *apara*, crooked, deformed).

[4] In the original *Ubaia*, a myrtle with a healthy wholesome fruit (*uba*, a fruit, and *aia*, good).

The youth turned towards her. His lip was silent, but his eyes spoke. One tear coursed down his manly cheek, like the drops which during the summer heat trickle over the scarped rock.

Cauby walked on and disappeared in the dense foliage.

The bosom of Araken's daughter heaved like the overflowing billow fringed with surf, and she sobbed aloud. But in her soul, so dark with sorrow, burned a faint spark which lit up her cheeks. Thus in the blackness of night a firedrake glimmers over the white sands of the high-land plateau.

"Stranger, take the last smile of Iraçéma—and fly!"

The warrior caught her in his arms and placed his lips to hers. They were as twin fruits of the Araça [1] shrub, both sprung from the womb of the same flower.

The voice of Cauby called the stranger by name, and Iraçéma remained clinging for support to the trunk of a palm.

CHAPTER X.

In the silent wigwam meditates the old Pagé.

Iraçéma leans against the rugged trunk that serves as a stay. Her large black eyes, fixed on the forest clearings, and sunk with sorrow, gaze with long and tremulous looks, threading and unthreading the seed-pearl of teardrops that bedew her cheeks.

The Ará, perched on the opposite shelf, views with sad green eyes her beautiful lady.

From the day that saw the white warrior tread Tabajára land she had been forgotten by Iraçéma. The rosy lips of the maid never opened now to let

---

[1] *Araça*, a Brazilian shrub with fruit of the guava family.

her pick from them the fruity pulp or the paste of green maize,[1] nor ever now did the sweet hand caress her or smooth the golden plumage of her head.

If she spoke the beloved name of her mistress, the smile of Iraçéma was never bent upon her, nor did the ear of the mistress even appear to know the voice of that companion and friend, which had once been so dear to her heart.

Woe to her! The Tupy nation called her Jandáia,[2] because in her joy she made the plains resound with her vibrating song. But now, sad and silent because disdained by her mistress, she appeared no more the beautiful Jandáia, but rather the homely Urutão,[3] which knows only to groan.

Low sloped the sun over the Serra heights; its rays hardly gilded the highest crests. The hushed melancholy of evening which precedes the silence of night began to oppress the various sounds of the prairie. Here and there a night-bird, deceived by the thicker darkness of the forest, screeched aloud.

The old man raised his bald forehead.

"Was it not the cry of the Inhuma bird[4] that awoke the ear of Araken?" said he, wondering.

The maiden trembled. Already she was out of the wigwam, and back to answer the Pagé's question.

"It is the War-cry of Cauby the brave!"

When the second screech of the midnight bird

---

[1] Indian-corn, *milho*.

[2] *Jandáia*, also written *Nhendáia* and *Nhándaia*, which is an adjective that qualifies the ará or macaw, from *nheng*, to speak, *antan*, hard, rough, strong, and *ará*, the agent who acts, *nh'ant'-ará*. *Ceará* in Tupy means "the song of the jandáia," from *cemo*, to sing loud, and *arára*, paroquet.

[3] *Urutão*, a night-bird.

[4] *Inhuma*, a bird which sings regularly about midnight with a harsh unpleasant note. The orthography is *anhuma*, from *anho*, solitary, and *anum*, a well-known aotophagus, which the aborigines regarded as a bird of augury. Thus it would mean the "solitary *anum*," the unicorn-bird.

reached her ear, Iraçéma ran towards the forest, fleet as a doe pursued by the hunter: she never drew breath till she had reached the clearing, which lay in the wood like a long lake.

The first thing that met her eye was Martim, sitting tranquilly upon a Sapopema [1] bough and eyeing all that occurred. Opposite him a hundred Tabajára warriors with Irapúam at their head formed a circle. The brave Cauby, his eye flashing with anger and his weapons grasped in his muscular arm, stood up before them all.

Irapúam had demanded the stranger, and the guide had answered him simply—

"Slay Cauby first."

The daughter of the Pagé flew like an arrow. Behold her graceful form shielding Martim from the blows of the braves. Irapúam roared with rage, as roars the ounce attacked in its lair.

"Daughter of Araken," said Cauby in a whisper, "lead the stranger to the wigwam. Araken alone can save him."

Iraçéma turned towards the white warrior.

"Come!"

He remained immovable.

"If the stranger will not come, Iraçéma will die with him."

Martim arose; but far from following the maiden, he walked straight towards Irapúam. His sword flashed in the air.

"Chief! the Braves of my race have never refused combat. If he whom thou beholdest did not seek it, it was because his fathers have forbidden him to shed blood in the land of hospitality."

The Tabajára chief yelled with joy; his powerful arm wielded the tomahawk. But the two champions

---

[1] *Sapopema*, a tree with thick branches. The wood is hard, and is much prized for furniture.

had scanty time to measure each other with the eye. When the first blow was being struck, Cauby and Iraçéma were between them.

In vain the daughter of Araken besought the Christian. Vainly did she throw her arms round him, endeavouring to withdraw him from the combat. On his side, Cauby as vainly strove to provoke Irapúam, and to draw upon himself the wrath of the chief.

At a sign from Irapúam, the warriors seized the brother and sister, and the combat began.

Suddenly the hoarse sound of the War-trumpet thundered through the forest. The sons of the Serra trembled as they recognised the boom of the Sea-shell and the War-cry of the Pytiguáras, those Lords of the Shores, which the fallen trees shade. The echo came from the Great Wigwam, which perhaps the enemy was at that moment attacking.

The warriors flew there, carrying with them their Chiefs. With the stranger only remained the daughter of Araken.

CHAPTER XI.

THE Tabajára warriors, rushing to the Taba, awaited the enemy in part of the Caiçára or Curral.[1]

The foe not coming, they went forth to seek him.

They beat the forests all around and scoured the plains. There was no trace of the Pytiguáras ; yet the well-known War-boom of the Shell from the shores had sounded in the ears of the mountain braves. Of this none doubted.

Irapúam suspected that it was a stratagem of the daughter of Araken to save the stranger, and he went

---

[1] *Caiçara*, from *cai*, a bit of burnt wood, and the desinence *çara*, what *is* or is made. "What is made of burnt wood," *i.e.*, a strong enclosure of pointed stakes—a Curral.

straight to the wigwam of the Pagé; as the Guará[1] runs along the skirts of the forest when following the trail of the escaping prey, so did the wrathful warrior hurry his steps.

Araken saw the great Tabajára chief enter his cabin, but he did not move. Sitting on his hammock with crossed legs, he was giving ear to Iraçéma. The maiden related the events of the evening; beholding the sinister countenance of Irapúam, she sprang to her bow and placed herself by the white warrior's side.

Martim put her gently away and advanced a few steps.

The protection with which the Tabajára maid surrounded *him*, a warrior, annoyed him.

"Araken! the vengeance of the Tabajáras demands the white warrior; Irapúam comes to fetch him."

"The Guest is the beloved of Tupan; who so molests the Stranger shall hear the voice of his Thunder."

"It is the Stranger who has offended Tupan, robbing him of his Virgin who keeps the dreams of the Juréma draught."

"The mouth of Irapúam lies like the hiss of the Giboia,"[2] exclaimed Iraçéma.

Martim said—

"Irapúam is vile, and unworthy to be the Chief of braves."

The Pagé spoke slow and solemnly—

"If the Virgin has yielded the flower of her Chastity to the white warrior, she will die; but the Guest of

---

[1] *Guará*, a wild dog, the Brazilian wolf. The word decomposed with *g*, the relative *u*, to eat, and *ara* for *a*, the emphatic desinence is *g-u-ára*, "comedor," or "voracious eater."

[2] *Giboia*, the wild people so called the boa-constrictor, the largest snake in the Brazils, which can easily swallow a stag. The word comes from *gi*, a hatchet, and *boia*, any snake (the root of our "boa"), because the serpent strikes with its fangs like the blow of a hatchet.

Tupan is sacred; none shall touch him; all shall serve him."

Irapúam raged; his hoarse growl rumbled within his muscular chest like the noise made by the Sucury [1] in the depths of the river.

"The wrath of Irapúam's anger will not let him hearken to the old Pagé! It will fall upon *him* if he dare to withdraw the Stranger from the vengeance of the Tabajáras."

At this moment the venerable Andíra, brother of the Pagé, entered the cabin. He grasped the terrible tomahawk, and a still more terrible fury gleamed in his eyes.

"The vampire comes to suck Irapúam's blood, if indeed it *is* blood and not honey [2] that runs in the veins of him who dares to threaten the old Pagé in his wigwam."

Araken stayed his brother.

"Peace and silence, Andíra!"

The Pagé raised his tall thin stature, and appeared like the angry viper [3] who crouches on the ground the better to spring upon his victim. His wrinkles waxed deeper, whilst his shrunken lips displayed his white and sharpened teeth.

"Let Irapúam venture one step more, and the wrath of Tupan shall crush him with the weight of this lean and withered hand!"

"At this moment Tupan is not with the Pagé," replied the Chief.

The Pagé laughed, and the sinister laugh seemed

---

[1] *Sucury* or *Sucurin*, a gigantic serpent which lies in deep rivers, and can swallow an ox. The word comes from *suu*, an animal, and *cury* or *curu*, a snorter, "the snorting or hissing beast."

[2] *Si é que tens sangue e não mel nas veias.* The meaning of the word *Irapúam* is "round honey." It must be remembered that Irapúam taunted Andira farther back about *his* name, which means "old vampire," and this was *his* retort.

[3] In the original *Caninana*.

to roll round the enclosure like the bark of the Ariranha.[1]

"Hear his thunder,[2] and let the warrior's soul tremble as the earth in its depths!"

Araken pronouncing these terrible words, advanced to the middle of the wigwam. There he lifted up a great stone and stamped with force upon the ground, which suddenly clave asunder. A frightful noise, which seemed torn from the bowels of the earth, issued out from the dark cavern.

Irapúam neither trembled nor turned pale, but he felt his sight growing dim and his lips lost their power of speech.

"The Lord of Thunder is for the Pagé; the Lord of War will be for Irapúam."

The grim warrior left the wigwam, and soon his mighty form disappeared in the twilight.

The Pagé and his brother resumed their conversation in the doorway.

Martim, still surprised at what he had beheld, could not take his eyes off the deep cavern, which the stamp of the old Pagé had opened in the ground. A dull sound, like the distant boom of the waves breaking upon the shore, still echoed through the depths.

The Christian warrior reflected; he could not believe that the God of the Tabajáras had given such immense power to his priest.

Araken perceiving what was passing in the mind of the stranger, lit the Caximbo and seized the Maracá, or mystic rattle.

---

[1] *Ariranha,* the largest species of Brazilian otter.
[2] *Ouve seu trovão.* This was a stratagem practised by the Pagés to rule their votaries by terror. The hut was built upon a rock which contained a subterraneous passage, communicating by a narrow aperture with the plain. Araken had taken the precaution to block up the two entrances with stones, and thus to hide them from the people. Removing one stone from each end caused the air to rush through the narrow spiral channel with a loud noise, as the sea-shell murmurs when applied to the ear.

"It is time," he said, "to appease the wrath of Tupan and to hush the voice of his thunder."

So saying he left the cabin.

Iraçéma then approached the youth with laughing mouth and eyes sparkling with joy.

"The heart of Iraçéma is like the rice-plant, glad in the waves of the river.[1] None can hurt the white warrior in the wigwam of Araken."

"Keep away from the enemy, Tabajára maid," replied the stranger in a harsh voice. And retiring quickly to the opposite side of the wigwam, he hid his face from the tender complaining looks of the virgin.

"What has Iraçéma done that the white warrior should turn away his eyes from her as if she were the worm of the earth?"

The maiden's words, gently whispered, reached Martim's heart. Thus whisper the murmurs of the breeze in the fan-leaves of the palm-tree. The youth felt anger against himself and sorrow for her.

"Dost thou not hear, beautiful virgin?" exclaimed he, pointing to the speaking cave.

"It is the voice of Tupan!"

"Thy god speaks by the mouth of his Pagé: *If the virgin of Tupan yield to the stranger the flower of her chastity, she shall die.*"

Iraçéma hung her head.

"It is not the voice of Tupan that the pale-faced warrior hears, but the song of the white virgin that calls to him."

Suddenly the strange sounds which came from the depths of the earth ceased, and there was so deep a silence in the wigwam, that the pulses throbbing through the warrior's veins and the sighs that trembled on the virgin's lips were heard.

---

[1] In the original *abati*, or *abaty n'agua*. *Abati* is rice, which thrives when in water, and which Iraçéma used as a symbol of her joy.

CHAPTER XII.

The day darkened; night was already coming on.

The Pagé returned to the wigwam, and again poising the slab of stone, closed with it the mouth of the subterranean passage.

Cauby also arrived from the great Taba, where he and his brother braves had retired after beating the forest in search of the Pytiguara enemy.

In the centre of the wigwam, amidst the hammocks, slung and squared, Iraçéma spread the mat of Carnaúba palm, and served the remains of the game with the wines made during the last moon. The Tabajára brave alone relished the supper; the gall which is wrung from the heart by sorrow did not embitter his palate.

The Pagé drew from his calumet the sacred smoke of Tupan, which filled the depths of his lungs. The stranger greedily inhaled the fresh air to cool his boiling blood. The maiden seemed to sigh her soul away, like honey dropping from the comb, in the frequent sobs that burst from her trembling lips.

Cauby soon retired to the great Taba; the Pagé still inhaled the smoke which prepared him for the mysteries of the Sacred Rite.

There arises in the night silence a vibrating cry which ascends to the sky. Martim raises up his head and listens. Again a similar sound is heard. The warrior whispers, so that only the maiden could hear him—

"Hast heard, Iraçéma, the Seagull's cry?"

"Iraçéma has heard the cry of a bird which she does not know."

"It is the Atyaty,[1] the Heron of the Sea, and Iraçéma is the mountain-maid who has never trodden upon the white beach upon which the waves break."

[1] *Atyaty*, seagull.

"The beach belongs to the Pytiguaras, the Lords of the Palm groves."

The warriors of the great tribe who inhabited the seaboard called themselves Pytiguaras, Lords of the Valleys; but the Tabajáras, their enemies, contemptuously termed them Potyuáras, or Shrimp-Eaters.

Iraçéma did not wish to offend the white warrior, and therefore, when speaking of the Pytiguaras, she gave them the warlike name which they had chosen for themselves.

The stranger reflected, and retained for a moment, on the lip of prudence, the word which he was about to utter.

"The Seagull's song is the War-cry of the brave Poty, the friend of thy guest."

The maiden trembled for her brethren. The fame of the fierce Poty, brother of Jacaúna, had spread afar, from the sea-shore to the heights of the Serra. Scarcely was there a wigwam which had not panted with a lust of vengeance; in almost all of them the blow of his unerring tomahawk had laid a warrior low in his Camocim.

Iraçéma thought that Poty came at the head of his braves to deliver his friend. Doubtless it was he who had sounded the Sea-shell at the time when the combat began. It was therefore in a tone of mixed sadness and sweetness that she replied—

"The stranger is saved; the brethren of Iraçéma will die, for she will not speak."

"Cast out this grief from thy soul, Tabajára maid! The stranger in leaving thy prairies will not leave in them, like the famished tiger, a trail of blood."

Iraçéma took the hand of the white warrior and kissed it.

"The stranger's smile," she continued, "blunts the remembrance of the harm they wish me."

Martim rose and walked to the door.

"Where goes the white warrior?"

"To seek Poty."

"The guest of Araken may not leave this wigwam, for the warriors of Irapúam will kill him."

"A warrior owes his life to God and to his weapons only. He will not be protected by old men and women!"

"What is one brave against a thousand? The Tamanduá[1] is brave and strong, yet the cats of the mountains kill and eat him because they are so many. The arms of the white warrior only reach as far as the shadow of his body—those of the Tabajáras fly high and straight as the Anajê."[2]

"Every warrior has his day."

"The stranger would not see Iraçéma die, yet he would make her behold his death."

Martim hesitated, perplexed.

"Iraçéma will go and meet the Pytiguára Chief, and will bring to her guest the words of his warrior friend."

The Pagé finally awoke from his reverie. The Maracá rattled in his right hand; the bells rang in time to his stiff slow step.

He called his daughter apart.

"If the braves of Trapúam fall upon the wigwam, lift up the stone and hide the stranger in the bosom of the earth."

"The guest must not be left alone. Wait till Iraçéma returns. The inhuma has not yet sung."

The old man again sat upon his hammock. The maiden went forth after fastening the door of the wigwam.

[1] *Tamanduá*, ant-eater.
[2] *Anajé*, a powerful hawk, the local eagle.

CHAPTER XIII.

The daughter of Araken advances in the darkness; she stands and listens. For the third time the cry of the Seagull sounds in her ears; she bends her steps straight to the place whence it came, and arrives at the edge of a lake. Her glance pierces the darkness, but finds nought of what it seeks. The tender voice, soft as the hum of the colibri bird, breaks the silence.

"Poty, the brave's white brother calls him by the mouth of Iraçéma!"

Echo only answered her.

"The Daughter of his Foes comes to seek him, because the stranger loves him, and she loves the stranger."

The smooth surface of the lake clove, and a figure appeared swimming towards the margin and rising from the water.

"Was it Martim who sent Iraçéma, since she knows the name of Poty, his brother in war?"

"The Pytiguára chief may speak; the white warrior is waiting."

"Then Iraçéma will return and tell him that Poty has come to save him."

"The stranger knows, and sent Iraçéma to hear Poty's tidings."

"The words of Poty will leave his mouth only for the ear of his white brother."

"He must wait then till Araken leaves and the wigwam remains deserted; then will Iraçéma guide him to the presence of the stranger."

"Never, daughter of the Tabajáras! has a Pytiguára brave crossed the threshold of a foeman's wigwam save as a conqueror. Bring here the warrior of the sea."

"The vengeance of Irapúam hovers around the wigwam of Araken. Has the stranger's brother brought Pytiguára warriors enough to defend and to save him?"

Poty reflected.

"Relate, Maid of the Mountains, all that has happened in these prairies since the Warrior of the Sea planted foot upon them."

Iraçéma related all—how the wrath of Irapúam had burst forth against the stranger, until the voice of Tupan, invoked by the Pagé, had appeased his fury.

"The anger of Irapúam is like that of the bat; he fears the light and flies only in the dark."

The hand of Poty suddenly closed the maiden's lips; his words sank to a whisper.

"The Virgin of the Forest must hold her breath and hush her voice; the foeman's ear listens in the dark."

The leaves gently rustled as if trodden upon by the restless Nambú. The sound at first came from the skirts of the forest and then swept towards the valley. The valiant Poty gliding along the grass, like the clever prawn from which he took his name and quickness, disappeared in the deep lake. The water without a murmur buried him in its limpid wave.

Iraçéma returned to the wigwam; on the way she perceived the shadows of many warriors who were crawling on the ground like the Intanha frog.[1]

Araken, seeing her come in, left the wigwam.

The Tabajára maid related to Martim all that had passed between herself and Poty. The Christian warrior rose up impetuously to rescue his Pytiguára brother. Iraçéma threw round his neck her beautiful arms.

"The Chief does not want his brother. He is the son of the waters, and the waters will protect him. Later, the stranger's ear shall listen to the words of his friend."

---

[1] *Intanha*, commonly called the *ferrador*, the blacksmith frog.

"Iraçéma, it is time that thy guest should leave the wigwam of the Pagé and the plains of the Tabajáras. He does not fear the braves of Irapúam; he fears the eyes of the Virgin of Tupan."

"He will fly from them?"

"The stranger *must* fly from *them* as the Oitibó does from the morning star."

Martim hastened his steps.

"Ungrateful brave! go slay, first brother, then self. Iraçéma will follow him to the happy plains where wend the shades of those that were."

"Kill my brother, sayest thou, cruel maid?"

"Thy trail will guide the enemy to his hiding-place."

The Christian halted suddenly midway in the wigwam, and there remained silent and still. Iraçéma, fearing to look upon him, fixed her eyes on his shadow, which the bright embers of the fire threw on the broken wall of the wigwam.

The shaggy dog lying close to the hot ashes gave signs that a friend was approaching. The door interwoven with the fronds of the Carnaúba palm was opened from without. Cauby entered.

"The Cauim wine has disturbed the spirit of the braves. They are coming to slay the stranger."

The maiden arose impetuously.

"Lift up the stone which closes the throat of Tupan, that he may conceal the guest."

The Tabajára brave uphove the enormous slab, and poised it on the ground.

"The son of Araken shall lie across the Wigwam-door, and if a brave pass over his body, let him rise no more from the ground."

Cauby obeyed. The maiden fastened the door.

A few moments passed. The war-cry of the braves sounds closer; the angry voices of Irapúam and Cauby rise above the rest.

"They come, but Tupan will save his guest."

At this moment, as if the thunder-god had heard the words of his virgin, the cave, which till then was still, roared with a dull roar.

"Listen! It is the voice of Tupan!"

Iraçéma presses the warrior's hand and leads him into the cave. They descend together into the bowels of the earth.

CHAPTER XIV.

The Tabajára braves, excited by their copious libations of foaming Cauim, were inflamed by the voice of Irapúam, who had so often led them to victory.

Wine appeases the thirst of the body, but breeds another and a wilder thirst in the savage mind.

The braves yell vengeance against the audacious stranger who had defied their arms, and who had offended the God of their fathers and their War Chief, the greatest of the Tabajáras.

Then they leapt with rage and rushed about in the darkness. The red light of the Ubirátán[1] which shone in the distance guided them to the cabin of Araken.

From time to time the foremost of those who came to spy the enemy raised themselves up from the ground.

"The Pagé is in the forest," they murmured.

"And the stranger?" inquired Irapúam.

"In the cabin with Iraçéma."

The great chief leaps up with a terrific bound, and reaches the Wigwam-door followed by his warriors.

The face of Cauby appears at the entrance. His arms guarded a space in front of him—say within the reach of a Maracajá's spring.[2]

---

[1] The iron wood of *ubira* (from *pái*, wood, and *antan*, hard).
[2] *Maracajá* is a wild cat. It must not be confounded with

"Dastardly are the braves who attack in herds like the Caetetús.[1] The Jaguar,[2] Lord of the Forest, and the Anajê, Lord of the Clouds, combat the enemy alone."

"Dirt be in the vile mouth which raises its voice against the bravest of the Tabajára braves."

Saying these words, Irapúam brandished his fatal tomahawk, but his arm stopped in the air. The bowels of the earth again rumbled as they had rumbled when Araken awoke the awful voice of Tupan.

The braves raise a cry of fear, and, surrounding their Chief, force him away from the funest spot and the wrath of Tupan, so evidently roused against them.

Cauby once more lay down across the threshold; his eyes sleep but his ears keep watch.

The voice of Tupan became silent.

Iraçéma and the Christian, lost in the depths of the earth, descended into a deep grotto. Suddenly a voice arising from the cavernous depths filled their ears.

"Does the Sea-Warrior listen to the words of his brother?"

"It is Poty, the friend of thy guest," said the Christian to the maid.

Iraçéma trembled.

"He speaks by the mouth of Tupan."

Martim then answered the Pytiguára—

"The words of Poty enter into the soul of his brother."

---

the *Maracujá* or passion-flower, which represents all the instruments of our Saviour's passion, as the pillar, nails, scourges, and crown of thorns.

[1] *Caetetús* is the wild pig of the forest, from *caeté*, large virgin forest, and *suu*, game, which euphony changes to *tu*.

[2] *Jaguar*, amongst the aborigines, was applied to all the animals that devoured them, especially the ounce. *Jaguareté* meant "the great eater." It is derived from *ja*, "us," and *guara*, "the voracious."

"Does no other ear listen?"

"None save those of the Virgin who twice in one sun has saved the life of thy brother."

"Woman is weak; the Tabajára is revengeful; and the brother of Jacaúna[1] is prudent."

Iraçéma sighed and lay her head upon the youth's breast.

"Lord of Iraçéma, stop her ears that she may not listen."

Martim gently put away the graceful head.

"The Pytiguára Chief may speak; the ears that listen are friendly and faithful."

"His brother orders and Poty speaks. Ere the sun shall rise over the Serra, the Sea-Warrior must seek the river-plain of the Herons' Nests. The Dead Star will guide him to the white beach. No Tabajára brave will follow him, because the Inubia of the Pytiguáras will sound from the mountain-side."

"How many Pytiguára braves accompany their valiant Chief?"

"Not one. Poty came alone with his arms. When the bad spirits of the forest separated the Sea-Warrior from his brother, Poty followed his trail. His heart would not let him return to call the braves of his Taba; but he sent his faithful dog to the great Jacaúna."

"The Pytiguára Chief is alone; he must not sound the Inubia, which will raise all the Tabajára braves against him."

"He *must* do it to save his white brother. Poty will mock at Irapúam, as he mocked him when he fought with a hundred men against his white brother."

The daughter of the Pagé, who had listened silently, now bent towards the Christian's ear.

"Iraçéma would save the stranger and his brother; she knows her thoughts. The Pytiguára Chief is

---

[1] *Jacaúna* was the celebrated Chief, brother of Poty, and a friend to Martim Soares Moreno. His name is that of a black tree, also called in Brazil Jacarandá.

staunch and brave. Irapúam is crafty and treacherous as the Acauan.[1] Before the stranger can reach the forest he must fall, and his brother must also fall with him."

"What can the Tabajára maid do to save the stranger and his brother?" asked Martim.

"One more sun and another must rise, then the moon of flowers[2] will appear. It is the feast-time when the Tabajára braves pass the night in the Sacred Wood and receive from the Pagé their happy dreams. When they are all sleeping, the white warrior will leave the plains of Ipú, and will vanish from the eyes of Iraçéma, but not from her soul."

Martim strained the maiden to his breast, but soon he gently repelled her. The contact of her beautiful form, sweet as the forest lily, warm as the nest of the Beijaflor,[3] was as a thorn in his heart. He remembered the awful warning of the Pagé.

The voice of the Christian repeated to Poty the project of Iraçéma; the Pytiguára chief, prudent as the Tamanduá, took thought, and then replied—

"Wisdom has spoken by the mouth of the Tabajára Virgin. Poty will wait the moon of flowers."

CHAPTER XV.

THE day was born and dead. The fire, companion of the night, already shone in the Wigwam of Araken. The stars, daughters of the moon, rolled their slow and silent courses in the blue heavens, awaiting the return of their absent mother.

---

[1] The *Acauan* is a Secretary-bird that destroys serpents. The word is from *caa*, wood, and *uan*, from *u*, "to eat"—a wood-eater.
[2] *A lua das flores*, the moon of flowers.
[3] *Beijaflor*, literally Kiss-flower, the humming-bird.

Martim gently rocked himself; and his soul, like the white hammock which waved from side to side, wavered between one and another thought. There the pale-faced virgin awaited him with chaste affection. Here the dark maiden smiled upon him with ardent love.

Iraçéma leant languidly against the head of the hammock; her large black eyes, tender as those of the Sabiá-thrush, sought the stranger and pierced his soul. The Christian smiled. The virgin, trembling like the Sahy-bird [1] fascinated by the serpent, bent her yielding form and reclined upon the warrior's bosom.

He strained her passionately to his heart, his lips sought her longing lip, and thus they celebrated in this sanctuary of the soul the hymen of love.

In a dark obscure corner sat the Pagé, plunged in the contemplation of things remote from this world. He heaved one long sad sigh. Did his heart forebode that which his eyes could not see? Or was it some ill-omened presentiment concerning the future of his race which re-echoed in the soul of Araken?

No one ever knew!

The Christian gently repelled the Indian girl. He would not leave a trail of disgrace in the hospitable Wigwam. He closed his eyes that he might not see her, and endeavoured to fill his thoughts with the name and the fear of God.

Christ!—Jesus!—Mary!

A calm returned to the warrior's breast, but every time his eye rested upon the Tabajára virgin he felt the blood course through his veins like liquid fire. Thus when the thoughtless child stirs the live embers, its sparks fly out and consume its flesh.

The Christian shut his eyes, but amid the darkness of his thoughts the Tabajára virgin ever arose, and ever more beautiful. In vain his heavy lids invoked

---

[1] *Sahy*, a beautiful blue bird.

sleep. They opened despite all his endeavours. An inspiration from Heaven at last descended upon his troubled mind.

"Beautiful maid of the desert! this is the last night of thy guest under the roof of Araken. Would that he had never come there! For thy sake and for his own, make his sleep glad and happy."

"Let the warrior command, and Iraçéma will obey. What can she do to make him glad?"

The Christian murmured low that the old Pagé might not hear him.

"The Virgin of Tupan keeps the dreams of the Jurema, which are sweet and pleasant!"

A sad smile was Iraçéma's answer.

"The stranger is going to live for ever encircling the white virgin.[1] Never more will his eyes behold the daughter of Araken; yet he wishes that sleep should close his lids, and that dreams should convey him back to the land of his brothers!"

"Sleep is the warrior's rest," said Martim, "and dreams are the gladness of his soul. The stranger would not bear sadness with him from the Land of Hospitality, nor would he leave it in the heart of Iraçéma."

The virgin sat unmoved.

"Go! and return with the wine of Tupan."

When Iraçéma came back, the Pagé was no longer in the Wigwam. She drew from her bosom the bowl which she had hidden under her Carioba [2] of cotton interwoven with feathers. Martim seized it from her hands, and drained the few drops of bitter green liquid. Presently the hammock received his torpid form.

Now he may live with Iraçéma, and gather the

---

[1] In the original *á cintura da virgem*. The savages call a successful lover *aguaçaba*, which literally means, the woman whom the man's arm encircles.

[2] *Carioba*, a cotton garment ornamented with parrots' feathers.

kisses from her lips which ripened there amidst smiles, like the fruit in the corolla of the flower. He may love her, and may savour the honey and perfume of this love without leaving its poison in the virgin's breast.

The joy was life, only more real and intense. The evil was a dream, an illusion; to him the maiden was an image, a shadow.

Iraçéma withdrew, silent and sorrowful. The warrior's arms opened, and his lips gently murmured her name.

The Juruty flitting about the forest hears the tender cooing of her mate. She flutters her wings and flies to meet him in the warm nest. Thus the virgin of the desert nestled in the warrior's arms.

When morning came, it found Iraçéma sleeping like a butterfly in the petals of the beautiful cactus. Her cheek was suffused with the blushes of modesty, and as the first sunbeam sparkles through the early dawn, on her brightened face shone the happy smile of the bride, the aurora of happy love.

Martim seeing Iraçéma still pressed to his heart, thought that the dream continued, and closed his eyes not to disturb it.

The Poçema-trump of the braves thundering through the valley awoke him from the sweet illusion. He knew then that he was alive and awake. His cruel hand smothered the kiss which expanded like a flower on the bride's lips.

"The kisses of Iraçéma are sweet in dreams. The white warrior fills his soul with them. But in life the lips of the Virgin of Tupan are bitter and painful like the Jurema-thorns."

The daughter of Araken hid her joy in her heart. She was hushed and startled like the bird which feels the coming storm. She quickly withdrew from the Wigwam, and plunged into the river according to custom.

The Jandaia never returned to the Wigwam, and Tupan no longer owned his Virgin in the Tabajára land.

CHAPTER XVI.

THE moon's white disc rose slowly above the horizon. The brightness of the sun pales the virgin of the heavens, as the warrior's love blanches the wife's cheek.

"Jacy!"[1] . . . "Our mother!" exclaimed the Tabajára warriors. And brandishing their bows, they chanted the song of the new moon, discharging at her showers of arrows.

"Thou art come into the heavens, O mother of the braves! Thou turnest thy face once more to behold thy sons. Thou bringest waters to fill the rivers, and pulp to the Cujú-nut.

"Thou art come, O bride of the sun! Thy daughters, the virgins of the earth, smile at thy approach. May thy soft light bring love into the hearts of the brave, and make fruitful the young mother's bosom."

The evening was falling. The women and children sported in the vast Ocara. The youths who had not yet won their name by notable deeds were running races in the valley.

The warriors followed Irapúam to the Sacred Wood, where the Pagé and his daughter awaited them for the mysteries of the Jurema.

Iraçéma had already lit the fires of joy![2]

---

[1] *Jacy*, the moon, literally our mother. Amongst the savages the moon was a month, and at the change they held their feast.
[2] *Fogos de alegria*. The savages called their fire-faggots *tory* and *toryba*. A joy-feast was a great number of fires.

Araken remained statue-like and ecstatic in the centre of a cloud of smoke.

Each warrior on arriving placed at his feet an offering for Tupan. One brought the succulent game, another water-flour, a third Piracem [1] of the Trahira,[2] and so on each in turn. The old Pagé, for whom were the gifts, received them with disdain.

When all had taken seat round the Great Fire, the priest of Tupan commanded silence by a gesture, and three times pronounced aloud the dread name, as though to fill himself with the God who inspired him.

"Tupan! Tupan! Tupan!"

Three times the distant echoes answered the name.

Iraçéma came with the Igaçaba full of the green liquor. Araken decreed to each warrior his dreams, and distributed the wine of the Jurema, which was to transport the Tabajára brave to the happy land.

The mighty hunter dreamt that stags and Pácas [3] ran to meet his arrows and transfixed themselves; at length, tired of wounding them, he dug the Bucán [4] in the earth, and roasted so much game that a thousand warriors could not finish it in a year.

The conqueror of hearts dreamt that the most beautiful of the Tabajára virgins left their fathers' Wigwams to follow him, slaves to his will and pleasure. Never had the hammock of any chief witnessed the reality of such wild warm visions.

The hero's vision was of tremendous struggles and fearful combats, whence he always issued victorious and covered with fame and glory.

[1] In the original *farinha d'agua*. This is a sort of flour like tapioca, which the Indians used to eat mixed with water.
[2] *Piracem de trahira*. Trahira is a river fish. *Pira caém* means fish roasted.
[3] *Pácas* (*Cavia páca*), a small rodent in Brazil like a pig two months old; its flesh is eaten.
[4] *Bucan* is a Tupy word for a way of grilling flesh, which the French of Maranhão turn into *boucaner*, and whence comes our English *buccaneer*.

The old man saw his youth renewed in his numerous offspring, like the dry trunk acquiring new strength and sap, and still sprouting into buds and flowers.

All felt such lively, such lasting happiness, that in one night they lived many moons.

Their lips murmured, their gestures spoke; and the Pagé, who saw and heard all, gathered from their unveiled souls their most secret thoughts.

When Iraçéma had offered to each brave the wine of Tupan, she left the wood. The rites did not permit her to be present at the sleep of the warriors, nor hear and see their dreams.

She went her way straight to the cabin, where Martim awaited her.

"Let the white warrior take up his arms. It is time to go."

"Lead me to my brother Poty."

The bride made straight for the valley, the Christian following her. They reached the rock base, which fell sloping with clumps of foliage upon the margin of the lake.

"Let the stranger call his brother."

Martim imitated the cry of the seagull.

The stone which closed the entrance of the grotto fell, and the figure of Poty the brave appeared in the gloom.

The two brothers pressed forehead to forehead and breast to breast, showing that they had but one heart.

"Poty is happy because he sees his brother, whom the bad spirit of the forest had borne away from his sight."

"Happy is the brave who has a friend at his side like the valiant Poty; all the other warriors will envy him."

Iraçéma sighed, thinking that the affection of the Pytiguára sufficed to the happiness of the stranger.

"The Tabajára braves sleep. The daughter of Araken will guide the strangers."

D

The bride led the way; the two warriors followed behind. When they had gone about the distance of a heron's flight, the Pytiguára chief began to be uneasy, and whispered in the ear of the Christian—

"My brother had better send the daughter of the Pagé back to the Wigwam of her father. The warriors could march quicker without her."

Martim felt a sudden sadness; but the voice of prudence and friendship prevailed in his heart. He advanced to Iraçéma and spoke softly to soothe her sorrow.

"The deeper the root in the earth, the harder it is to withdraw the plant. Each step Iraçéma takes on the road of farewell is a root which she plants in the heart of her guest."

"Iraçéma would accompany him as far as the borders of the Tabajára land, in order to return with more calmness in her breast."

Martim did not answer. They continued their march, and as they walked the night fell, the stars paled, and finally the freshness of dawn gladdened the forest; the morning clouds, purely white as cotton, appeared in the heavens.

Poty looked at the forest and stopped. Martim understood, and said to Iraçéma—

"Thy guest no longer treads on the land of the Tabajáras. It is the right moment to bid him farewell."

CHAPTER XVII.

Iraçéma placed her hand upon the bosom of the white warrior.

"The daughter of the Tabajáras has now left the land of her fathers, and she may speak."

"What keepest thou within thy bosom, beautiful daughter of the forest?"

She gazed with brimming eyes at the Christian.

"Iraçéma cannot tear herself from the stranger."

"Yet thus it must be, daughter of Araken. Return to the cabin of thine old father, who awaits thee."

"Araken has no longer a daughter."

Martim turned towards her with a harsh and severe gesture.

"A warrior of my race never leaves the Wigwam of his host widowed of its joy. Araken will embrace his daughter, and shall not curse the ungrateful stranger."

The girl hung her head; veiled in the long black tresses which hung about her neck, she crossed her beautiful arms over her bosom, and stood robed in her modesty. Thus the rosy cactus, before opening into a lovely flower, retains within its breast the perfumed bud.

"Thy slave will accompany thee, white warrior, because thy blood sleeps in her bosom."

Martim trembled.

"The bad spirits of the night have disturbed the spirit of Iraçéma."

"The white warrior was dreaming when Tupan abandoned his Virgin, because she betrayed the secret of the Jurema."

The Christian hid his face from the light.

"O God!" exclaimed his trembling lip.

Both remained silent.

At last Poty spoke—

"The Tabajára warriors awake."

The heart of the bride, like that of the stranger, was deaf to the voice of prudence. The sun arose in the horizon, and his majestic glance descended from the wooded uplands to the forest. Poty stood like a solitary tree-trunk waiting for his brother to give the signal for departure. It was Iraçéma who broke silence.

"Come! the life of the warrior is in danger until he treads the Pytiguára land."

Martim followed the girl silently, and she flitted before him amongst the trees like the timid Acoty.[1] Sorrow preyed upon his heart, but the perfume wafted on the air by the passage of the beautiful Tabajára fanned the love in his warrior-breast. Still his step was slow and his breathing was oppressed.

Poty reflected. In his youthful brain had lived the spirit of an Abaeté.[2] The Pytiguára Chief thought th love is like Cauim, which, drunk with moderation, fortifies the brave, but in excess weakens the hero's courage. He knew how fleet was the Tabajára's foot, and he expected the moment when he must die defending his friend.

As the shades of evening began to sadden the day, the Christian stopped in the middle of the forest. Poty lit the fire of hospitality. The bride unfolded the white hammock of cotton fringed with the feathers of the Toucan,[3] and hung it to the branches of a tree.

"Husband of Iraçéma, thy hammock awaits thee."

The daughter of Araken then went and sat afar off on the root of a tree, like the solitary doe who has been driven forth from the sunny plain by her ungrateful mate. The Pytiguára warrior disappeared in the thickest of the foliage.

Martim sat silent and sorrowful, like the trunk of some tree from which the wind has torn the beautiful Cipó[4] which embraced it. The passing breeze at last bore on it one murmur—

"Iraçéma!"

It was the cry of the mate. The wounded doe flew back to the sunny plain.

---

[1] *Acoty*, generally written *cutia*, a racoon.
[2] *Abaeté* means a good, strong, wise, clever man.
[3] *Tucano*, a well-known bird with gorgeous plumage, black, green, scarlet, and orange, with a large beak.
[4] *Cipó*, a Lliana or climbing plant.

IRAÇÉMA.

The forest distilled its sweetest fragrance and was vocal with its most harmonious music; the sighs of the heart mingled with the whispers of the wilderness. It was the feast of Love, the song of Hymen.

Already the morning light pierced the dense thicket, when the solemn and sonorous voice of Poty sounded amidst the hum and the buzz of waking life.

"The Tabajáras walk through the forest!"

Iraçéma sprang from the arms that encircled her and from the lips which held her captive—sprang from the hammock lightly to the ground, like the agile Zabelê,[1] and seizing the weapons of her spouse, led him into the depths of the bush.

From time to time the prudent Poty laid his ear to the face of earth, and his head inclined from side to side, as the cloud on the summit of a rock waves with every puff of the coming storm.

"What does the ear of the warrior Poty hear?"

"It listens to the flying step of the Tabajára. He comes like the Tapyr[2] tearing through the forest."

"The Pytiguára warrior is like the Ostrich[3] which flies along the earth; we will follow him like his wings," said Iraçéma.

The Chief shook his head anew.

"Whilst the Sea-Warrior slept the enemy ran. Those who first set out are now near, as the horns are to the bow."

Shame gnawed the heart of Martim.

"Let the Chief Poty fly and save Iraçéma. The bad warrior, who would not listen to the voice of his brother and the wish of his bride, can only die."

Martim began to retrace his steps.

"The soul of the white warrior does not listen to

---

[1] *Zabelê*, a small bird somewhat like a partridge.
[2] *Tapyr*, a well-known animal about the size of a calf. The hide is useful, and of buff colour. It is also called *Tapijerete*, *Tapy'ra*, and *Tapy'ra caapóra*.
[3] In the original *Ema*, the South American ostrich.

his mouth. Poty and his brother have but one life."

The lip of Iraçéma spoke not—only smiled.

CHAPTER XVIII.

The forest literally trembled as it echoed the career of the Tabajára braves.

The form of Irapúam the Great first looms amidst the trees. His suffused eye caught sight of the white warrior through a cloud of blood; a hoarse and tiger-like roar burst from his brawny chest.

The Tabajára Chief and his tribe were about to fall upon the fugitives like the swollen waves which break on the Mocoribe's[1] flank.

But hush!—in the distance sounds the bark of the Indian dog.

Poty gave a cry of joy.

"It is Poty's hound that guides the warriors of his Taba to save his brother."

The hoarse sea-shell of the Pytiguáras bellowed through the forest. The great Jacaúna, Lord of the Sea-shores, was marching from the river of the herons with the best of his braves.

The Pytiguáras receive the first assault of the foe on the jagged heads of their shafts, which they loosed in showers like the porcupine[2] raising his quills. Presently resounded the War-Poçema of the Tabajáras; the space between the enemies was narrowed, and the hand-to-hand combat began.

Jacaúna attacked Irapúam. The horrible fight

[1] *Mocoribe*, now called *Mucuripe*, means "to make glad;" it is a hill of sand in a bay of the same name, a league from Fortaleza, the great seaport town of Ceará.
[2] In the original *Coandú*, porcupine.

was that of ten braves, yet it did not exhaust the strength of the two great chiefs. When their tomahawks clashed, the battle trembled to the heart as one man.

The brother of Iraçéma came straight to the stranger who had taken the daughter of Araken from the hospitable Wigwam; the trail of vengeance led him; the sight of his sister maddened him. Cauby the brave furiously assaults the enemy.

Iraçéma remained by the side of her warrior and spouse. She saw Cauby from afar and cried—

"Let the Lord of Iraçéma listen to the prayer of his slave; let him not shed the blood of the son of Araken. If the warrior Cauby must die, let it be by the hand of Iraçéma, not by his."

Martim looked at the savage with eyes of horror.

"Would Iraçéma slay her brother?"

"Iraçéma would see the blood of Cauby stain her hand rather than the hand of her lord, because the eyes of Iraçéma dwell upon him, and not upon herself."

The battle still rages. Cauby fights with fury. The Christian hardly defends himself, but the poisoned arrows from the young wife's bow save him from the blows of the enemy.

Poty had already laid low the old Andira and all the braves who during the struggle had encountered his good tomahawk. Martim leaves to him the son of Araken and seeks out Irapúam.

"Jacaúna is a great Chief; his War-collar[1] thrice encircles his neck! This Tabájara belongs to the white warrior."

"Revenge is the honour of warfare, and Jacaúna loves the friend of Poty."

The great Pytiguára chief upraised his formidable

---

[1] *Seu collar de guerra.* The collar which the savages made of the teeth of vanquished enemies (taking from each one tooth), was a blazon and a proof of valour.

tomahawk. The duel between Irapúam and Martim began. The Christian's sword was shivered by the savage's tomahawk. The Tabajára Chief advanced upon his unarmed adversary.

Iraçéma hissed like the Boicininga,[1] and threw herself between her warrior and the Tabajára; at once the massive weapon trembled in his powerful right hand and his arm fell inanimate by his side.

The Poçema of victory sounded. The Pytiguára warriors, headed by Jacaúna and Poty, swept the forest. The Tabajáras snatched, as they fled, their Chief from the hatred and vengeance of the daughter of Araken, who had the power of conquering him, as the Jandáia prostrates the tallest and strongest palm-tree by nibbling the core.

The eyes of Iraçéma, scanning the forest, saw the ground strewed with the bodies of her brethren, and in the distance the remnant of their war-party flying in a black cloud of dust. That blood which stained the ground was the same brave blood which now lit up her cheeks with shame.

The grief-drops moistened her beautiful cheek. Martim withdrew that he might not embarrass her sorrow. He wished her naked woe to bathe itself in tear-floods.

CHAPTER XIX.

POTY returned from pursuing the foe. His eyes filled with delight when he saw the white warrior safe.

The faithful dog followed him closely, still licking from its hairy mouth the Tabajára blood, of which it had drunk its fill. Its master caressed it, pleased by its courage and devotion. It had saved Martim by guiding so diligently the warriors of Jacaúna.

[1] A large species of boa.

IRAÇÉMA.

"The bad spirits of the forest may again separate the white warrior from his Pytiguára brother. The dog will henceforth follow him, so that even from a distance Poty may hear his call."

"But the dog is thy companion and faithful friend."

"It will be Poty's companion and friend still more when it serves his brother than when it serves him. The white warrior shall call it 'Japy,'[1] and it will be the fleet foot with which from afar they will run to each other."

Jacaúna gave the signal of departure.

The Pytiguára warriors marched for the glad banks of the Heron's River, where rose the great Taba of the Prairie Lords.

The sun declined and again soared in the heavens. The warriors arrived where the sea-range fell towards the midlands. Already they had passed that part of the mountain which, being scant of tree and shorn like the Capivára,[2] the people of Tupan had called Ibyapina.[3]

Poty took the Christian where grew a leafy Jatobá,[4] that overtopped the trees of the Serra's highest point when waving before the wind; it seemed to sweep the sky with its immense dome.

"On this spot the white warrior's brother was born," said the Pytiguára Chief.

Martim embraced the enormous trunk.

---

[1] *Japy* means "our foot."

[2] *Capivára, capiuára* (that which lives on Capim, the coarse grass of the country), is a kind of water-hog. The Peruvian people of Rio Branco wear the teeth of this animal as earrings.

[3] *Ibyapina* means "bald land."

[4] *Jatobá*, an enormous and royal-looking tree. The place where this scene took place is now called Villa Viçosa, where tradition says Poty, afterwards Camarão, was born. Jatobá is the name of a river and of a Serra in South Quiteria, and Jatobá was the name of the father of Poty and Jacaúna.

"Jatobá, thou that sawest my brother Poty come into the world: the stranger embraces thee!"

"May the lightning wither thee, O tree of the warrior Poty! when his brother abandons him."

Then the chief spoke as follows:—

"Then Jacaúna was not yet a warrior. Jatobá, our greatest Chief, was leading the Pytiguáras to victory. As soon as the full waters began to run, he marched straight for the Serra. Arriving here, he sent for the whole Taba, that it might be nearer the enemy, to vanquish them again. The same moon which saw their arrival shone upon the hammock in which Sahy, his wife, gave him one more warrior of his blood. The moonlight played amongst the leafage of the Jatobá, and the smile upon the lips of the great and wise Chief who had taken its name and might."

Iraçema approached.

The turtle-dove,[1] feeding in the sands, leaves its mate, who flits restlessly from branch to branch, and coos that the absent one may reply. Thus the forest girl wandered in search of her prop, softly humming a gentle, tender song.

Martim received her with his soul in his eyes, and leading his wife on the side of his heart, and his friend on the side of his strength, returned to the Ranch[2] of the Pytiguáras.

CHAPTER XX.

THE moon waxed rounder. Three suns had passed since Martim and Iraçema had been in the lands of the Pytiguáras, Lords of the banks of the rivers

---

[1] In the original *Rôla*.
[2] *Rancho* is a shed made of mud and sticks, and thatched with Sapé leaves or roofed with tiles.

Camocim and Acaráu.[1] The strangers had hung their hammocks in the large cabin of the great Jacaúna. The brave Chief claimed for himself the pleasure of being the white warrior's host.

Poty abandoned his wigwam that he might accompany his brother of war to the cabin of his brother by blood, and to enjoy every moment that the sea-warrior could spare to devote to friendship from the love of Iraçéma.

Darkness had already left the face of the earth, but Martim saw that it had not left the face of his wife since the day of the combat.

"Sorrow lives in the soul of Iraçéma!"

"The wife's gladness can come only from her husband. When thy eyes leave Iraçéma's, tears fill them."

"Why weeps the daughter of the Tabajáras?"

"This is the Taba of the Pytiguáras, enemies of her people. The sight of Iraçéma still sees the skulls of her brothers staked round the Caiçára, her ears still listen to the death-song of the Tabajára captives, her hand still touches arms dyed with the blood of her fathers."

The bride placed her two hands on the warrior's shoulders and reclined upon his breast.

"Iraçéma will suffer all for her warrior and lord. The Atá fruit[2] is sweet and pleasant, but when bruised it sours. Thy wife would not that her love sour thy heart. She would fill it with the sweetness of honey."

"Let calm return to the breast of the daughter of the Tabajáras. She shall leave the Taba of her people's foes."

The Christian marched straight to the cabin of Jacaúna. The Great Chief was joyful on seeing his

---

[1] Two rivers of Ceará, discharging into the ocean.
[2] The *Atá*, custard-apple.

guest arrive, but joy soon fled from his warlike brow when Martim said—

"The white warrior is going to leave thy cabin, Great Chief."

"Then there is something wanting to him in the cabin of Jacaúna?"

"Thy guest hath wanted nothing. He was happy here; but the voice of his heart sends him to another place."

"Then leave, and take all that is needful for the journey. May Tupan fortify my brother, and bring him back again to the cabin of Jacaúna, that he may celebrate his wellcoming."

Poty arrived: hearing that the sea-warrior was going, he said—

"Thy brother will accompany thee."

"Will not Poty's warriors need their chief?"

"Unless my brother desires that they go with Poty, Jacaúna will lead them to victory."

"The cabin of Poty will be deserted and sad."

"The heart of the white brave's brother would be still more desert and sad without him."

The sea-warrior left the banks of the River of the Herons, and marched towards the land where the sun sets. His wife and friend followed his steps. They went beyond the fertile forest range, where the abundant fruits breed a swarm of flies, from which it takes the name of Meruoca.[1]

They crossed the little streams which discharge their waters into the River of the Herons, and they sighted on the far horizon a high mountain-range. The day expired; a black cloud seemed to be advancing from the sea. It was the Urubús,[2] that feast on the dead which the ocean throws up on the beach, and return with the night to their nests.

[1] *Meru-oca* means "the Fly's House." It is a Serra close to Sobral, fertile in all that is useful as food.

[2] *Urubú*, the Brazilian turkey-buzzard.

The travellers slept at Uruburetama.[1] When the sun reappeared, it found them on the banks of the river which rises in the Serra-gap, and descends winding like a serpent into the plain. Its mazes deceive, at every step, the pilgrims who follow its tortuous course; for which reason it was called the Mundahú.[2]

Following its cool banks, Martim, on the second sun, beheld the green seas and the white beaches, where the murmuring waves now sob, and then, raging with fury, break in flakes of foam.

The eyes of the white warrior dilated at the vast expanse, his chest heaved. This same sea also kissed the white sands of the Potengi,[3] his cradle, where he first saw the light of America. He threw himself into the waves, and revelled in the thought that he bathed his body in the waters of his native country, and his soul in yearning for it.

Iraçéma felt her heart weep, but soon her warrior's smile reassured her.

Meantime Poty from the top of a palm tree arrowed the savoury Camoropim,[4] which sported in the little bay of Mundahú, and prepared the Moquem for their refection.

CHAPTER XXI.

THE sun had already left the zenith. The travellers reach the mouth of that river where the savoury Tra-

---

[1] *Uruburetama*, a high mountain-range which swarms with vultures' nests.
[2] *Mundahú*, a tortuous river rising in the Serra of Uruburetama; from *mundé*, a snare, and *hû* or *û a* river.
[3] *Potengi*, the river that waters the city of Natal, a seaport town of Rio Grande do Norte, where Martim Soares Moreno was born.
[4] *Camoropim*, a large fish, tasting like a codfish.

hira [1] salmon breeds abundantly, and whose banks are peopled by fishermen of the great Pytiguára race.

They received the strangers with that generous hospitality which was a law of their religion, and Poty with the respect due to so great a warrior, and to a brother of Jacaúna, the most powerful Chief of the Pytiguáras.

To rest the travellers, and to dismiss them with proper ceremony, the Chief of the Tribe received Martim, Iraçéma, and Poty in the Jangada, and spreading a sail to the breeze, bore them far down the coast. All the fishermen in their rafts followed their Chief, and filled the air with a song of lament, accompanied by the murmurings of the Uraça,[2] which imitates the sobbing of the wind.

Beyond the fishing tribe, and nearer the Serras, was the hunting tribe. They occupied the borders of the Soipé,[3] covered with forests, where abounded deer, the fat Paca, and the slender Jacu.[4] Hence the dwellers of these regions had named it the Hunting-Ground.

Jaguarassú, or Great Tiger, the Chief of these hunters, had a Wigwam on the banks of the lake formed by the river as it nears the sea. Here the travellers met with the same warm reception which they had received from the fishermen.

After leaving Soipé, the travellers crossed the river

---

[1] *As saborosas trahiras.* The river Trahiry, from *trahira*, name of a savage fish, and *oy* water or river, is thirty leagues north of the capital of Ceará.

[2] *Uraça*, a sort of flute which they made of big shells.

[3] *Soipé*, hunting-ground, from *soo*, "game," and *ipé*, "the place where." Now it is called Siupé, and its river and village belong to the parish and township of Fortaleza. It is situated on the banks of marshes called Jaguarassú, at the mouth of the river.

[4] *Jacu (Crax Penelope)*, a large bird, of which there are four different kinds; it tastes and looks, when cooked, somewhat like, but much better than, our pheasant.

Pacoty,[1] on whose borders flourished the leafy banana, waving its green plumes.

Farther on is the Iguápe[2] stream, whose waters encircle the dunes of sand.

In the distance, crowning the horizon, appeared a high sand-hill, snowy white as the ocean foam. The summit overhung the palms and cocos, and appeared like the bald head of the Condor,[3] there awaiting the storm blowing up from the ocean bounds.

"Poty knows the great hill of sand?" asked the Christian.

"Poty knows all the land that belongs to the Pytiguáras, from the banks of the great river which forms an arm of the sea,[4] to the banks of the stream where the Jaguar lives. He has been already to the height of Mocoribe, and thence he has seen, far at sea, the big Igáras[5] of the white warriors, the enemies of my brother, who dwell in Mearim."

"Why callest thou the great sand-hill Mocoribe?"

"The fisherman of the beach, who puts out to sea in Jangádas, there where the Aty[6] flies, is sad because he is far from his cabin where sleep the children of his blood. When he returns, and his eyes first behold the hill of sand, gladness returns to the man's breath. Then he says that the hill of the sands gives joy."

---

[1] *Pacoty*, river of the Pacobas. It rises in the Serra of Baturité, and empties itself into the ocean, two leagues north of Aquirás. *Pacoba*, also called *Pacoeira* and *Musa*, is the indigenous banana of Brazil, a shrubby growth some ten or twelve feet high, and as thick as a man's thigh, yet so soft that it may be cut down with a single stroke of the sword.

[2] *Iguápe*, a bay distant two miles from Aquirás. The word, which is common in Brazil, means "water which encircles."

[3] The well-known and monstrous bird of the eagle species, with a very hard, sharp beak that will pierce a bull's hide.

[4] *Rio que forma um braço do mar*. This is the Parnahyba, the main river of Piauhy, and literally means "arm running from the sea."

[5] *Igáras*, big canoes, meaning the ships of the French.

[6] *Aty*, seagull.

"The fisherman says well; thy brother, like him, is happy when he sees the mountain of sand."

Martim and Poty ascended the head of Mocoribe. Iraçéma followed, with her eyes, her spouse, wandering like the Jaçanan [1] round the beautiful bay, which earth formed to receive the sea. On her way she collected the sweet Cajús, which appease the warriors' thirst, and gathered delicate shells to ornament her neck.

The travellers dwelt in Mocoribe three suns. Then Martim directed his steps beyond it. The wife and friend followed him to the bank of a river, whose banks were overflowed and covered with mangrove. The sea entering into it formed a basin of clear crystalline water, which appeared almost scooped out of the stone like a vase of pottery.

Whilst reconnoitring this place the Christian warrior began to reflect. To the present time he had marched without any object, and he had allowed his steps to guide him where they would. He had no other thought except to absent himself from the Taba of the Pytiguáras, that he might the better soothe the sorrow in Iraçéma's heart. The Christian knew by experience that travel cures a Saudade, because the soul rests whilst the body moves. But now seated on the beach he pondered.

Poty came.

"The white warrior thinks; the breast of his brother is open to receive his thought."

"Poty's brother thinks that this is a better place than the margins of Jaguaribe for the Taba of the warriors of his race. In these waters the big Igáras that come from the far-off land may lie sheltered from wind and sea: hence they can fall upon Mearim and destroy

---

[1] *Jaçanan*, a bird called in Africa a lily-trotter: here a waterhen, scarlet and green.

the white Tapuios,[1] the allies of the Tabajáras, enemies of Poty's nation."

The Pytiguára chief reflected and replied—

"My brother may go and bring his warriors. Poty will plant his Taba close to the Mayry[2] of his friend."

Iraçéma drew nigh. The Christian made a gesture of silence to the Pytiguára chief.

"The voice of the husband is silent, and his eyes fall when Iraçéma comes. Shall she depart?"

"Thy husband wants thee nearer, that his voice and eyes may penetrate still deeper into thy soul."

The beautiful savage was radiant with smiles, as the ripening flower opens its petals, and she leant upon the shoulder of her warrior.

"Iraçéma listens to thee."

"These plains are joyful, and will be more so when Iraçéma dwells in them. What says her heart?"

"Iraçéma's heart is ever glad when she is with her lord and warrior."

The Christian followed the bank of the river and chose a place for his Wigwam. Poty felled the Carnaúba to make props of its trunks; the daughter of Araken weaved, fanlike, the fronds of the palms to thatch the roof and cloth the walls. Martim dug the trenches, and made a door of laths and layers of bamboo.

When night came, the lovers slung their hammock in their new cabin, and the friend slept in the porch which faced the rising sun.]

---

[1] *Brancos tapuios;* in Tupy, *Tapuitininga.* A name the Pytiguáras gave to the French, to distinguish them from Tupinambás. The word means the "Deserters of their village."

[2] *Mayry,* city, comes from *mayr,* stranger, and was applied to the settlements of the whites to distinguish them from the Indian villages; in fact, a strangery.

E

CHAPTER XXII.

Poty saluted his friend and spoke as follows:—

"Ere the father of Jacaúna and Poty, the valiant warrior Jatobá, ruled over all the Pytiguára warriors, the Great Tomahawk of the Nation was in the right hand of Batuireté,[1] the Head Chief, Sire of Jatobá. It was he who came along the sea-beach to the river of the Jaguars, and expelled the Tabajáras into the interior, and dictated to each tribe the limits of its lands. Then he entered the inner regions as far as the Serra which takes his name.

"When his stars were many,[2] so many that his Camocim no longer contained all the nuts that mark the number of his years, his body began to incline earthwards, his arm stiffened like the branch of the unbending Ubiratan, and his eyes grew dark. He then called the warrior Jatobá and said, 'Let my son take the Tomahawk of the Pytiguára Nation. Tupan wills not that Batuireté should carry it any more to war, since he has taken from him the strength of his body, the use of his arm, and the light of his eyes. But Tupan has been good to him, since he gave him a son like the warrior Jatobá.'

"Jatobá took the Tomahawk of the Pytiguáras. Batuireté assumed the staff of his old age and set out. He crossed the vast uninhabited regions to the luxuriant prairies, where run the waters that come from the quarter of the night. As the old warrior dragged his limbs along their banks, and the light of his eyes would not let him behold nor the fruits, nor

---

[1] *Batuireté*, "celebrated snipe." The soubriquet of this great Chief signifies that he was a "brave swimmer." It is also the name of a very fertile Serra, and the region which he occupied.
[2] *Suas estrellas erão muitas.* The savages counted their years by the heliacal rising of the Pleiades, and also by keeping a cashew-nut of each spring.

the trees, nor the birds of the air, he said in his sadness, 'Ah! my bygone days!'"

"The people who heard him wept over the ruins of the Great Chief; and since then, whoever passes by that spot repeats his words, 'Ah! meus tempos passados;' for which reason the river and the prairie are called Quixeramobim.[1]

"Batuireté came from the 'Path of the Herons'[2] as far as that Serra which thou seest in the distance, and there he first lived. On the topmost peak the old warrior made his nest, as high as flies the hawk, to pass the remnant of his days speaking with Tupan. His son already sleeps under the earth, whilst he, even during the last moon, was thinking at his cabin door, to await the night which brings the Great Sleep. All the Pytiguára warriors, when the voice of war awakes them, visit and beg the old man that he will teach them to conquer; for no other warrior ever knew to fight as he did. Thus the tribes call him no more by his name, but know him as the Great Wise Man of War—Maranguab.[3]

"The chief Poty wants to visit the Serra to see his mighty Grandsire; but before day falls he will be back in the cabin of his brother. Has he any other wish?"

"The white warrior will accompany his brother. He wants to embrace the Great Chief of the Pytiguáras, Grandfather of Poty, and to tell the old man that he lives again in his grandson."

Martim called Iraçéma, and they both set out,

---

[1] *Quixeramobim*, translated into Portuguese, means, "Ah! meus outros tempos;" in English, "Ah! my other times."

[2] *Caminho dos garças*, or flight of the herons, in Tupy is *Acarapé*, a village in the parish of Batuireté, nine leagues from the capital of Ceará.

[3] *Maranguab* means "to war" and "wise man." Maranguape, five leagues' distant from the capital, is noted for its beauty and fertility.

guided by the Pytiguára, to the Serra of Maranguab, which loomed above the horizon. They followed the course of the river to the place where it is joined by the stream of Pirapora.[1]

The cabin of the old warrior was close to one of those beautiful cascades where the fish leap in the midst of the bubbling foam. The waters here are fresh and sweet, like the sea-breeze in the hour of heat, murmuring amongst the palm-leaves.

Batuireté was sitting upon one of the cascade rocks; the burning sun-rays fell full upon his head, which was bald and wrinkled as the Genipapo.[2] Thus sleeps the Jaburú[3] at the edge of the tank.

"Poty has arrived at the cabin of the great Maranguab, father of Jatobá, and has brought his white brother to see the greatest Warrior of the Nations."

The old man only opened his heavy eyelids, and passed a long but feeble look from the grandson to the stranger. Then his chest heaved and his lips murmured—

"Tupan wills that these eyes should see, before being quenched, the White Hawk side by side with the Narseja."[4]

The Abaeté dropped his head on his chest, and spoke no more, nor moved again.

Poty and Martim, supposing that he slept, respectfully withdrew, not to disturb the repose of one who

---

[1] *Pirapora*, a river of Maranguape, noted for the freshness of its waters and the excellence of its baths. They are in the environs of the Cachoeiras (rapids, cataracts, or waterfalls), and are called the "Baths of Pirapora." The word means "fish-leap."

[2] *Genipapo*, a well-known Brazilian tree, whose fruit produces a dark dye with which the Indians used to tattoo themselves.

[3] *Jaburú*, a large crane.

[4] *O gavião branco*, the white hawk, whilst *Narseja* is the snipe. Batuireté thus calling the stranger, and speaking of his grandson as a snipe by comparison, prophesied the destruction of his race by the whites. It was the last word he spoke.

had done such deeds during his long life. Iraçéma, who had bathed in the nearest Cachoeira, came to meet them, bringing combs of the purest honey in a leaf of the Taioba.[1]

The friends wandered about the flourishing environs till the shade of the mountain darkened the valley. They then returned to the spot where they had left the Maranguab.

The old man was still there in the same attitude, with his head bent on his chest and his crossed knees supporting his forehead. The ants were running up his body, and the Tuins [2] were fluttering around him and settling upon his bald head.

Poty placed his hand on the old man's head, and felt that he was dead. He had died of old age.

The Pytiguára Chief then intoned the Song of Death; presently he went into the cabin to fetch the Camoçim, which was filled to overflowing with nuts of Cajú. Martim counted five times five handfuls.

Meanwhile, Iraçéma gathered in the forest the Andiroba,[3] with which to anoint the body of the old man in the Camoçim, where the dutiful hand of his grandson placed him. The Funeral Vase remained suspended to the cabin roof.

They then planted the Ortiga, or large stinging nettle, before the doorway, to defend against animals the abandoned Oca.[4] Poty bade a sorrowful farewell to these scenes, and returned with his companions to the borders of the sea.

[1] *Taioba*, a bush with large leaves, from *ca*, tree, and *oba*, dress, clothing.
[2] *Tuins* in Brazil is a kind of little parrot.
[3] *Andiroba*, a large tree, native of Brazil, which is of an aromatic nature, and gives a bitter oil.
[4] *Oca*, house, cabin, wigwam.

CHAPTER XXIII.

Four moons had lighted the heavens since Iraçéma had left the plains of Ipú, and three since she had dwelt in the Wigwam of her husband by the shore of the sea.

Gladness dwelt within her soul. The daughter of the forest was happy as the swallow that abandons its paternal nest and goes forth to build a new home in the land where the flower-season begins. Iraçema likewise found there, on the sea-shore, a nest of love—the heart's new country!

She wandered over the beautiful plains like the humming-bird hovering amongst the flowers of the acacia. The light of early morning found her already clinging to the shoulder of her husband, ever smiling, like the Enrediça,[1] which twines round the tree-trunk, and which covers it with a new garland every morning.

Martim went out to hunt with Poty. He then separated himself from her in order to have the pleasure of returning to her.

In the middle of a green pasture hard by was a beautiful lake, to which the wild girl used to direct her light step. It was the hour of the morning bath. She would cast herself into the water, and swim with the white herons and the scarlet Jaçanans. The Pytiguára warriors who chanced to come that way called this the "Lake of Beauty," because it was bathed in by Iraçéma, the most beautiful of the race of Tupan.

And from that time till now, mothers come from afar to dip their daughters in the waters of the Por-

---

[1] *Enrediça*, a creeper which entwines and entangles round a tree-trunk.

angába,[1] which they suppose have the virtue of making the virgins beautiful and beloved by the braves.

After the bath Iraçéma wandered to the skirts of the Serra of Maranguab, where rises the river of the Marrecas.[2] There in the cool shade grew the most savoury fruits of the country; she would collect a plentiful supply, and rock herself in the branches of the Maracujá-tree, waiting for Martim to return from hunting.

Her fancy did not always, however, lead her to the Jerarahú,[3] but often to the opposite side, close to the lake of the Sapiranga,[4] whose waters are said to inflame the eyes. Near it was a wood, thick and leafy, with clumps of Muritys, which formed in the middle of the plateau a large island of beautiful palms. Iraçéma loved the Murityapúa,[5] where the wind blew softly. Here she stripped the pulp from the red Coco to make refreshing drinks, mixed with the bee-honey, which the warriors liked to drink in the great heat of the day.

One morning Poty guided Martim to the chase. They marched towards a Serra which towers on the opposite side to Maranguab, its twin sister. The highest peak bends like the hooked beak of the macaw, and hence the warriors named it Aratanha.[6]

---

[1] *Porangaba* means beauty; it is a lake in a delightful spot, distant one league from the City. Now it is called Arronches; on its banks is a decayed village of the same name.

[2] *Marrecas*, wild ducks.

[3] *Jerarahú*, "river of the wild ducks." This place is even now notable for its delicious fruits, especially the beautiful oranges known as the oranges of Jerarahú.

[4] *Sapiranga*, which means "red eyes," and they also call by this name a certain ophthalmia in the North. It is a lake close to Alagadiço Novo, about two leagues from the Capital.

[5] *Murityapúa*, where there is now a small town. The word is from *murity*, palm, and *apúam*, an island or clump.

[6] *Aratanha*, from *arara*, a macaw, and *tanha*, teeth. A fertile and cultivated Serra, which is a continuation of Maranguape.

They mounted by the side of Guaiuba,[1] whence the waters descend into the valley, and they went to the stream where the Pacas are to be found.

The sun shone on the Macaw's Beak only when the hunters descended from Pacatuba[2] to the plateau. From afar they saw Iraçéma, who came to wait for them on the margin of her lake, the Porangába. She came towards them with the proud step of the heron stalking by the water's edge. Outside her Carioba she wore a belt of Maniva, the flowers of which are an emblem of fruitfulness. A festoon of the same flowers twined round her throat and fell over her marble bosom.

She seized the hand of her husband and carried it to her lips.

"Thy blood lives in the bosom of Iraçéma. She will be the mother of thy son."

"*Son* saidst thou?" exclaimed the Christian with joy.

Kneeling down, he threw his arm around her and kissed her, mutely thanking God for this great happiness.

When he arose Poty spoke—

"The happiness of the young brave is a wife and a friend; the first gives gladness, the second gives strength. The warrior without a spouse is like a tree lacking leaves and flowers; never shall he behold its fruit. The brave without a friend is like the solitary tree waving in the midst of the prairie with each blast of wind; its fruit never ripens. The happiness of the strong man is the offspring which is born to him, and which is his pride. Every warrior of his blood is one branch more to raise up his name to the sky, like the

---

[1] *Guaiuba*, which means "whence come the waters of the valley," is a river rising in the Serra of Aratanha, and crossing the village of the same name, six leagues from the capital.

[2] *Pacatuba*, "bed of the Pacas." There is now a new but important village in a beautiful valley of the Serra of Aratanha.

top branch of the cedar. Beloved by Tupan is the warrior who has a wife, a friend, and many sons. He has nothing more to desire save a glorious death."

Martim pressed his bosom to that of Poty.

"The heart of both husband and friend speaks by the mouth of Poty. The white warrior is blest, O Chief of the Pytiguáras, Lords of the Sea-shores; and happiness was born to him in the Land of the Palm-trees, where the Baúnilha perfumes the air; it was begotten by the blood of thy race, who bear on their faces the colour of the sun's ray. The white warrior no longer desires any other country save the land of his son and of his heart."

At the break of dawn Poty set out to gather the seeds of the Crajurú,[1] which yields a most beautiful red dye, and the bark of the Angico, whence is extracted a lustrous black. On the way his unerring arrow brought down a wild duck sailing in the air, and he took from its wings the longest feathers. He then ascended Mocoribe and sounded the Inubia. The sea-breeze carried far the hoarse sound. The Shell of the Fishermen of the Trahiry and the Horn of the Hunters of the Soipé gave answer.

Martim bathed in the river waters, and walked on the beach to dry himself in the wind and sun. By his side ran Iraçéma, collecting the yellow ambergris[2] cast up by the sea. Every night the wife perfumed her body and the white hammock, that the love of the warrior might remain captivated.

Poty returned.

[1] *Crajurú*, a tree whose seeds give a scarlet dye.
[2] *Ambar.* The sea-beach of Ceará was at that time full of ambergris, cast up by the sea. The savages call it *Pirarepoti*, "the secretion of a fish."

CHAPTER XXIV.

It was customary amongst the race of Tupan for the brave to wear on his body the colours of his nation. They first traced upon the skin black lines like those of the Coaty,[1] whence came the name of the War-painting art. They also varied the colours, and many warriors were covered with emblems of their deeds.

The stranger having adopted the country of his spouse and his friend, was expected to pass through this ceremony in order to become a redskin warrior and a son of Tupan. With this intention Poty had provided for himself the necessary objects.

Iraçéma prepared the dyes, the Chief dipping in them the feathers, traced over the warrior's body the red and black lines, the Pytiguára colours. He then drew on his forehead an arrow, and said—

"As the arrow pierces the hard trunk, so the warrior's eye penetrates the soul of the people."

On the arm a hawk.

"As the Anajê swoops from the clouds, so falls the warrior's arm upon the enemy."

On the left foot the root of a palm tree.

"As the little root supports in the ground the lofty palm tree, thus the firm foot of the warrior sustains his frame."

On the right foot a wing.

"As the wing of the Majoy[2] cleaves the air, thus the fleet foot of the warrior has no equal in the race."

---

[1] *Coaty*, a small fox-like animal, a racoon, whose hide has a red ground with black stripes. *Coatyara*, he who paints; *coatyá*, to paint; *coatyabo*, he who is painted. History mentions the fact that Martim Soares Moreno painted and dressed like the savages of Ceará whilst he was living amongst them.

[2] *Majoy*, swallow.

Iraçéma then took the feather-vane, and painted a leaf with a bee upon it: her voice murmured through her smiles—

"As the bee makes honey in the black heart of the Jacarandá, so sweetness is in the breast of the bravest warrior."

Martim opened his arms and lips to receive the body and soul of his wife.

"My brother is a great warrior of the Pytiguára nation. He wants a name in the language of his new country."

"The name of thy brother shall be called by whatever part of his body thou imposest thy hand upon."

"Coatyábo!" exclaimed Iraçéma.

"Thou hast said it. I am the painted warrior, the warrior of the wife and of the friend."

Poty gave to his brother the bow and the tomahawk, which were the noble arms of a brave. Iraçéma had prepared for him the plumes and ornamented belt worn by illustrious Chiefs.

The daughter of Araken fetched from the cabin the meats of the feast and the wines of the Genipapo and Mandioca. The warriors drank copiously and danced joyous dances. Whilst they revolved round the bonfires they sang songs of gladness.

Poty chanted.

"As the Cobra-Snake which has two heads and only one body, so is the friendship of Coatyábo and Poty."

Iraçéma took up the refrain.

"As the oyster which leaves not the rock until after death, so is Iraçéma joined to her husband."

The warriors chanted.

"As the Jatobá in the forest, so is the warrior Coatyábo between his brother and spouse; his branches entwine with those of the Ubiratan, and his shade protects the humble grass."

The fires of joy burnt until morning came, and with them lasted the Feast of the Warriors.

CHAPTER XXV.

Joy still reigned in the cabin during the whole time whilst the ears of corn ripened and waxed yellow.

Once at break of day the Christian was strolling by the borders of the sea. His soul was weary.

The humming-bird satiates itself with honey and perfume; it then sleeps in its little white nest of cotton, until another year comes round with its Moon of Flowers. Like it, the warrior's soul is sated with happiness; it wants sleep and repose.

Hunting and excursions in the mountains with his friend by his side, the tender caresses of the wife awaiting his return, the pleasant Carbeto[1] in the Wigwam porch, no longer awakened in him emotions as they were wont to do. His heart began to speak.

Iraçéma was sporting on the beach. His eyes wandered from her over the sea's vast expanse.

Large white wings were seen hovering over the blue waste. The Christian knew that it was a big Igára of many sails, such as were constructed by his brethren, and the Saudade of his country wrung his breast.

High rose the sun; the warrior on the shore followed with his eyes the white wings as they fled. In vain the wife called him to the hut, in vain she displayed to his eyes her graces, or offered him the best fruits of the country. The warrior never moved until the sail disappeared behind the horizon.

Poty returned from the Serra, where for the first time he had been alone. He had left serenity on his brother's countenance, and now he found there sorrow. Martim went forth to meet him.

"The great Igára of the white Tapúia is on the sea. The eyes of Poty's brother saw them flying

---

[1] *Carbeto*, a sort of evening meeting of the Indians in a large cabin where they used to converse.

towards the banks of the Mearim. They are the allies of the Tupinambás [1] and the enemies of his and my race."

"Poty is lord of a thousand bows; if Coatyabo wishes, he will accompany him with his braves to the banks of the Mearim to conquer the Tapúitinga, and his friends the treacherous Tupinambás."

"When it is time, Poty's brother will tell him."

The warriors returned to the cabin where Iraçéma was. The sweet song to-day was silent on the wife's lips. She wove amidst her sighs the fringe of the maternal hammock, broader and thicker than the marriage-cot. Poty, who saw her thus occupied, spoke.

"When the Sabiá sings, it is the season of love. When, silent, it makes the nest for the little one: it is the time for work."

"My brother speaks like the Ran [2] announcing the rain, but the Sabiá which makes its nest does not know if it will sleep in it."

The voice of Iraçéma trembled. Her eye sought Martim. He was thinking. The words of Iraçéma passed over him like the breeze upon the smooth surface of the rocks, noiseless and echoless.

The sun still shone on the sea-beach, and the sands reflected its ardent rays, but neither the light which came from heaven nor that which earth gave could drive darkness from the Christian's soul. Every moment the twilight deepened on his forehead.

Arrived from the banks of the Acaraú a Pytiguára warrior, sent by Jacaúna to his brother Poty. He had followed the warriors' trail as far as the Trahiry, whence the Fishermen had guided him to the Wigwam.

---

[1] *Tupinambás* means fathers of the Tupys, a formidable nation, the primitive branch of the great Tupy race. After an heroic resistance, not being able to expel the Portuguese from Bahia, they migrated to Maranhão, where they formed alliance with the French, who overran these regions.

[2] *Ran*, frog.

Poty was alone in the porch. He rose up and bent his head, to listen with more gravity and respect to the words which his brother had sent him by the mouth of the messenger.

"The Tapuitinga who was in the Mearim came through the forests as far as the beginning of the Ibyapába, where he had made an alliance with Irapúam to fight the Pytiguára nation. They are coming down the Serra to the banks of the river where the herons drink, and where Poty raised the Tabá of his warriors. Jacaúna now summons him to defend the lands of our fathers, and his people want their greatest warrior."

"The warrior must return to the banks of Acaraú, and his foot must not rest until it has trodden the floor of Jacaúna's Wigwam. When he arrives, he will say to the great chief, '*Jacaúna's brother has arrived at the Taba of his warriors*'—and he will not lie."

The messenger departed.

Poty aroused himself, and walked towards the plains, guided by the trail of Coatyabo. He met him far beyond, wandering amongst the reeds and rushes which border the banks of Jacaratuy.[1]

"The white Tapuia is in the Ibyapába, to help the Tabajáras against Jacaúna. Poty is hastening to defend the land of his brothers, and the Taba where sleep the Camocins of his fathers. He will know how to conquer quickly, in order to return to Coatyábo."

"Poty's brother goes with him. Nothing separates two warrior-friends when sounds the Inubia of war."

"My brother is great like the sea, and good like the sky."

The two friends embraced, and marched with their faces turned to the quarter of the rising sun.

---

[1] *Jacaratuy*, a lake near the present town of Ceará.

CHAPTER XXVI.

Walking—ever walking—the braves arrived at the borders of a lake which was in the plateau-land.

The Christian suddenly stopped and turned his face towards the sea. The sadness left his heart and rose to his forehead.

"My brother's foot has taken root in the Land of Love," said the Chief. "Let him remain. Poty will quickly return."

"Poty's brother will accompany him. He has said it, and his word is like the arrow of Poty's bow; when it whistles, it has already pierced the mark."

"Does my brother then wish that Iraçéma should accompany him to the banks of the Acaraú?"

"We go to fight her brothers. The Taba of the Pytiguáras would only be to her a scene of pain and sadness. The daughter of the Tabajáras should remain."

"What then does Coatyábo await?"

"Poty's brother is afflicted because the daughter of the Tabajáras may be sad, and abandon the Wigwam without awaiting his return. Before departing, he would wish to soothe the spirit of the wife."

Poty took thought.

"The tears of Woman soften the warrior's heart as the morning dew softens the Earth."

"My brother is wise. The husband must go without seeing Iraçéma."

The Christian advanced. Poty bid him stop. From the Aljava[1] which Iraçéma had adorned with black and red feathers, and had placed on her husband's shoulders, he selected an arrow.

The Pytiguára drew the bow; the fleet arrow pierced

---

[1] *Aljava*, Arabic and Portuguese word for quiver.

a Goiamum[1] which was running on the banks of the lake, and stopped only where the feathers would not allow it to enter farther.

The warrior thrust the arrow into the ground with the prey transfixed and turned towards Coatyábo.

"My brother may now set out contentedly. Iraçéma will follow his trail; arriving here, she will see his arrow and obey his will."

Martim smiled; and breaking a branch of the Maracujá—the flower of remembrance—he twined it round the arrow and advanced, followed by Poty.

Soon the two warriors disappeared amongst the trees; the heat of the sun had already dried their footsteps on the banks of the lake. Iraçéma became uneasy, and followed her husband's trail as far as the tableland. Gentle shades already mottled the prairies when she reached the brink of the lake. Her eyes detected the arrow of her husband thrust into the ground, and the pierced Goiamum with the broken branch, and they filled with tears.

"He commands Iraçéma to go backwards like the Goiamum, and to keep his remembrance like the Maracujá, which retains its flower until death."

The daughter of the Tabajáras slowly retraced her steps backwards without turning her body, and never taking her eyes off the arrow of her warrior till she reached the cabin. Here she sat down on the threshold, and bent her forehead on her knees, till sleep soothed the pain in her breast. Hardly had the day broken, when she directed her hasty steps to the lake, and arrived at its bank. The arrow was still there, as it had been the evening before. Then he had not returned.

From this time till the bath hour, instead of seeking the lake of beauty, where hitherto she had bathed with such pleasure, she came to that which had seen

---

[1] *Goiamum*, a large Brazilian crab which courses backwards.

her husband abandon her. She would sit down close to the arrow until night came, and then seek the cabin.

She would set out in early morning, as hurriedly as she would return slowly in the evening. The same warriors who had seen her so joyous in the waters of Porangába now met her sad and alone, like the widowed heron on the river-banks. Hence they called the spot, "of the Mocejana,"[1] or "of the forsaken."

One day when the beautiful daughter of Araken was lamenting on the brink of the Mocejana Lake, a strident voice from the top of a Carnaúba cried out her name—

"Iracéma! Iracéma!"

Raising her eyes, she saw amongst the palm-fronds her beautiful Jandáia flapping its wings and ruffling its feathers with the joy of seeing her.

The remembrance of her country, extinguished by love, burned again in her thoughts. She saw the beautiful plains of the Ipú; the sides of the mountain-range where she was born, and the Wigwam of Araken; and she felt Saudades; but even at this moment she did not repent of having abandoned them.

Her voice gushed forth in song. The Jandáia opened its wings, fluttered around, and settled on her shoulder. It stretched its neck and rubbed itself against her throat; it smoothed her hair with its black beak, and pecked her small red lips, as if it mistook them for a Pitanga.[2]

Iracéma remembered how ungrateful she had been to the Jandáia, forgetting it at the time of her happiness, and now it came to console her in her sorrow.

This evening she did not return alone to the cabin,

---

[1] *Mocejana* is a lake and village two leagues from the capital of Ceará. The word means "what made abandon," "the place of abandoning," and "occasion of abandoning."

[2] A small red fruit in Brazil, the *Pitanga* myrtle berry.

and all next day her agile fingers wove a beautiful cage of straw, which she lined with the soft wool of the Monguba,[1] to receive her companion and friend.

On the following dawn the voice of the Jandáia awoke her. The beautiful bird left its mistress no more, either because it could never weary of seeing her after so long an absence, or because instinct told it that she needed a companion in her sad solitude.

CHAPTER XXVII.

ONE evening Iraçéma saw from afar two warriors advancing on the sea-beach. Her heart beat more quickly.

An instant afterwards, she forgot in the arms of her husband the many days of yearning and desolation which she had passed in the solitary Wigwam.

Again her graces and endearments filled the eyes of the Christian, and gladness once more dwelt in his soul.

Like the dry plain, which, when the thick fog comes, grows green again and is spangled with flowers, so the beautiful daughter of the forest revived at the return of her husband, and her beauty was adorned with soft and tender smiles.

Martim and his brother had arrived at the Taba of Jacaúna as the Inúbia was sounding. They led Poty's thousand bowmen to the combat. Again the Tabajáras, in spite of the alliance with the white Tapuias of the Mearim, were overcome by the brave Pytiguáras.

Never had such an obstinate fight been fought,

---

[1] *Monguba*, a tree with its fruit full of downy cotton, like that of the Sumaúma, only black, which gives its name to part of the Serra of Maranguape.

nor had so disputed a victory been won on the plains watered by the Acaraú and the Camoçim. The valour was equal on both sides, and neither nation would have been victor, had not the God of War already decided to give these shores to the race of the white warrior allied to the Pytiguáras.

Immediately after triumphing, the Christian returned to the sea-beach where he had built his Wigwam. He felt anew in his soul the thirst of love, and he trembled to think that Iraçéma might have deserted the place which had formerly been peopled by happiness.

The Christian loved the Daughter of the Forest once more, as at first, when it appeared that time could not exhaust his heart. But a few short suns sufficed to wither these flowers of a heart exiled from its country.

The Imbú,[1] son of the mountains, if it spring up in the plains where the wind or the birds have borne its seed, finding good and fresh ground, may perhaps one day dome itself with green foliage and bear flowers. But a single breath of the sea suffices to wither it; the leaves strew the ground, the blossoms are carried away by the breeze.

Like the Imbú on the plains was the heart of the white warrior in the savage land. Friendship and love had accompanied him and sustained him for a time; now, however, far from his home and his people, he felt himself in a desert. The friend and the wife did not suffice any longer to his existence, full of great and noble projects of ambition.

He passed the suns, once so short, now so long, on the beach, listening to the moaning of the wind and the sobbing of the waves. His eyes, lost in the immensity of the horizon, sought, but in vain, to espy

---

[1] *Imbú*, a fruit growing abundantly on the Serra of Araripe, not on the shore; it is savoury, and resembles the Cajá (see note 1, page 12).

upon the transparent blue the whiteness of a sail wandering over the seas. At a short distance from the cabin, at the edge of the ocean, was a dune of sand. The fishermen called it Jacarécanga,[1] on account of its resemblance to a crocodile's head. From the bosom of the white sands scorched by the ardent sun flowed a pure fresh water; thus pain distils sweet tears of relief and consolation. To this hill the Christian would repair, and remain there meditating upon his destiny. Sometimes the idea of returning to his own country and people would cross his mind, but he knew that Iraçéma would accompany him, and this thought gnawed his heart. Each step that took Iraçéma farther from her native plains, now that she no longer could nestle in his heart, was to rob her of a portion of her life.

Poty knows that Martim desires to be alone, and discreetly withdraws. The warrior knows what afflicts his brother's soul, and hopes all things from time, which alone hardens the warrior's heart, like the core of the Jacarandá.

Iraçéma also avoids the eyes of her husband, because she already perceives that those eyes, so much loved, are troubled at her sight, and, instead of filling with delight at her beauty as formerly, now seem to turn wearily away. But *her* eyes never tire of following apart, and at a distance, her Lord and Warrior, who had made them captive.

Woe to her! . . . The blow had struck home to her heart, and, like the Copaiba,[2] wounded in the core, she shed tears in one continuous stream.

---

[1] *Jacarécanga*, a hill of white sand on the beach at Ceará, famed for a fountain of pure fresh water. The word means "crocodile's head."

[2] *Copaiba*, a sort of sovereign balsam—copayva.

CHAPTER XXVIII.

Once the sobs of Iraçéma reached the Christian's soul. His eyes sought her all around, and could not find her.

The daughter of Araken was sitting at some distance upon the turfy grass in the midst of a green clump of Ubaias; weeping veiled her beautiful face, and the teardrops that rolled down her cheeks one after another fell upon her bosom where the offspring of love already breathed and grew. Thus fall the leaves of the flourishing tree before the ripening of its fruit.

"What wrings the tears from the heart of Iraçema?"

"The Cajueiro[1] weeps and is sad when it becomes a dry trunk. Iraçéma lost her happiness when her Lord separated from her."

"Am I not near thee?"

"The *body* of Coatyábo is here, but his soul flies to the Land of his Fathers, and seeks the white virgin who awaits him."

Martim was grieved. The large black eyes that the Indian fixed on him pierced him to the heart's core.

"The White Warrior is *thy* husband; he belongs to *thee*."

The beautiful Tabajára smiled in her sorrow.

"How long is it that he has withdrawn his spirit from Iraçéma? Once his feet guided him to the cool Serras and the glad tablelands; his foot loved to tread the land of happiness and to follow the steps of his wife; now he seeks alone the scorching sands, because the sea which murmurs there comes from the plains where he was born, and the hill of sand, because from its top he can descry the passing Igára."

[1] The tree of the *Cajú*.

"It is his anxiety to fight the Tupinambá which guides the warrior's steps to the borders of the sea," said the Christian.

Iraçéma continued—

"His lip has dried towards his wife, as the sugar-cane when the great suns burn; it then loses its sweet honey, and the withered leaves play never more in the wind. Now he only speaks to the sea-beach breeze, that it may carry back his voice to the Cabin of his Fathers."

"The voice of the White Warrior is only calling his brothers to defend the cabin of Iraçéma and the land of his son when the enemy shall come!"

The wife shook her head.

"When Coatyábo walks in the plains, his eyes avoid the fruit of the Genipapo, and seeks the white thorn; its fruit is savoury, but it has the colour of the Tabajáras. The thorn bears a white flower, like the cheeks of the pale virgin. If the birds sing, his ear no longer cares to listen to the sweet song of the Graúna, but he opens his soul to the cry of the Japim,[1] because it has golden feathers like the hair of her whom he loves."

"Sorrow dims the sight of Iraçéma and embitters her lip. But gladness will soon return to the wife's soul, as the green leaves bud again on the tree."

"When the White Warrior's son has left the bosom of Iraçéma she will die, like the Abaty[2] after it has yielded its fruit. Then he will have nothing to detain him in a foreign land."

"Thy voice burns, daughter of Araken, like the winds which blow in the great heat from the deserts of Ico.[3] Wouldst thou abandon thy husband?"

"Does the white warrior see that beautiful Jacarandá which rises to the clouds? At its feet still lies the

---

[1] *Japim*, a golden bird with black specks, whose name signifies "to suffer."

[2] *Abaty* means rice.

[3] *Ico*, a south-eastern portion of the province of Ceará.

dry root of the leafy myrtle, which every winter bears foliage and red berries to embrace and cover its brother tree. If it did not die, the Jacarandá would not have sun enough to reach that height. Iracéma is the Folha escura[1] which creates darkness in Coatyabo's soul. She must fall, that gladness may shine within his breast."

The Christian threw his arms round the waist of the beautiful Indian and strained her to his heart. His lips sought hers in a kiss, but it was harsh and bitter.

CHAPTER XXIX.

Poty returned from the bath. He follows the trail of Coatyábo in the sand, and ascends the height of Jacarécanga. Here he finds the warrior on the summit, standing upright, with his eyes straining, and his arms stretched towards the broad seas.

The Pytiguára follows his gaze, and discovers a large Igára ploughing the green waters and driven on by the wind.

"It is the great Igára of my brother's Nation sent to seek him."

The Christian sighed.

"They are the White Warriors, enemies of his race, who seek, for a war of vengeance, the shores of the brave Pytiguára nation. They were routed with the Tabajáras on the banks of the Camoçim. Now they come with their friends the Tupinambás by the way of the sea."

"My brother is a Great Chief. What thinks he that his brother Poty should do?"

[1] *Folha escura*, the myrtle which the Indians call Capixuna or dark-leaved. Iracéma used it as a symbol of the ennui she produced in her husband.

"Summon the Hunters of the Soipé and the Fishers the Trahiry. We will hasten to encounter them."

Poty awoke the voice of the Inubia, and the two warriors set out for Mocoribe.

Soon they saw hastening from all parts the braves of Jaguarassú and Camoropim to respond to the War-cry. The brother of Jacaúna warned them of the enemy's approach.

The great Maracatim [1] flew upon the waters along the coast, which extends as far as the margins of the Parnahyba.[2]

The moon began to increase; when the ship left the waters of the Mearim, contrary winds drove it into the high seas, far beyond its destination.

The Pytiguára warriors, in order not to startle the enemy, hide themselves amongst the Cajueiros, and follow the great Igára along the shore. During the day the white sails are conspicuous, and by night the ship's lights pierced the sea's darkness like fireflies lost in the forest.

Many suns they marched thus. They pass beyond the Camoçim, and at last they tread the beautiful shores of the Bay of Parrots.[3]

Poty sends a warrior to the great Jacaúna and prepares for the combat. Martim, who had mounted the hill of sand, knew that the Maracatim would seek shelter under the lee of the land, and warns his brother.

The sun was already rising. The Guaraciaba [4] warriors and their friends the Tupinambás run along

---

[1] *Maracatim* is a large ship which rises at the prow. Little boats or canoes were called Igára, meaning "lady of the water."

[2] *Parnahyba*, a large river of Piauhy, on the north coast of Brazil.

[3] *Bahia dos papagaios*. It is the Bay of Jericoacoara, and means "Bay of the plain of the parrots," and is one of the best parts of Ceará.

[4] *Guaraciaba* means "yellow-haired." These were the French settlers at Maranhão.

the waves in light Pirogos[1] to make the shore. They form a great arch, like a shoal of fish crossing the current of a river.

In the middle are the fire-warriors,[2] who carry the lightning; on each wing the warriors of Mearim, who brandish the tomahawk. But no nation ever drew the bow so unerringly as the great Pytiguáras, and Poty was the greatest Chief of all the Chiefs who carried the Inubia of war. At his side marches his brother, as great a Chief as himself, and learned in the stratagems of the white race, with hair like the sun.

During the night the Pytiguáras had by his directions fixed into the beach a strong Caiçára, or stockade of thorns, and had raised against it a wall of sand, where the "lightning" might cool and extinguish itself. Here they await the foe. Martim orders other warriors to man the tops of the highest palms, and there, screened by the broad fronds, to make ready for the moment of attack.

The arrow of Poty was the first which left the beach, and the Guaraciába chief was the first hero that bit the dust upon the strange soil.

The thunders roar from the right of the white warriors, but the bolts only burrow themselves in the sand or dive into the sea.

The Pytiguára arrows now fall from the heavens, then they fly from the earth and bury themselves in the enemies' hearts. Each warrior falls riddled with many arrows, like the prey for which the Piranhas[3] fight in the waters of the lake.

The enemy once more embark in the canoes, and return to the Maracatim to fetch bigger and heavier thunders, which neither one man nor two could manage.

[1] *Pirogos*, canoes.
[2] *Guerreiros do fogo*—the French, from their guns.
[3] *Piranha*, a fresh-water fish, a ferocious kind of salmon. It lives in lakes and dead waters, and has teeth which bite like scissors.

When they were returning, the Chief of the Fishers, who swims in the sea-waters like the agile Camoropim, from whom he took his name, casts himself into the waves and dives. Before the foam had passed away from the place where he disappeared, the enemy's canoe had sunk as if it had been swallowed by a whale.

The night came and brought with it repose.

At dawn of day, the Maracatim was flying in the horizon towards the banks of the Mearim. Jacaúna arrived, not in time for the fight, but for the feast of victory.

At the same hour that the songs of the Pytiguára warriors were celebrating the conquest of the Guaraciábas, the first son born to this Land of Liberty begotten by the blood of the white race, saw the light in the plains of Porangába.

CHAPTER XXX.

IRAÇÉMA thought that her bosom would burst. She sought the banks of the river where grows the Coqueiro-palm, and clasped the trunk of the tree till a tiny cry inundated her whole being with joy.

The young mother, proud of so much happiness, took the tender one in her arms, and with him cast herself into the limpid waters of the river. Then she gave him the delicate breast, and her eyes devoured him with sorrow and love.

"Thou art Moacyr,[1] the fruit of my anguish."

The Jandáia perched at the top of the palm tree repeated "Moacyr;" and from that time the friendly bird united in its song the names of both mother and son.

[1] *Moacyr* or "son of suffering," from *moacy*, pain, and *ira*, a desinence meaning "that comes from."

The innocent slept; Iraçéma sighed.

"The Jaty makes honey in the sweet-smelling trunk of the Sassafrax;[1] during the month of flowers it flies from branch to branch collecting the juice to fill the comb, but it does not taste its sweetness's reward, because the Irára[2] devours in one night the whole swarm. Thy mother, also, child of my sorrow, will never taste the joy of seeing the smile on thy lips."

The young mother fastened over her shoulders a broad swathe[3] of soft cotton, which she had made to carry her child always fastened upon her hip. She then followed over the sands the trail of her spouse, who had been gone three suns. She walked gently, not to awake the little one, that slept like a bird under the maternal wing.

When she arrived at the great hill of sand, she saw that the trail of Martim and Poty continued along the beach, and guessed that they were gone to the war. Her heart sighed, but her eyes sought the face of her babe.

She turned her face back towards the Mocoribe.

"Thou art the Hill of Gladness, but for Iraçéma thou bringest nothing but sorrow."

Returning, the mother placed the still-sleeping child in his father's hammock, widowed and solitary, in the cabin centre. She lay down upon the mat where she had slept since the time her husband's arms had ceased opening to receive her.

The morning light entered the cabin. Iraçéma saw the shade of a warrior come in with it.

Cauby was standing in the doorway.

---

[1] *Sassafrax*, a well-known tree, growing both in North and South America, much used in medicine.
[2] *Irára*, a kind of bush-dog, which attacks beehives and devours the honey.
[3] *Faxa*, vulgarly called *Typoia;* swathing or swaddling clothes.

The wife of Martim sprang up with one bound to protect her child. Her brother raised his sad eyes from the hammock to her face, and spoke with a still sadder voice.

"It was not vengeance which drew the warrior Cauby to the plains of the Tabajáras; he has already forgiven. It was a longing to see Iraçéma, who took away with her all his gladness."

"Then welcome be the warrior Cauby to the cabin of his brother," said the wife, embracing him.

"The fruit of thy bosom sleeps in this hammock, and the eyes of Cauby long to behold it."

Iraçéma opened the fringe of feathers and showed the babe's fair face. Cauby contemplated it for some time, and then laughing said—

"He has sucked the soul of my sister,"[1] and he kissed in the mother's eyes the image of the child, fearing lest his touch might hurt it.

The trembling voice of the girl cried—

"Does Araken still live upon the earth?"

"Hardly; since my sister left him his head bent upon his bosom, and it rose up no more."

"Tell him that Iraçéma is already dead, that he may be consoled."

Cauby's sister prepared food for the warrior, and slung in the porch the hammock of hospitality, that he might repose after the fatigues of the journey. When the traveller was refreshed, he arose with these words—

"Say, where is Iraçéma's husband and Cauby's brother, that the braves may exchange the embrace of friendship?"

The sighing lips of the unhappy wife moved like the petals of the cactus-flower stirred by a breeze,

---

[1] *Chupou tua alma.* A child in Tupy is called *Pitanga*, from *piter*, to suck, and *anga*, soul—suck-soul. Cauby meant that it resembled the mother, and had absorbed a portion of her spirit.

and remained speechless. But tears rolled from her eyes in big drops.

Cauby's face clouded.

"Iraçéma's brother thought that sadness remained in the plains she had abandoned, because she took with her all the smiles of those who loved her!"

Iraçéma dried her eyes.

"The husband of Iraçéma has left with the warrior Poty for the shores of the Acaraú. Before three suns shall have illuminated the earth he will return, and with him gladness to the soul of the wife."

"The warrior Cauby awaits him, to know what he has done with the smile which lived on Iraçéma's lips."

The voice of the Tabajára grew hoarse, and his restless step walked at random up and down the cabin.

CHAPTER XXXI.

Softly sang Iraçéma, rocking the hammock to soothe her son.

The beach sands cracked beneath the strong firm foot of the Tabajára brave, who came from the sea-border with an abundance of fish.

The young mother crossed the fringes of the hammock that the flies might not tease her sleeping babe, and went forth to meet her brother.

"Cauby will return to the mountains of the Tabajáras!" she said gently.

The warrior's brow clouded over.

"Iraçéma sends away her brother from her Wigwam that he may not see the sorrow which fills it."

"Araken had many sons in his youth. Some were carried off by war, and they died like braves; others chose wives, and begot in their turn numerous offspring. Araken had but two children of his old age. Iraçéma is for him like the dove which the hunter has stolen from its nest. Alone remains with the old Pagé the warrior Cauby, to sustain his bent frame and to guide his tremulous steps."

"Cauby will depart when the shade shall leave the face of Iraçéma. As lives the night-star, so lives Iraçéma in her sorrow. Only the eyes of her husband can banish the darkness from her brow. Go, in order that his sight may not wax dim at the sight of Cauby!"

"Iraçéma's brother will depart to please her, but he will return every time the Cajueiro flowers to feel in his heart the child of her bosom."

He entered the cabin. Iraçéma took the child from the hammock, and both mother and son remained pressed to the heart of Cauby. He then passed through the door, and soon disappeared amid the trees.

Iraçéma, dragging along her trembling steps, accompanied him for some distance, till he was lost to sight on the skirts of the forest. Then she stopped; when the cry of the Jandáia, accompanied by the infant's wail, recalled her to the cabin; only the cold sand upon which she had sat, kept the secret of the tears which it had drank.

The young mother gave her child the breast, but the babe's moan was not hushed. The scanty milk refused to flow.

The blood of the unhappy girl had been thinned by the ever-flowing tears of which her eyes had not wearied, and none came to her bosom, where the first nourishment of life is formed.

She dissolved the white Cariman[1] and prepared

---

[1] *Cariman*, strained mandioca—a porridge of mandioca; from *caric*, to run, and *mani*, manioc.

over the fire the Mingáo [1] to nourish her son. When the sun gilded the mountain-crests she set out towards the forest, carrying on her bosom the sleeping child.

In the thickness of the wood was found the lair of the absent Irára; the pups, still small, were whining and rolling over one another. The beautiful Tabajára crept softly up to it. She made for her child a cradle of a soft bough of the Maracujá, and sat down near it.

She took one by one into her lap all the pups of the Irára, and abandoned to their famished mouths her bosom, beautiful as the red Pitanga, which she had anointed with the honey of the bee. The hungry young ones fastened upon it, and greedily drained her breasts.

Iraçéma felt pain hitherto unknown to her; they seemed to exhaust her life. At last, however, her bosom began to swell, and the milk, still tinged with the life-fluid of which it is formed, gushed forth.

The happy mother cast away the little Iráras, and, full of joy, appeased the hunger of the babe. He is now doubly Moacyr, the son of pain, once born of Iraçema, and secondly nourished by her.

The daughter of Araken at last began to feel that her veins were drying up, and withal her life, embittered by sorrow, rejected the nourishment which might have restored her strength. Tears and sighs had alike banished the smile and the appetite from her beautiful mouth.

[1] *Mingáo*, a sort of porridge of which the Brazilians are very fond; it is made of mandioca-flour, sugar, eggs, cinnamon, &c., &c.

CHAPTER XXXII.

THE sun declines. Japy springs out of the forest and runs towards the Wigwam-door.

Iraçéma, sitting with her child upon her bosom, basks in the sun's ray, for she feels the cold shivering through her frame. On seeing the faithful messenger of her husband, hope revived in her heart. She would have arisen to meet her Lord and Warrior, but her weak limbs refused to obey her will.

She fell helpless against a Wigwam-prop.

Japy licked the inanimate hand, and jumped playfully, to make the child laugh, with little barks of joy. At times it rushed to the forest skirts and barked to call its master, and then it ran back to the cabin to fondle the mother and the child.

At this time Martim was treading the yellow prairies of Tauapé;[1] his inseparable brother, Poty, marched by his side.

Eight moons[2] had sped since he had left the beach of Jacarécanga. After conquering the Guaraciábas in the Bay of the Parrots, the Christian warrior left for the banks of the Mearim, where lived the savage allies of the Tupinambás.

Poty and his warriors accompanied him. After they had crossed the flowing arm of the sea which comes from the Serra of Tauatinga[3] and bathes the plains where men fish for Piau,[4] they finally saw the

---

[1] *Tauapé* means "place of yellow clay." It is on the road to Maranguape.
[2] *Moons* are months, as suns are days.
[3] *Tauatinga*, a Serra in the province of Piauhy where rises the Parahyba river.
[4] *Piau*, a fish which gives its name to the river and province of Piauhy.

beaches of the Mearim, and the Velha Taba [1] of the barbarous Tapuia.

The race of the Sunny-hair gained more and more the friendship of the Tupinambás, the number of the white warriors increased, and they had already raised in the island the great Itaoca [2] to send forth their lightning.

When Martim had seen what was wanted, he retraced his way to the prairies of the Porangába, which he now treads. Already he hears the hoarse grating of the tide on the beach of the Mocoribe; already the breath of the ocean wave fans his cheek.

The nearer his step approaches the Wigwam, the slower and more heavy it becomes. He dreads to arrive; he feels that his soul is about to suffer, when the sad heart-weary eyes of his wife shall pierce it.

Long ago had speech deserted his parched lip; the friend respects this silence, which he well understands. It is the stillness of the waters running over the dark deep places.

As soon as the two warriors reached the river-banks, they heard the barking of the dog calling them and the cry of the Jandáia in lamentation.

They were now very near the Wigwam, which was hid only by a slip of forest. The Christian stopped, pressing his hand to his bosom to still his heart, which beat like the Poraquî.[3]

"The bark of Japy is of gladness," quoth the chief.

"Because he has arrived; but the voice of the Jandáia is of sadness. Will the absent warrior find peace in the bosom of the deserted wife, or will Saudades have killed the fruit of her love?"

The Christian moved forward his dilatory step.

---

[1] *Velha Taba* is the Portuguese of Tapui-tapera, and was the name of one of the Tupinambá settlements in Maranhão.

[2] *Itaoca*, house of stone—fortress.

[3] *Poraquî*, electric fish which jumps; of flat, broad, and ugly shape.

Suddenly, between the branches of the trees, his eyes beheld sitting at the Wigwam-door Iraçéma with her boy in her lap, and the dog playing about them. His heart carried him there with a bound, and his whole soul rushed to his lips—

"Iraçéma!"

The broken-hearted wife and mother could only open her eyes on hearing the beloved voice. Only with a great effort she can raise the babe in her arms and present it to the father, who gazes at it with ecstatic love.

"Receive the son of thy blood. Thou hast arrived in time; already my breasts have no nourishment for him."

Placing the child in the paternal arms, the unhappy mother fainted away, like the Jetyca[1] with its uprooted bulb. The husband then saw how pain and sorrow had withered her form; but beauty still dwelt there, like perfume in the fallen flower of the Manacá.[2]

Iraçéma rose no more from the hammock where the afflicted arms of Martim had placed her. The husband, whose love was born anew with paternal joy, surrounded her with caresses, which filled her soul with its former happiness. But they could not bring her back to life. The stamen of her flower was broken for ever.

"Let the body of thy wife sleep at the foot of the palm-tree which thou lovedst. When the breeze of the sea shall sigh amongst its leaves, Iraçéma will think it is *thy* voice whispering through her hair."

Her lip became silent for ever; the last spark faded away from the darkening eyes.

Poty supported his brother in his great sorrow. Martim felt how precious in misfortune is a true

---

[1] *Jetyca*, a tree which gives gum.
[2] *Manacá*, a flower well known in Pará. They also call by this name the most beautiful girl in a tribe, or anything of pleasure connected with a feast.

friend; he is like the hill which shelters from the hurricane[1] the trunk of the strong hardy Ubiratan, pierced by the Copim.[2]

The Camoçim received the corpse of Iraçéma, which, steeped in aromatic spices and sweet herbs, was buried at the foot of the palm tree on the river-banks. Martim broke a branch of myrtle, the leaf of sadness, and laid it on the last resting-place of his wife.

The Jandáia, perched at the top of the palm tree, sadly repeated—

"Iraçéma!"

From that time the Pytiguára warriors who passed by the deserted Wigwam, and who heard the plaintive voice of the devoted bird incessantly calling for its mistress, withdrew with their souls full of sadness from the palm-tree where sang the Jandáia.

And thus it happened that one day, the river where the palm-tree grew, and the prairies through which the river winds, came to be called Ceará.[3]

CHAPTER XXXIII.

THE Cajueiro flowered four times since Martim had left the shores of Ceará, bearing with him in the fragile bark his little son and the faithful dog. The Jandáia would not leave the land where rested its friend and mistress.

---

[1] In the original *Vendaval*, which is the wind that brings ships home from the West Indies. It is not constant, as the trade-wind, yet it generally ranges between the south and north-west.

[2] *Copim*, a white ant, composed of *co*, a hole, and *pim*, a sting.

[3] *Ceará* is composed of *cemo*, to sing loud, and *ará*, a parroqueet. The above is the legend which gave the province its name.

The first Cearense, still in his cradle, thus became an Emigrant from his Fatherland. Did this announce the destinies of the race to be?

Poty with his warriors awaited on the river-banks. The Christian had promised to return; every morning he climbed the sand-hill and strained his eyes, hoping for a friendly sail to whiten the sea-horizon.

Martim at last returned to the land which had once seen his happiness, and which now sees his bitter regret. When his foot pressed the hot white sand, there spread through his frame a fire which burned his heart: it was the fire of consuming memory.

The flame was extinguished only when he stood on the place where his wife slept, because at that moment his heart overflowed like the trunk of the Jetahy[1] in the great heats, and refreshed his grief with a shower of tears.

Many warriors of his race accompanied the white Chief to found with him the Christian Mayri. There came also a Priest of his Faith, black-robed, to plant the Cross upon this savage soil.

Poty was the first who knelt at the foot of the Sacred Wood. He would not allow anything again to part himself and his white brother; for this reason, as they had but one heart, he wished that both might have the same God.

He received in baptism the name of the Saint[2] whose day it was, and of the King he was about to serve; besides these two, his own translated into the tongue of his new brethren.

His fame increased, and it is still the pride of the land in which he first saw the light.

The Mayri which Martim founded on the river-banks within the shores of Ceará flourished. The word of the true God budded in the savage land, and

---

[1] *Jetahy*, a kind of Hymenæa from which a yellow gum exudes.

[2] Antonio Phelipe Camarão.

the holy Church-bells re-echoed through the valleys where once bellowed the Maracá.

Jacaúna came to inhabit the plains of the Porangába, to be near his white friend. Camerão (Poty) placed the Taba of his warriors on the banks of the Mocejána. Later, when Albuquerque,[1] the Great Chief of the White Warriors, arrived, Martim and Camarão made for the banks of the Mearim, to chastise the ferocious Tupinambá and to expel the white Tapuia.

The husband of Iraçéma never could behold without the deepest emotion the shores where he had been so happy, and the green leaves under whose shade slept the beautiful Tabajára girl.

Often he would go and sit upon these soft sands, to meditate, and to soothe the bitter Saudade in his heart.

The Jandáias still sang upon the crests of the palm-tree, but no more remembered the sweet name of Iraçema.

On *this* Earth all things pass away!

[1] Jeronimo de Albuquerque, Chief of the Expedition to Maranhão in 1612.

FINIS.

No. 1

MANUEL DE MORAES

A Chronicle of the Seventeenth Century

BY

J. M. PEREIRA DA SILVA

TRANSLATED BY

RICHARD F. AND ISABEL BURTON

LONDON
BICKERS & SON, 1 LEICESTER SQUARE
1886

TWO WORDS TO THE READER.

AUTHOR'S PREFACE.

THE "Biographia Luzitana" of the Abbade Diogo Barbosa supplies the following short notice of the life of Manuel de Moraes:—

He was born in São Paulo (Brazil) at the end of the sixteenth or at the beginning of the seventeenth century; he wrote a History of America, which is now wholly lost, and a Memoir advocating the acclamation of Dom João IV., published (1641) at Leyden with the title of "Prognostico y Respuesta à una pergunta de un Caballero muy ilustre sobre las cosas de Portugal" ("Forecast and Reply to the Question of an Illustrious Personage upon the Affairs of Portugal"). He was condemned by the Tribunal of the Holy Office, and he was "relaxed" in effigy at the Act of Faith of April 6, 1643, his crimes being apostasy from the Catholic creed and intermarriage with a schismatic. Finally, he died at Lisbon, a natural death, according to some, whilst others, not less informed, declare that he lost his life by violence. Innocencio Francisco da Silva adds to this, in his

"Diccionario Biographico e Bibliographico Portuguez e Brazileiro," that Manuel de Moraes belonged to the Company of Jesus at São Paulo, and that he was garotted at the Act of Faith, December 15, 1647.

Other writers, who have sought to preserve his name, especially myself, in the supplement to my "Varões Illustres do Brazil durante os tempos coloniaes" ("The Worthies of Brazil in her Colonial Days"), have done nothing but repeat the notices given by the Abbade Diogo Barbosa. The fact is, that, despite all our research, we have been unable to procure other details.[1]

Thus, though the existence of Manuel de Moraes cannot be contested, it is evidently impossible to write a regular biographical study of his career. We want precise information to set off and to describe

---

[1] The "Historia Geral do Brazil," by M. F. A. de Varnhagen (Laemmert, Rio de Janeiro, 1854), prints (vol. i. p. 410) a document addressed to the Crown by the citizens of São Paulo, strongly complaining of the Jesuits interfering with the slaves. We read: "In all the villages about Pernambuco there was not an Indian or a Gentile who did not go over to the (Dutch) enemy; and with them was their spiritual guide, the Padre Manuel de Moraes, who induced and persuaded them to commit this outrage, making himself the greatest heretic and apostate that the Church of God has known in those days." Vol. ii. p. 42 informs us that "Padre Manuel de Moraes, who from a Jesuit became a Calvinist, and intermarried with *women* of that sect, was therefore burnt in effigy at the Auto da Fé of Lisbon on April 6, 1642. He afterwards repented, and gave himself up to the (Portuguese) restorers of Pernambuco; the latter recommended him to Lisbon, where he was condemned perpetually to wear the heretical dress with the usual flames, and was for ever suspended from holy orders by the Act of Faith of December 15, 1649." The latter also found guilty of "Judaism" five other inhabitants of Pernambuco.—*Translator's Note.*

the physiognomy, the life, and the deeds of a man who appears to have been of some eminence in his day.

Desirous, however, of presenting him to the reading world, and of filling up the outlines of a character whose individuality was so original and characteristic, I have resolved to treat the Paulista author in the same way as I proceeded with the Portuguese poet Jeronymo Cortereal; in the latter case, however, older authors had left for me a biography far less defective.

The Chronicle of Cortereal will thus be supplemented by that of Manuel de Moraes. The former offered a picture of the Portuguese people and society during the last days of Dom Sebastião, until Spain imposed upon us her yoke. The latter will contain descriptions of the stirring events which distinguished the seventeenth century in São Paulo, and in the Jesuit Missions of La Guayra; in Pernambuco, and in the wars with the Hollanders; in the Low Countries, and in the emigration of the Portuguese Jews; in Portugal, and in the blood-stained tyranny of the Inquisition. Upon the same page the realities of history and the vagaries of fancy must meet and greet one another. But is not this the most popular branch of our modern literature, the formula in highest esteem with the public of the nineteenth century?

J. M. PEREIRA DA SILVA.

A WORD BY THE TRANSLATOR.

TURNING over some old and almost forgotten manuscripts, I lately lit upon the translation here offered to the public. Four happy years spent in the Highlands of the Brazil have left the most pleasant memories; and these pages, describing familiar scenes, speak of days which we would fain recall. May some portion of the charm which the little volume has for us find its way to the reader's heart!

The version is not literal—indeed far from it. The genius of the Portuguese language is far too flowery, too tautological, and too fond of metaphor for our rough Northern speech and our directness of thought and expression. What should we feel if told, for instance, of a man past forty "fading away like a rose upon its stem?"

Yet I have avoided taking liberties with our author, especially in matters to which he himself would object. My excuses are due to him for having translated his tale without permission being duly asked and given; the fact is, our attempts to meet him at Rio de Janeiro were in vain. Moreover, he has himself courted this injury: *tous les droits sont reservés*, would have saved him from the liberty thus taken by a stranger.

Translations, the publishers assure us, are not popular in England. So much the worse. Surely a good tale imported from a foreign source is worth a dozen of the flimsy "sensation novels," run off for the use of the moment, ephemera which have only the dubious merits of exciting a morbid interest, and of being read in three volumes within three hours.

Trieste, *November* 30, 1884.

MANUEL DE MORAES.

CHAPTER I.

OLD SÃO PAULO.

THE Brazilian traveller of our modern day who runs up by the Santos and Jundiahy Railway to São Paulo, the capital of a great province also so named, finds but little that can suggest what was that very heroic city in the earlier years of the seventeenth century. There is the same enchanting atmosphere, at times portentously lustrous and transparent; the same grateful mixture of tropical and temperate vegetation, the banana rustling in the cool shadow of the pine and the palm; the same glorious day under the Tropic of Capricorn, whose line passes within a mile or two of the suburbs, and the same bright healthful night of Central Europe colouring the cheeks and strengthening the frames of the inhabitants.

But the streets are now laid down with macadam; the old stockades and walls, which defended the young settlement, have made way for house and homestead; the rivers and rivulets have been bridged; the tenements, formerly restricted to a door and a single window outside, and inside to a "but and a ben," have become double storeys, with painted façades, and metal balconies, and glass pineapples; the baby village has grown up to cityhood, and the city is fast extending itself towards its northern and eastern faubourgs, the "Luz" and the "Braz."

The people have changed even more. The long hose, the trunk-breeches, the slashed doublets, and the flapped felt hats of two hundred years ago are now gone—clean gone. The men affect Bismarck hats and *pantalons collants;* whilst the fair sex appears in the shape-improvers, the chignons, and the pink and white pigments proper to this our section of the seventeenth century.

The celebrated Martim Affonso de Souza, afterwards the hero of Portuguese India, first visited this charming site in 1532. Guided by the friendly Red Man, he scaled the formidable granite heights known as the "Serra do Mar," the Eastern Ghats of Middle Brazil, and following the course of the streams which turned inland towards the far west, he reached the now famous plains of Piratininga, and the wigwams inhabited by his ally, the Cacique Tyberiçá.

Presently Martim Affonso, created Donatory of a grant which, with a hundred leagues of maritime frontage, extended to an unknown depth in the interior, built the fortified village of São Vicente at the mouth of a stream, or rather a lagoon channel, which enters the Bay of Santos. It was peopled by natives and laborious settlers, many of them scions of illustrious families; and all were entitled to boast that they had founded the first Portuguese colony in the Brazil.

São Vicente, however, soon gave precedence to Santos, which, originally a Misericordia,—a hospital organised like that of Lisbon,—became a port on the northern or sheltered side of the island, separated from *terra firma* by a river-like sea-arm. Thus it was less exposed to the fury of the Atlantic, which had swept away old São Vicente, and to the attacks of pirates, English, Spanish, and Netherlanders, who periodically plundered and harried the coast.

Their base-line laid down, the Portuguese settlers proceeded to occupy the interior. With a thousand difficulties, they scaled the terrible heights of Paraná-piassába—"the chain which looks towards the ocean"—loftiest of the maritime range that half encircles the Santos basin with its rocky arms and regular crest. They swarmed up cliffs, they let themselves down from crags that invaded the upper strata of ether, and they compared the country with the "region of the moon." Those slopes, whose trees seem from afar to rise in the gentlest steps and on the most regular gradients, proved heart-breaking steeps of rock and tree, of roots and of soft humus, the decay of vegetation, into which men sank to the knee. They swam the river-courses, and they bridged the torrents and rapids with trunks felled upon the banks. Night and day they spent in an atmosphere now torrid and humid, then raw and frigid; sleeping upon the ground or in hammocks slung to the branches. What fancy could have traced, in those times, the line of rail which now bears the traveller over all these terrors and hardships, occupying three hours to perform what to former generations cost at least as many days?

The metamorphosis has, on the other hand, caused the traveller to lose much of the poetry of the primeval forest and of the eternal sea. We no longer, from the Alto da Serra of the mule-road, view, as with a bird's eye, the superb panorama of the lowlands; the thin white surf-line breaking in far perspective on the yellow sands; the manifold surface-drains and sea-arms, winding like ribbons of silver amongst the netherlands, and the islands forested with the sombre green mangrove; the infinite varieties of town and village, of field and plantation; the slopes with gigantic timber falling below our feet, and on one side the roaring, dashing cataract of the "Rio dos Pedros," a snowy sheet torn to rags and strips by the black fangs of its rocky bed.

The Povoação, or village of São Paulo, showed by its position the master-hand of the Jesuits, who, after years of stormy discussion, had succeeded in transferring to it the rights and privileges of the ruined township Santo André; and thus the religious had thriven by the death and decay of the laical settlement. The site of the successful rival was a ridge of red clay, about a mile in length by half that breadth, bounded on the north by the wide and often flooded valley of the Tiété, or "Good-water river," an affluent of the mighty Paraná-Plata. On the east, under a precipitous slope, flows the Tamanduátahy—"the stream of the ant-eater"—a narrow but deep and dangerous feeder of the main artery; while to the west is the valley of a similar but even smaller feature, the Anhangabahú—Black-devil water—a branchlet of the Tamanduatahy.

During the first thirty years of the seventeenth century, São Paulo contained only three or four hundred houses, for the most part simple cottages, walled with pisé or rough concrete, and roofed with thatch or tile; of these, hardly one in ten belonged to families in easy circumstances, whilst four or five large churches made the mean habitations look meaner still. No neat "chacara" or villa rose from the orchard and the garden which now combine the jasmine and the rose, the pink and the myrtle. The long streets were traced with tolerably straight lines; the cross-alleys were compelled by the slopes to use the rudest steps of granite and "bullock's blood," a deep-red sandstone brought from the neighbouring mountains. Wheeled vehicles were, of course, unknown, and the mules were sometimes engulfed in the mud-holes that yawned between the pavement slabs.

Commanding the eminence, whose feet were washed by the Tamanduatahy, and on the highest and most picturesque site rose the convent of the Company of Jesus, now the palace of the President and hall of the Chamber of Deputies. The double-storeyed frontage, tasteless and almost barbarous, as indeed appear to be all the architectural efforts of the Jesuits in the Brazil, formed two sides of the main square. On the north was the habitation of the Fathers; to the east, at right angles, stood the modest church of the Order, with its short and substantial belfry. Behind their long and rambling building the riverine valley-banks were planted with fruit-trees, especially the orange, the guava, and the delicious Jaboticába-myrtle. From this vantage-ground the eye ranged across the valley of the Tiété, bound on the east by the heights which bear the Penha church, and on the north by the Serra da Cantereira—"of the potter's wife"—the last offsets of the great and famous Mantiqueira range.

In those days the population consisted of about three thousand souls; a few were pure Portuguese, some were "Mamelucos" or half-breeds, white and Indian; others were mulattoes and negro slaves, whilst the majority were free and catechised aborigines. Already the monastic orders had built for themselves houses; the most important, however, was the Institute of Saint Ignatius de Loyola; and stringent orders from the home-capital had recommended to the authorities, civil and military, the support and protection of the Jesuits as the apostles of the Indians and the firmest stays of the altar and the throne.

The several classes were distinguished by their professions and habits. The Portuguese, either born in Europe or in the Brazil, busied themselves with commerce and barter, with building houses and laying out plantations, and with similar primitive industries; the slaves were confined to husbandry and to personal services. Although held the least respectable of all classes, the "Mamelucos" were the audacious explorers of the far western wilds. They continually excited European covetousness by discovering mines of gold and other metals, and by bringing back with them thousands of captives, or, as the term then was, "rescued men," whose lives they were by law permitted to purchase.

Frequent and furious were the contests between these laymen and the Jesuits, who strove to defend the hapless indigens and to preserve the rights and privileges of the savage freeman. The Regulars never feared to resist their brother "Conquistadores," who, under a variety of pretexts, converted to their own use the persons and property of the "Indians and Gentiles." The Fathers were assisted by the respect of the people, by the superstitious belief of the age, and, at first, by the public conviction of their pure intentions. But presently the successors of the early Thaumaturgi and Apostles showed that their defence of the "native" was limited to preserving him from all except themselves; whilst hands were wanting to others, their own lands were tilled and their coffers were filled to overflowing. This monopoly of precious labour led to discontent, and the latter engendered a succession of tumults, which ended in the first expulsion of the Jesuits from São Paulo.

The catechised Indians, known as "Caboclos," formed a separate class, at once submissive and devout; simple, active, and industrious. It was composed chiefly of mechanics, agriculturists, musicians and singers. All learned the offices and delighted in the feasts of the Church, in splendid ceremonies, and especially in long and pompous processions; briefly, in all things which appealed to the eye of sense. They obeyed and revered the Jesuits as their fathers and friends, their masters and protectors, their medicine-men and their guardian angels. They listened to their counsels, they attended the schools in which the Portuguese language and grammar were taught: they sought to understand the explanation of the

Roman Catechism, and they applied themselves with especial ardour to the song and the sacred music with which the Jesuits softened and polished their faith and manners. They sent their children immediately after infancy to the church-choirs, where they studied instrumental performance and the sundry harmonious services of their religion.

The captaincy of São Vicente, now known as the province of São Paulo, was then governed by the heirs of the first grandee, who appointed as their representatives authorities entitled lieutenants and captains-major (capitães-móres). All did homage in temporal matters to the Governor of Rio de Janeiro.

In its earliest days São Paulo had fought with valour and success against the Tamoyo tribe of Rio de Janeiro, who had taken the part of the French invader. This race made incessant attacks upon its southern neighbours, robbing and slaying them without ruth or regard to age or sex; and its violence terrified the milder Carijós and Goyanázes, who inhabited the plains and forests of our captaincy. At length, by the valour of the Paulistas and their Indian auxiliaries, the Tamoyo name ceased to be a byword in the land.

But what groans and sorrow, what prayers in the temples, what genuflexions before the altars followed the evil report that the Hollanders, having seized the city São Salvador da Bahia, and soon afterwards of Pernambuco, threatened to drown the Brazil in a flood of calamities, and to raise upon the ruins of the Roman religion the cold and lifeless abstraction of a Reformed faith, whose apostles were Luther, Calvin, and their herd of followers. Hearing the hateful successes of these heretics, all the people of the town and its environs, guided by the Jesuits and by the authorities, flocked to implore mercy and salvation from the Eternal. Curses loud and deep mingled with the tears of the whites and the Mamelucos, of the Gentiles and the slaves, who violently beat their breasts, severely scourged themselves, and wearied out every saint of the calendar with petitions for pity and protection. And how describe the joy and enthusiasm with which they heard the triumph of Portugal and Spain united under the sceptre of Philip of Castile?

Such was the state of affairs when, on an April evening of 1628, two men walked down the slope upon whose summit rose the Jesuit convent, and began to pace to and fro under the myrtle avenues bordering the Tamanduatahy.

Both wore the habit of the Jesuits; one, however, had passed the age of forty, at which time men begin to die; his hair was already waxing iron grey, and his head somewhat bald. A sympathetic and amiable countenance, eyes full of loving-kindness, and gentle manners distinguished from his fellows this Father Eusebio de Monserrate.

Conversing with his companion, who had little exceeded the first score of years, the priest now fingered the big black beads of a lengthy rosary, ending in a large metal cross; then stopped for a moment the better to listen and to reply with short and guarded words. Now he raised his eyes to heaven, then he fixed them upon the youth as if to read the secrets of his soul. Tall, vigorous, and framed for activity was the junior, still a Novice in the Company; but now, weighed down by sorrow, he was apparently readier to confess himself than to keep up a regular and consecutive exchange of thoughts.

Lingeringly died out the daylight after the sun had buried itself behind tall Jaraguá, the saddle-back fronting the Penha mound. The latest splendours of the west were reflected eastwards in bands of pink and green, which seemed to rise and spire upwards as the crimson glow waxed cooler; and presently they gave way to a soft neutral tint, based upon a vaporous grey, and tinged with the faintest emerald, where it met the rose-colour of the zenith. A sweet sea-breeze from the east, sporting with the flowers and the leaves, refreshed an atmosphere still heated by the breath of noon, and dispersed the mists which began to gloom over the humid lowlands. Nature prepared to take her rest; the timid dove, flushed by the softest sound, arose from the path, and sought amid the branches a safe roosting-place, whilst upon the boughs of a blasted pine-tree the large dark-brown buzzards gathered to repose their pinions after the long laborious flights of the hours of light.

The bells of the Jesuit Campanile struck seven as the two men whom we have described neared the stream. Both, reverently raising their felt hats with enormous flaps, broke off speech to address the Most High. Having crossed themselves after prayer, the Father took the hand of the Novice and thus addressed him:—

"Thou wouldst then quit the house of God and give up the service of religion and the Company?"

"I feel no calling for the ghostly state," replied the youth, attempting to kiss the hand that was withdrawn. "Doth not the Lord guide His own creation?" he resumed after some moments of silence. "If He grant not to me the will and the vocation, it is that He destineth me for another career."

"Thine end will be miserable, my son," rejoined the Padre. "The Almighty ordaineth no tyranny. Hardly He granteth conviction that the stray sheep may be gathered into the fold of the Church. He createth men free that they may be responsible for will and deed. But thou wilt be wretched. The Catholic Church is the divine reason, the sole salvation of mankind; and there can be no rest for him who abandoneth her, and who plungeth into the depths of this world of woe."

"Why then did not God sow in my heart the seed of longing and ardent aspiration for a priestly life and for the rigorous discipline demanded by the holy Institute?" inquired the youth with an outburst of bitterness that betrayed the excitement of his spirit.

"That thou mayest learn to subdue the passions which agitate mankind," replied the elder. "The greater is his gain who sacrificeth himself in the struggle, and who conquereth the unruly instincts of nature and youth!"

"And of what value can be such mock piety?" murmured the youth.

The Jesuit smiled sadly, reading the depths of his companion's thoughts, and, reaching a fallen tree, he sat upon it, drawing to his side the unhappy Novice.

"Listen to me," said the Father, with kindly accents. "I too have passed through thine age; I too have felt boiling in my bosom the passions which I perceive in thee—passions which drove me from the path of true happiness here, and which threatened to do so hereafter. I also, like saintly Ignatius de Loyola, the founder of our holy Institution, found myself engaged in the extravagant and disorderly struggles of life. I too have fought like a soldier, have travelled like a pilgrim, have suffered hunger and thirst, peril, imprisonment, and exile. I, as well as others, learned to my cost, was taught by the experience of evil, sincerely to repent me of my misdeeds, and the Eternal took pity upon me. He opened for me in due time the eyes of reason, and He led me to seek refuge and repose of body and soul in His sacred house. May God be merciful to thee also, and show thee in eternity His infinite compassion!"

"Ah! let me also taste the joys of my youth," exclaimed the Novice. "Let Nature follow in my case, as she did in thine, her legitimate career."

The Padre looked at him, and saw, despite the words which betrayed a firm resolution, tears starting from his eyes. He judged this exaltation of fancy to be rather the green longings of inexperience than the cold settled purpose of an evil will. He felt deep pity for the youth, and the sentiment was increased by the memories of his own past. Presently with a close and friendly embrace he said, "Religion gaineth nothing by doubts and struggles of the spirit, nor will the Company of Saint Ignatius accept involuntary service. Go thy ways. My conscience biddeth me bless thy speeding forth, and entreat Almighty God that He may befriend thee in thy rough and stony path. May He open to thee the treasures of His ineffable grace in time to save thee from all dangers!"

The Novice fell upon his knees and humbly received the benediction of the Religious. At the parting, the Padre felt his eyes fill with tears, which rolled down cheeks that were pale and drawn by grief. He followed with his glance the youth who left the enclosure and disappeared in the shades of night. He then arose from the tree-trunk, and mechanically climbed the hill towards the convent. Reaching the summit, he turned him round and sought once more to see the Novice.

Vain attempt! He had vanished from that scene for evermore.

During a few minutes the good Father prayed in silence; he then answered the porter's greeting and entered the establishment. Taking the way to the church, he fell prostrate before the altar, and in that position he prayed two long hours for the soul's weal of that unhappy Novice, torn from a religious vocation by the temptations of the world, the flesh, and the devil.

CHAPTER II.

THE NOVICE.

MEANWHILE Manuel de Moraes, for such was the name of our Novice, after leaving the Jesuits' Close, walked quickly towards the centre of the settlement.

Born in the earlier years of the seventeenth century, the youth had been brought up by his father, José de Moraes, for the laborious life of a Jesuit missioner. It was the parent's settled conviction that this was the happiest condition of man, and the position at once the most brilliant and the most useful to society open to the only son with whom Providence had blessed him.

José, a native of Minho in Portugal, had there married Ignez da Dôres, and, driven by poverty from home, he had sought fortune with her in distant Brazil. Guided by the Jesuits, whom he fervently admired, he had applied himself to agriculture in the captaincy of São Vicente, and he had achieved the reputation of an honest man. His family numbered, besides Manuel, three young daughters, whose tender minds were trained by their mother to tread the paths of honour and religion.

José had himself intrusted his beloved son to the care of the Company, and more especially to Padre Eusebio de Monserrate, his old friend and protector.

The boy had shown early talent. No student excelled him in acuteness and penetration, in desire to please, and in willingness to learn. He had won the esteem of his teachers by his scholarly turn of mind and by the regularity of his life, although he had often incurred their blame by opposing and resisting the discipline and the mystic devotion inculcated by the Fathers of the Company.

Eusebio de Monserrate attempted to bend this lofty will, and to modify the evidently mundane tendencies of the Novice. He failed, as we have seen. Manuel de Moraes resolved to fly the holy house, and he hoped to obtain the parental consent by showing his father that advice and warning were in vain.

The night became stormy. The sunset breeze presently fell to a profound calm. Lightning from the south-east flashed over the horizon, and rose in gerbes and jets, in balls and globes of fire, as though produced by art—an appearance which the electric fluid often assumes in the Highlands of the Brazil. At first a thin warm rain drizzled through the air, but the drops soon became heavier, and the black clouds threatened a torrential downfall.

Grave thoughts haunted the Novice, whom the important step which he had just taken had made more than usually susceptible of impressions from without. How would he be received by his father when the latter came to learn his headstrong plans and projects? Had Padre Eusebio broken the tidings to his parent? What career, what adventures, awaited him now that he no longer belonged to the flock of Saint Ignatius? Would this entire liberty, this plunge into the depths of laical society, a world to him utterly unknown, be really what his fancy painted it? Would it be better suited to his character and ambition than the religious community which had sheltered him to the age of twenty-four?

Descending a steep slope which led to the hill where his father's house stood on the edge of the settlement, he heard loud cries and unusual sounds proceeding from the lower depths of a wretched alley.

Though unarmed, he was dressed in the black soutane of the Order; and his high spirit hurried him at once in the direction of the voice, which seemed to call for assistance. And did not the Jesuit garb lend him a moral force superior to all physical strength?

Turning the corner of a gloomy by-street, he found himself fronting a group of four men and a girl, whilst the dense shade prevented more minute observation. Approaching them suddenly, he cried out, showing the cross of his rosary—

"Stop, ye sinners! in the name of God, stop!"

More effectual than the sword was the Novice's resolute exclamation. Three of the men at once took to flight; the fourth fell upon his knees before the young priest, and the woman who, uttering loud shrieks, had been dragged along the ground, hastened to follow his example. Both poured forth at the same time expressions of gratitude and kissed the Jesuit habit.

"What hath happened?" inquired Manuel de Moraes in consoling accents, hastening to raise them.

"Padre," exclaimed the man in a calmer tone, "I am a poor Carijó, and this maiden is my daughter. Here was our abode," pointing to a pauper shanty. "Three whites burst in the door, tore my Cora from her bed, and dragged her into the street. I awoke with a start, and embraced my girl with a father's arms, which are stronger than the best of weapons. We were struggling when your Reverence came up and saved us."

"And whose blood is this?" asked Manuel, seeing red stains upon the Indian's head, face, and cotton shirt.

"It is a small matter, O my preserver!" exclaimed the Indian, pressing his lips to the hand of his deliverer. "Only a few traces of the cudgel. It is nought since my Cora hath escaped from her persecutors."

"Hast thou recognised the robbers?" asked the youth.

"They are dogs," was the Carijó's reply. "I could not well see their faces, but I hold them to be none but certain bad white neighbours who kidnap in São Paulo without respect for the voice of the holy Missionaries or fear of the Eternal God's chastisements. We are poor weak Pagans, and only the Padres can succour and preserve us!"

They walked towards the wretched hovel where the Indians lived, and found its only door torn from its hinges and lying upon the ground. All three entered. The Carijó struck fire with a flint, and with a few dry splints lighted up the interior. Hereupon Manuel recognised the Cabóclo as one of the most faithful followers of his religion and frequenters of the Company's Church.

The man wore a shirt and short drawers of undyed cotton; his feet were naked, but his aspect was not that of a slave. Cora was dressed in a large-sleeved gown of the same material, girt tightly round the waist. Her thick black locks, shining like polished jet, fell upon her shoulders. Eyes almond-shaped, with the darkest pupils set in bluish white—eyes to which a fringe of curving lashes lent the softest expression —admirably harmonised with the flush of youthful cheeks, with the delicate pink of the mouth, with the pleasing lines of the features, and with the bending of the Indian form.

A large coarse print of the Blessed Virgin adorned the walls of the hovel, which were of clay, whilst tamped earth formed the floor.

Manuel aided the Indian to replace the door of the shanty, calmed him with advice how to guard against the future, and exhorted the maiden to persevere in the paths of virtue. Then he took leave and resumed his way, meditating on the struggle of the two races thus placed faced to face, one fated to disappear from the surface of earth, the other destined to break away from the prestige and authority with which the Fathers of the Company attempted to repress its semi-barbarous instincts.

He dimly felt that, in the battle of life, the weaker brain and body must make room for the stronger, and that their destruction was but a matter of time. The sentimental feeling in favour of a doomed race stole over him. He was tempted to return into the bosom of an Order whose object was to save so many helpless souls, and to protect so many lives rendered interesting by their feebleness and by their innocency of life and faith.

But either false shame forbade him to retrace his steps, or an innate but ill-defined aspiration, which blinded his reason and attracted his ambition to the unknown world of society, compelled him to work out his fate.

Immersed in such reverie he reached his home. A profound quiet hovered over the settlement; not a light shone in the streets; not a door nor a window stood open. The sky waxed still more gloomy; the rain became thicker; the wind blew in sudden gusts; the lightning gleamed with lurid fire, and the thunder, still distant, muttered its ominous promise to approach.

The family of José de Moraes was not rich in the gifts of fortune, yet it knew no want; the industry of its Chief supplied it with all the necessaries and with some of the comforts of life. The father, whose age might have been between forty-five and fifty years, was seated in a *Rede* or net-hammock, and around him stood his wife and three young daughters apparently listening to his words. The furniture consisted of a few stools and benches, a *Girão* or rough platform on four poles; some wooden hooks to which were suspended various implements, and a large water-jar of red pottery occupied the corner. Finally, a table of rough planking near the middle of the room supported a lighted candle in a wooden candlestick, and the cold remnants of a meal.

The frugal supper had just ended, and the family was receiving the blessing of its Chief before retiring to rest.

"Louvado seja nosso Senhor Jesu Christo!" (Blessed be our Lord Jesus Christ!) ejaculated the son, using the normal Jesuit formula, and reverently kissing the hands of his father and mother.

"What! out of the Holy House at such untimely hours? Thou bringest to us bad tidings of evil."

The sudden question, which sounded like a dire omen, caused Manuel to turn pale. How announce his desertion of the Company to a father whose mind clung so lovingly to the blessedness of ecclesiastic life, to the conviction that nothing equalled the religious mission?

Before attempting a reply he tried to deprecate the effects which must result from his disclosures by affectionate inquiries addressed to the family after three days of absence.

José de Moraes assured him in a few curt words that all were in full health of soul and body, and again demanded the cause of this unexpected visit.

The son felt that the tale must be told as briefly as possible. Already José de Moraes had been displeased by his unwillingness to exchange the noviciate for the brotherhood, the second degree of the Order, and the necessary preliminary to the Priesthood. The father had ever kept his son, even from the earliest age, at the most respectful distance, breeding fear where love should have been; yet, when profoundly irritated at times by the reports of the Jesuits which reached his ears, he expected the youth to open his heart as to a friend, and he chafed as at a grievance when this was not done.

"Before answering you, my beloved father," said Manuel, kneeling upon the ground in the presence of his parent, and clinging to his hand with extreme affection, "before answering you, I venture to implore your pardon!"

Hearing these words, José de Moraes snatched away the hand which his son was still holding to his lips, rose to his feet, and retiring a few steps, assumed the sternest aspect, and exclaimed in his harshest tones, "What crime hast thou committed to dishonour my blood? I must know it before God may permit me in my ignorance to pronounce thy pardon!"

The unhappy Manuel then became certain that Padre Monserrate had not prepared his father for the blow about to fall upon him. Terrified by this unforeseen circumstance, he stood silent for some minutes, and the voice which attempted to utter a reply expired on his lips.

Nothing remained for José de Moraes but to order, after a glance which seemed to dive into his son's thoughts, that the truth and the whole truth be at once told.

Bending his head in deep grief, whilst tears rolled slowly down his cheeks, Manuel ejaculated, with the most painful effort, "Father, I have sinned against thy will; I have failed in my own desire to obey thee."

The parent raised his hand to a brow from which time had already bared the hair. Despite his sudden affliction he drew himself up proudly, his eyes gleamed, his lips set firmly, and the expression of his countenance foretold the coming storm.

"Then they have expelled thee from the Company?" he presently cried in despair.

"No, Senhor," replied Manuel, whose voice suddenly recovered something of its firmness. "My conduct in the house of the holy Fathers has ever been correct. They will themselves assure you that I bear amongst them a spotless name."

"The greater then thy offence," retorted the old man. "Thou hast covered with dishonour thy father, thy family, and thyself by some horrible misdeed committed outside the cloister."

"No, Sir," continued Manuel, yet more tranquilly. "I have ever trodden the paths of virtue, even as you taught me to tread them."

"I understand thee not," exclaimed José de Moraes, much relieved by hearing this formal denial of his suspicions and the horrible ideas bred by his own thoughts.

"I have committed no crime, Sir; I have done no unworthy deed," continued Manuel; "but I have broken your commands; I have disobeyed your will: however much I wished to satisfy you, my nature forbade it!"

More and more confused waxed the brain of José de Moraes as he heard these simple words uttered by his son with the gest and tone of one resolved to front the worst. What then could have happened so greatly to afflict a father's heart? In what had Manuel so despised the commands and disobeyed the paternal will to an extent that required a pardon to be asked before the offence was known? Not a gleam of intelligence supplied to him the key of the secret or lit up the dark significance of his son's words. Though still disquieted, he began to show less exasperation.

The agonised mother stood motionless as a statue, without a word, without a movement; her eyes, drowned in tears, roved from son to husband, from José to Manuel, without daring to dwell upon either countenance.

The two elder daughters embraced the little one, who might have numbered six summers; and, retiring into a corner, formed a group of terrified innocents, whose breathing was hushed by the terror of the scene.

"What, then, hast thou done?" asked with more

composure José de Moraes, approaching his son, and yielding to him after a struggle the hand which the Novice seemed to implore. At length the father gave way, less, however, to prove affection than to encourage the youth in telling the whole truth.

"Father, pardon me first," repeated Manuel. "Promise me your forgiveness, and I will open to you all my heart."

"Confess thou first!" exclaimed the old man, again retiring from his son, and showing evident signs of a fresh outbreak of wrath.

Silence reigned in the room.

Neither the son dared to speak, because the father had not encouraged him with a gesture or by a word of kindness; nor would the old man, after thus giving expression to what he meant, deign to continue the dialogue.

Meanwhile the house-dog, whose tail began to wag as the noise of angry voices subsided, approached Manuel to welcome him home after the faithful fashion of its hardly used kind.

"Be off!" cried the wrathful old man, with a fierce glance at the affectionate beast, which he drove with a kick from one end of the room to the other.

The dog, restraining a howl, rose slowly and crept sadly towards the street door, its usual station. There it crouched down, still, however, keeping a watchful eye upon the scene, whose purport it seemed to divine.

At length, with the desire and hope of ending the cruel scene, in which he took so prominent a part, Manuel resolved to speak out. He humbly bent his head, and with frequent pauses thus expressed himself:—

"I never found in myself a vocation for the peaceful life of the Cloister, for the career of the Religious. Many years have I struggled to overcome my will, to bend my spirit, to repress my longings for the world and for worldly existence; to stifle the cries of my soul, to silence the voice that summoned me to another destiny. I cannot belong to the Company of Jesus, as you, Sir, have resolved, and as I in obedience ought to do. Father, I prefer to abandon the Soutane, to leave the Order, and to assist you in the labours of your life."

"Never!" cried the old man with vehemence. "I have dedicated thee to Missionary life for thy good, for the service of God, for the love of Religion, and for the honour of thy family."

"That life, Sir, I will no more lead. This Soutane now belongs to me not, this garb is no longer mine. I have left the house of the Company; I have bidden it farewell for ever. God refuses to accept vows which are not from the heart and soul."

These decided terms, expressed in a voice not less firm, excited to the highest degree the irritation of José de Moraes. Without hesitating a moment, he replied to his son's retort by one even more stubborn and determined.

"I no longer own thee to be my child. Fly from my presence; leave at once this house which thou hast disgraced, and whose door shall for ever be shut against thee."

Manuel would have spoken, but the fierceness of his father made his heart sink. He looked towards his mother, who dropped sobbing upon a bench; towards his sisters, who, like doves in the presence of the hawk, cowered and clung together closer and closer.

"My dearest mother!" were the tearful accents which burst from his lips.

The mother half rose to embrace her son, when the old man, who with outstretched arm stood pointing to the door, frightened her once more to her seat.

"O Manuel!" cried the miserable parent, "obey thy father, return to thy duties, and——"

"It cannot now be," murmured the Novice.

"Silence, Senhora!" cried the father, cutting short the thread of her words. "He who standeth there is a lost man; he is no more our son. Be with him his father's curse and the unfailing wrath of Heaven."

Dona Ignez could say no more. She sat overwhelmed in submissive grief, like the Virgin of the Dolours, whose soul was rent by woe ineffable, whilst full of that evangelic and holy resignation of which only the scions of celestial birth are capable.

Then Manuel rose from his knees. He attempted to approach his father, who drove him away forcibly. He tried to speak, when an expressive gesture commanded silence. Approaching his mother, he took her hand, but the old man tore it away instantly before the son could touch it with his lips.

"Go forth to thy fate, thou wretch!" cried the maddened father.

Manuel saw that such excitement could not be calmed, that naught remained but to quit the house. He opened the street door, and, before closing it for the last time, he turned again upon his parents eyes full of tears, a look praying for love and pity. A sudden burst of sobs and a cry of "Farewell!" and "God be with thee!" in the voice of a broken heart were the response. The old man ended the scene by running to the door, and fastening it upon his son, who found himself homeless and in the street.

CHAPTER III.

THE RAID OF MATHEUS CHAGAS.

MEANWHILE the tornado raged its fiercest; Nature was in mourning, and the blackness of night veiled the road where not illuminated by the momentary flashing of the sheet-lightning, and by the forks and zigzags of the rapid discharges. But for these the Novice would assuredly have lost himself in the web of dark and narrow lanes, whose mud and dust he had trodden since his infancy.

Slowly, and feeling, as it were, the path, he walked northward towards the riverine valley-plain beyond the settlement. After some three-quarters of an hour, passing at rare intervals some wretched hovel, he reached the place now known as the "Luz," or northern suburb, because it was chosen, long after the date of our tale, for a Chapel and Convent of that invocation.

Though his soutane dripped lines of rain, and his coarse shoes had been buried deep in mud, Manuel went on for about half an hour, till he reached a rough tenement belonging to a friend of his earliest years, from whom he expected food and shelter.

Antonio da Costa, startled by the sudden appearance at such at time, supplied the Novice with a change of clothing and induced him to taste a slender meal. Our new personage was a man of two-and-twenty, but already looking older than his age. Living solitary in the little *sitio* or farm, the scanty portion left to him by his parents, and endowed with an ardent imagination and noble sentiments, he vegetated in a hopeless and enforced idleness, which, preying on his vitals, made life hateful.

Manuel frankly summed up for his friend the events of the evening and the state of his affairs; whilst Antonio, applying the moral to his own case, understood that now was the time to link together their fortunes, and find means of facing the world so new to both.

Instead of sleeping, the young men spent the remnant of the night in conversation and reverie, and they had not come to any resolution before the first pale rays of dawn descended upon the glooms of earth. The storm had worked off, and the day promised to be bright and calm.

As they still sat upon the same bedstead in earnest talk, a loud noise was heard coming from the road, a confusion of brawling voices, all speaking at the same time and in the highest tones. Opening the nearest shutter, the friends saw tramping before them a little column composed of some thirty whites and " Mamelucos," followed by about double the number of Redskins. They were habited in wayfarers' costume, broad-brimmed hats of fibre or skull-caps of the thickest woollen stuff, cotton jackets, breeches, and sandals; their rough upper coats were twisted round their waists, and small canvas bags hung by their sides. All carried arms, long matchlocks, swords, and matchets or side-knives, and their reckless countenances and martial swagger showed what errand was theirs. The two youths at once understood that before them was a " Bandeira," a Commando of adventurers, such as the Portuguese of São Paulo had in those days begun to organise.

The group halted in front of the cottage occupied by Antonio da Costa, and there began to debate some important matter with more of loudness and violence than before.

" No need of more prate," exclaimed a stentorian

THE RAID OF MATHEUS CHAGAS.

voice, drowning the lesser sounds about him. "Matheus Chagas ('of the Stigmata') knows the way best; he is a backwoodsman to the backbone; we ought to put ourselves in his hands. No Bandeira is of use without a head; let Matheus Chagas be acclaimed our Chief!"

Shouts of applause followed these words, and most of the adventurers cried, "Viva Matheus Chagas!"

Then broke through the crowd a short, stout figure, whose bullet-shaped head and bandy legs showed his strength, whilst a scar seaming a sunburnt face, whose breadth at the jaw was nearly double that at the eyebrows, proved that he had seen service. His horny hands grasped a mighty fire-piece, whilst a huge knife slung to his side hinted that he was ready to see service again. This personage was the Senhor Matheus Chagas, suddenly transformed by the acclamations of his companions into a Commandant.

"Friends!" he exclaimed with emphasis, after returning thanks for his promotion, "I will lead you all in a bee-line to Peru. We shall find our meat in the bush, our fish in the streams, water to quench our thirst, savoury fruits to refresh us, shady trees to shelter us from the sun, and Pagans in numbers to seize and to sell. I hope to Heaven we shall enter the land of the Spaniard more happily than Aleixo Garcia, whom they scandalously and cruelly robbed and murdered, and that we shall carry off many a load of gold and silver. Know ye not that the Cacique Taubixi advised the Portuguese of São Paulo to march upon all these riches, and to assist him against the Castilians, who wanted only to plunder the property of the Pagans, and to slay their wives and children?"

"Bravo! bravo! Viva Matheus Chagas!" And all applauded with voices rising in cadence to a scream and a yell.

"Form up, then, and forwards!" continued the

fiery speaker. "Thirty leagues hence our troubles begin. Till then a journey of roses. After that, Pagan rascals posted behind trees, charges of the jaguar on the bank, biting of the rattlesnake in the hollow. But never you fear! All these dangers are known to me. I served with one of the men whom Martim Affonso sent to the far west under the Captain José Sedenho[1] with the view of aiding Aleixo Garcia, and of whom few escaped the fray. Friends! let us be marching!"

Although only legends of Aleixo Garcia, and mere tales of the Peruvian Spaniards, superior to all in audacity, declared the existence of gold and silver mines in the bosom of the far west, and although of these not one had been discovered by the Portuguese; yet the idea obtaining general credence, spoke to their greed of gain, and drove them to endure the severest trials of life, to plunge into the densest forests, to cross the most dangerous rivers, and to climb the most precipitous mountains. Much owed the crown of Portugal to these bands of daring men. They conquered whole tracts of territory; they overlapped with their frontiers those of the Spaniards; they formed nuclei of villages and settlements, which, with time, became towns and cities; and they opened lines of road to the farthest west from the sea-shore upon which Europeans had begun to establish themselves. Many of these unknown braves ended their days in the desert; whole troops disappeared without

---

[1] Padre Ticho in his work upon Paraguay, and the "Historia Argentina" (lib. i. chap. v.), relates the fate of Aleixo Garcia, who, sent to explore by Martim Affonso, lost his life at the hand of Gaboto (Cabot), whilst the latter became master of the silver-mines. The same authors speak of the invitation of Taubixi, and Padre Ticho tells the tale of Sedenho and his sixty men, most of whom perished with their Chief. It is very unlikely that this most amiable of explorers, justly entitled "El buen Gaboto," would have been guilty of such an atrocity. —*Translator's Note.*

leaving a sign. They were not spared in combat by the poisoned shaft of the savage, nor after defeat by the terrible "tacapé," or tomahawk, with which the Red Man brained the prisoners doomed to become their horrid banquets. But the results of these expeditions of the Paulistas were extraordinary gains and advantages for the colonies, which increased wonderfully in extent, in population and in wealth.

Manuel de Moraes looked at his friend and said, "Doth not Heaven show us what we have to do? Why should not we accompany these men in their wanderings?"

And suddenly the same thought presented itself to Antonio da Costa, who replied, "So be it, and at once!"

They lost no time in further speech. The Novice donned his soutane, now dry, and his broad-brimmed felt. Antonio dressed himself in a jacket of coarse cotton, threw over it a rough woollen cape, covered his head with a straw hat, and caught up his sword and fire-piece. They both left the cottage, whose door they closed, and hastening after the band, which had already gained some distance, they came up with it upon the banks of the river Tiété. Antonio da Costa demanded to speak with the Chief, and offered himself and his companion to the Senhor Matheus Chagas.

"Ho! ho!" vociferated certain voices. "What is the use of these hobbledehoys, these mamma's darlings? We need stout fellows, ready to work and fight, not cockerels, who will only crow and give trouble."

"Silence there!" shouted Matheus Chagas. "I lead here, and I grant them leave to join us. Now we have priest and sacristan!"

Shouts of ribald laughter from the band followed this irreverent sally. The jest, in fact, suited the dress of Manuel de Moraes and the juvenile appearance of Antonio da Costa. A sudden blush mounted to the cheek of the Novice, who, turning to his friend, whispered that they had better withdraw. But the latter bade him disregard the jeering of the crowd; the die of destiny was now cast.

Then all resumed their way along the left bank of the Tiété, till, at a clearing farther down, they found six of the roughest craft, untrimmed tree-trunks lashed together with creepers as ropes, and resembling the modern Jangada or Catamarán of the North Brazilian coast. Upon these they embarked, slung their goods and provisions that they might not be washed off by the waters, and, casting loose the cords which bound the craft to their poles, slowly paddled down-stream.

The Tiété river wound its long length, like a gigantic serpent with immense horizontal folds, in reaches, bends, and horse-shoes, whose silvery, mirrory surface often glittered through the verd-obscure of the avenued vegetation. Here were lawn-like slopes, tenanted by patriarchal trees of Indian name, the wild fig, the Cabiuna or balm-tree, the towering Jatobá, the foliaged Gabiróba, the iron-wood, and the Jacarandá or rosewood. There ridges of high land sloped to the banks, and bore upon their backs crests of the densest primeval forest, whose columnar boles and mighty arms were laced and hung with a thousand llianas, beautiful parasites, lit up by sparks of flowers, and diffusing through the air delicious odours. The cries of the navigators and the splashing of the little fleet startled hosts of birds, which fled for refuge into the inner depths. Here moaned the Jurity-dove, as though lamenting the death of her young; there screamed the parroquet, winging his way high in air; there the vibrating and sudden note of the Arapónga or bell-bird resembled the stroke of the hammer upon the anvil. Now the nimble Cotiá[1] sprang

---

[1] The well-known Agouti, called by the Brazilian savages "Acuty."—*Translator's Note.*

frightened up the bank; then the chatter of the monkeys suggested the scoffs and jeers of a crowd which was amusing itself with seeing the adventurers pass by.

Every night the canoes were made fast to tree-trunks or to poles planted in the ground, and fires were lit against the damp night-air, and the ounce and boa, whilst the simple supper of maize, manioc, and wild meat made up for the fatigues of the day and supplied strength for the labours of the morrow. After setting a watch, the wearied men, wrapped in their cloaks, slept under the twinkling light of the stars. Again at dawn they rose, regained their Catamarans, and pursued their dangerous way.

Game was abundant, and it was not spared. Often during the day the sharp crack of the fire-piece and the whistle of the bullet rudely disturbed the silence of the wilderness. In the morning and at nightfall hooks were thrown out, and soon drew on shore a prodigious variety of delicious fish, especially the Surubim, or sturgeon of the Brazil, the Bagre, the Robále, and the Dourado or gold-fish. This lenten fare was varied with the flesh of gallinaceous birds, the Penelope and the Curassou, and with venison and the meat of large rodents, the Mocó, the Páca, and the Capivára or water-hog.

After eight days of sublime monotony, the adventurers reached the first Salto, or fall of the stream, across which ran a wall of rock, projected by buttresses on either side. A portage was here made; the dismantled catamarans, carried upon the men's shoulders to smooth waters below the leap, were once more put together. The breaks were rather rapids than falls or cataracts; but the arrowy waters, dashing and foaming through the steep-stoned breaches of the rock-wall, the hollow whirlpools and the heaped-up ridges of the current, would have dashed to pieces any craft clumsily handled whilst shooting the *mauvais pas*. The roughness of the banks and the necessity of cutting paths added much to the toils and fatigues of the band: the weaker, however, found strength and support in the energetic presence and in the personal experience of Matheus Chagas.

One day the piercing whistle of a wild beast rang through the luxuriant waste, and was answered by a second, which excited the attention of every man. Matheus Chagas rose, and commanding silence with a gesture, said in under-tones to his followers—

"The Red Man is near; beware of his ambush; he is cunning as the wolf, deadly as the serpent. Push on, and silence!"

Then making for the shore, the Chief chose out three Carijós whom he sent to reconnoitre the forest. These men plunged without delay into the matted underwood; they crept snake-like upon their stomachs; they sheltered themselves behind the tree-trunks, and their naked bodies, passing over the dried leaves, left no sound, and advanced with the rapidity of the deer.

Reaching the foot of a hillock, some five hundred yards from the place where the adventurers stood ready for offence or defence, the Carijós once more lay down at full length.

A sepulchral silence brooded over the scene; no cry of bird or beast, no murmur of the water, no whisper of the breeze. The burning sun darted his angriest beams, driving into the gloom of the forest every being that had life.

The Carijós applied their ears to the ground, and asked from it intelligence of the afar-off. Two are the Books which Savages study with profoundest attention;—Earth, which reveals what passes around them; Heaven, which tells them the vagaries of the atmosphere and the flight of time. After a quarter of an hour passed in the exercise of every perceptive faculty, the scouts arose slowly, and two of them responded with a movement of the head to the expressive gesture of the third. Then they inspected the soil to see what had lately passed over it. Finally, they returned to the adventurers cautiously as they had left them, and said to the Chief—

"The enemy is near, he is very near, he is exceedingly near. He is many in number, he is very many, he is exceedingly many."[1]

"And how can you know?" asked an inquisitive Portuguese.

"Silence there!" cried Matheus Chagas. "I lead here." Then he approached the Carijós, wishing to know how far they supposed the enemy to be lurking.

"They are three to six bow-lengths off. We heard upon the ground their tread; we saw on the earth their prints."

Hardly were the words spoken, when a bird, pierced by the six-foot Tupi shaft, crashed through the thick foliage and fell close to the band. A Carijó fetched the quarry, a Jacutinga or white-winged Penelope, and placed it in the Chief's hands.

There was no longer any doubt as to the neighbourhood of the savages. But Matheus Chagas, broken to forays and frays, was not the man to take alarm.

"The ambush! the ambush!" he cried. "Let the Padre go forth and speak to them; throw dust in their eyes, and count their numbers carefully. Now, fellows, dare to say the shaveling is of no use to you!"

Choosing two Portuguese, two Mamelucos, and four Carijós, he ordered them privily and from afar to follow Manuel de Moraes. He also advised the Novice to advance fearlessly upon the savages, to show his rosary cross, and to address them about Heaven. Thus they might believe that they stood, not before enemies, but in the presence of peaceful missionaries eager to catechise them.

Moraes prepared to obey with a stout heart, and Antonio da Costa, at his own request, was allowed by

[1] For this habit of threefold repetition, see Jean de Léry and Père Yves d'Évreux.—*Translator's Note.*

the Chief to accompany his friend. Both youths, with the eight adventurers concealed in the rear, took the direction pointed out to them by the Carijó scouts.

Presently Manuel and Antonio scaled a high and broken headland; and, reaching the summit, heard in the low ground beyond a prolonged whooping and yelling, which showed the savages to be near.

The Novice raised high his arms, clasping in his hands the cross and the rosary; then, closely followed by his friend, he straightway walked towards the voices. Not a sign of a human being appeared before or behind them.

The slope led to a level which ran along the river-bank. Hardly had they advanced five hundred yards when they found themselves the centre of a whooping swarm of savages, armed with stone knives and hatchets, clubs, tomahawks, and bows nearly eight feet long. All were naked and bronzed. The only dress was a tulip-shaped coronal of scarlet and yellow feathers, fastened by a string to their brows, and a similar kilt hanging from their waist.

Both the youths felt their blood run cold and their flesh creep in the presence of these cannibals, who seemed to regard them as meat for the Boucan.[1] Then Manuel, raising his head and hands, once more displayed the cross, and began in Portuguese a discourse, to which the Indians lent all attention, though apparently without understanding it. Humbly bending, and with arms crossed like a penitent upon his bosom, Antonio da Costa maintained a firm and resigned demeanour. Both thus represented the parts intrusted to them. The Pagans all pressed forward to examine their two visitors. Some applied themselves to the improvised Jesuit, felt his soutane, wondered at his hat, bent down to look at his big shoes, and were awed at his gestures and his incomprehen-

---

[1] The frame on which meat was smoked; hence our "buccaneer."—*Translator's Note.*

sible words. Others applied themselves to the acolyte, whom they treated with less ceremony, the chief amusement being to pull his beard.

"A man of peace," pompously exclaimed Manuel, "I would bring to you peace, and teach you the religion of the only God, the Creator of the universe. Leave, O savages! this wandering, erring life, which is so rapidly hurrying you to perdition. The only Son of God died upon Golgotha." . . .

The Pagans interrupted him by a few quick words in the Guaraní tongue. Some of their responses escaped Manuel, but he caught the general tenor of the communication, having studied that language in the house of the Company. The savages exchanged suspicions that the whole scene was a snare, intended to draw them to destruction. Manuel then addressed them in their mother-speech.

"Yes, I *have* companions, but they shall remain far from you, and they shall work you no harm. Messengers of peace and seeking to befriend you, we come here to address you."

"The Whites are bad, they are very bad, they are exceedingly bad. They are liars, very liars, excessive liars. We, we, we, do not believe you," responded one of them.

"Make yourselves easy," continued the Novice. "Those who come with me are good and kind."

Signs and signals passed between the savages, and some of them felt the two youths to ascertain if they bore concealed weapons. No arms being found, he who appeared to be the Chief of the tribe said to them resolutely—

"Pagé (father)! we are a strong Tribe, a large and a valiant: of a truth, we are a great Nation. Near us are our wigwams and our forts, our wives and children, our divining-rattles and our medicine-men. The Whites are bad, they are very bad, they are exceeding bad. But we will do you no hurt. Take your way, and go forth from amongst us; never come again, or be it at your peril: we will not look upon the pale face."

The Red-skins disappeared suddenly, as they had shown themselves; and the young men, recovering from their agitation, heard throughout the forest repeated strident whistlings, which showed that the foe, though unseen, was not off his guard. Then retracing their steps, they found hidden behind a tall tree the eight scouts that followed them.

"Have a care!" said a Carijó. "They are many hundred bows; if they doubt us, we die."

All returned in safety to the adventurers, who anxiously expected them. Matheus Chagas, hearing their account, gave orders to halt for a day and a night, until the savages should have retired far from the stream. Then they once more proceeded on their journey, vigilantly, and with every precaution known to the woodsman.

Already they had travelled two months upon the Tiété without meeting other adventures, when they perceived that the stream was widening out excessively, spreading over extensive plains, flooding the forests, and running with greater violence than usual.

Two days afterwards appeared in front a "broad" or lake of extraordinary dimensions, whose farther shore was not easily seen.

"'Tis the great river Paraná," said one of the Carijós; "we now enter its waters."

Impossible to describe the might and magnificence of this glorious stream. After traversing the lands of Matto-Grosso, Minas-Geraes, and the northern part of the captaincy of São Vicente, and receiving tributaries of an importance almost equal to its own, the Paraná formed, at the place discovered by our adventurers, a vast and beautiful bay, fed on one side by the Rio Tiété, on the other by the Sucuriú and the Pardo streams. The frail craft escaped the fury of the winds by hugging the left bank, and in calmer weather crossed the mouths of other great influents, such as the Aguapehi and the Santo Anastacio. When the adventurers approached the Paranápanema river, Matheus ordered them to exchange the main artery for the branch. They found it necessary to contend with pole and paddle against the downfall of the united currents. Four days of hard labour placed them at the embouchure of the Pirapó into the Paranápanema.

After some repose, which was much required, scouts were sent to reconnoitre the lands reached by the Bandeira. These on their return informed Matheus that they had met with certain signs of a neighbouring Indian village—tree branches cut, a want of game, and the trail of man. Once more the chief detached spies, who were ordered carefully to examine the neighbourhood.

These explorers, returning after some days, reported that they had found a large and important Aldeia or settlement of catechised Indians, with a stone church and ploughed fields, with herds of black cattle, horses, and sheep; and with other proofs that the people were not savage nomades.

Matheus Chagas at once concluded that he was near the Spanish settlement of La Guayra.

He was filled with joy by the thought that he had descended the Tiété river without the loss of a man or a brush with the Pagans, and that he had safely reached an Aldeia of the Guaranís. Here he expected, according to the reports bruited about São Paulo, to find immense hoards of gold and silver, which he could snatch from the Spaniards, even as the latter had robbed the Portuguese under Aleixo Garcia.

He at once formed his little troop into a military camp, and concealed it by the thickest bushes that grew nearest the settlement.

He then made every arrangement for the assault, and he resolved to glut himself with the spoils, and to bear them off in triumph to São Paulo.

CHAPTER IV.

THE NOVICE'S FIRST MISFORTUNE.

LORETO was the settlement that lay before the Paulista adventurers. It was one of the last built by the Jesuits, and one of the nearest to the disputed frontiers of Spain and Portugal. In 1557 the Government of Paraguay had founded Villa Real, at the junction of the rivers Paraná and Piquirí, and in 1577 Villa Rica on the Ivahy. These villages were stocked with Gentile Guaranís. As, however, their catechesis and civilisation prospered but slowly under the civil authorities, the Government of the metropolis ceded to the Jesuit missionaries the two Aldeias above mentioned, with authority to organise others.

The Jesuits soon prospered in the work of conversion, and presently dispersed their obedient flock over the upper regions of the Paraná. To their intrepid and exclusive efforts, during the first years of the seventeenth century, Santa Maria Maior on the Iguassú, São Francisco Xavier at the embouchure of the Imbiberabá, Arcanjos in Tayoba, Santo Ignacio on the Iquatemy, São Pedro on the Pinaes, and Loreto on the Pirajó owed their existence.

These children of Saint Ignatius did not spare themselves. Smiled upon them the idea of saving the souls and of championing the rights and liberties of Pagans made Catholics. They found the most fertile of soils, cut by numerous streams, and extending on both sides of the Paraná artery, from the Iguassú and the Igarcy rivers to the Paranápanena

and the Pardo. Immense numbers of wild tribes
became semi-civilised, and these communities began
to found an independent state in the heart of Portuguese and Castilian America. Thus rose the province of La Guayra, nominally subject to the crown
of Spain, but really, as will be seen, a theocratic des-
potism, perhaps the most actively evil of all governments, whose best action is rarely for good.

The Padres persuaded the Home Government to
forbid the entrance of Europeans, whatever might be
their nation, lest they should corrupt the innocent
savages. At the head of each settlement was placed
a "Cura," and as many Fathers and Brethren as were
necessary for its direction. The Curate was the principal authority, civil and ecclesiastic, and, as executive
Chief of the Mission, he administered the oath of obedience to the sundry functionaries chosen amongst
the converts. Each Aldeia possessed a Corregidor, or
Chief of Police, and his Lieutenant, two Alcaides, a
Standard-bearer, seven Administrators, a Secretary,
and various Caciques or Chiefs, besides officers of the
militia corps, organised, drilled, and disciplined by the
Padres. The little society was told off to its several
duties with military strictness. These applied themselves to agriculture, which consisted of sugar-cane,
maté or Paraguay tea, wheat, cotton, beans, maize,
indigo and tobacco; those worked in the farinha-
mills, in the smithies, at the carpenter's bench, and
at other handicrafts. Thus they formed a community
whose duties and rights were perfectly equal, being in
fact none; and in the dull routine of hopeless obedience they were permitted to make a certain progress,
which soon reached its *ne plus ultra*.

The Jesuits received, in their vast storehouses, all
the produce of the Aldeia. This material was rafted
down to Santa-Fé and Buenos Ayres, and at times it
was shipped directly to Spain, and bartered for articles
of necessity and comfort. A poll-tax of a dollar per

head was annually taken from each catechised savage. This sum rightfully belonged to the Home Government, but the Curas, who had charge of the statistics, defrauded the Crown by not including in their lists those in office, minors under twenty years, and even the sick. The remainder, a considerable amount, was remitted to the General of the Order, resident at Rome, and contributed to erect palatial buildings, and to extend far and wide the power and influence of the Institute.

At their labours, which were taskwork marked out day by day, men, women, and children were all apart; only the married occupied the same habitations, and separate quarters were provided for widows and bachelors, for girls and children.

The Curates in the "Reductions" of La Guayra were subject to the great Jesuit College of Asuncion, capital of Paraguay, which held authority over all the various nuclei of the Company settled in the valleys of La Plata and its tributaries.

When Córdoba was made the Head-quarters of the Order, the Principal, assisted by the ordinary and three extraordinary Councillors, there took up his residence, and thence extended his authority throughout South America. The colleges contained seminaries for instruction, secondary as well as primary, and presently the Spanish Captaincies of Buenos Ayres, Paraguay, and Tucuman could number in their bosom some three hundred Fathers and one hundred lay Brothers besides a host of Novices.

The Mission villages were all built on one and the same plan. The houses, of equal size and shape, with mud walls and red-tiled roofs, were surrounded by compounds. The streets were disposed in straight lines converging to a great square; on the right, and at the head of the latter, stood the church, with the campanile, the Jesuits' house, and the public magazines; whilst to the left were the cemetery and the habitations of the widows and the girls, who at the earliest age were taken from their fathers and their families. The *place* was adorned with a tall Cross in each corner, and with a central pillar supporting an image of the Blessed Virgin.

The men wore shirts and short drawers, pouches and cotton caps; the women dressed in the "tapay," long sleeveless gown, fitting close to the neck and waist. All went barefoot, and only the Caciques and the public functionaries were allowed to carry the staves which symbolised their several offices. A perfect equality was maintained in garb and ornaments, as in food and labour.

On Sundays the converts were taught the various arts of war, such as the use of the sabre, the gun, the bow, and the sling, with which they threw round stones. When drill ended, the weapons were replaced in the armoury, and the people remained without the means of offence or defence.

The Fathers taught, besides reading and writing, cyphering and instrumental music and chanting, so as to form artists for the Church festivals and the solemnities of the community. They found the "concord of sweet sounds" a powerful attraction to the Gentiles, who showed tolerably good taste and excessive fondness for the liberal art.

The converts were awakened by the ringing of the Church-bell, which announced the dawn and its prayer-meeting. Prime over, all repaired to their respective tasks, guarded by their overseers. The guilty were punished by a tribunal composed of the village authorities under the surveillance of the Cura.

Thus was governed the province of La Guayra at the time when Matheus Chagas attacked it with his Commando. The onslaught was one of the first organised by the filibusters of São Paulo upon the Jesuit Missions of the Paraná. Presently the invasions became so frequent and so destructive, that the

Fathers prevailed upon their flocks to abandon their homes, to fall back upon the lower river, and there to build new Reductions, less exposed to the raids of their Mameluco foes.

We have already said that Loreto was the outlying Mission village of the Spanish dominions. It contained eight streets with a total of about two thousand souls. The prairies around it were carefully cultivated, and showed all the signs of prosperity. Domestic animals fed in peace; the converts lived tranquilly under the communistic rule of the Fathers; and not a single accident had from the very beginning troubled the perfect order of peaceful and quiet Loreto.

Curious to say, the Portuguese of São Paulo, even the explorers and filibusters, knew nothing of the situation and the state of La Guayra, from the day when its Missions passed into the temporal, spiritual, and exclusive power of the Company. They still believed firmly in the last reports that the Gentiles longed for Portuguese aid against the Spaniards, and that the latter possessed stores of gold and silver, extracted without toil from the adjacent lands. The Castilians in point of morals were, perhaps, no better than the heathen, except that they were somewhat less cruel. The Paulistas, however, were animated by a furious hatred, engendered partly by the rival interests of neighbourhood in Europe and America, and partly because at that time their fatherland had been reduced to a province of the Spanish crown. In 1580 Philip the Second brought it violently under his yoke, and bequeathed it to his successors, with traditions of terror which, irritating the Lusitanian race against the rule of its rival and conqueror, continually excited them to rise and to strike the blow for independence.

The greatest inducement, then, for the Paulistas to attack the mission of La Guayra was to destroy the

Spaniards, not the converts; yet they had no intention of sparing the latter, nor of forfeiting the profits to be derived from enslaving and selling their captives.

Matheus Chagas, after learning from his spies the state of Loreto, forbade his comrades to betray their presence by the smallest sign, and he proposed to them an attack upon the village, which he believed to contain extraordinary wealth. All applauded the idea except Manuel de Moraes, who wished first to ascertain if the intended victims were friends or foes, and thus to avoid the possibility of committing an unscrupulous crime. The filibusters scoffed at his qualms of conscience. At length one morning, when Matheus Chagas saw the greater part of the population at work outside the village, and those inside it completely off their guard, he left some of his least useful men, and amongst them the Novice, to protect the camp, and he marched off prepared to give battle.

The Commando first met upon the open plain some fifty converts, who, at the sight of the enemy, fled to the village. They were followed by the filibusters, and all entered at the same time with an infernal din and outcry. The indigens defended themselves with the courage of despair, but their weapons were in the armoury; the foe never ceased to flesh his sword, and a few hours put the Portuguese in possession of the settlement, which was at once deserted by its owners. The sudden onslaught had terrified the Fathers and the Guaranís. Much blood had been spilt in the affray and in the pursuit, whilst many of the converts found themselves pinioned and barred up in their own homes. The adventurers then proceeded to examine the village which they had won. In the magazines they found rations, firearms, ammunition, weapons, cloth and clothes, ardent spirits and other valuable stores. They took from the Church, lamps and chandeliers of silver, and they hailed with loud vivas the appearance of such valuable booty. But they were disagreeably surprised not to see a trace of the Spaniards, whom they supposed also to inhabit the " Reduction."

Matheus Chagas gave the strictest orders for maintaining discipline. He summoned from his camp those left in charge. He counted and separated the captives, who were for the most part old Caciques, women, and children, all powerless to fly; and he placed the prisoners, divided into groups, under the charge of sentinels. He then proceeded to collect the booty, and to take the strongest measures against the possibility of desertion, and of losing the fruits of victory.

Well knowing, also, the imprudence of lingering in a hostile land, and wishing to quit the village as soon as possible, he proceeded to set apart what could be carried off. But when the booty, comprising jewels, arms, clothing, animals, and prisoners, came to be divided, all the adventurers agreed in preferring the same article, and their rivalry nearly led them to blows. The Chief at length managed to curb their pretensions and passions by opening a kind of lottery for the less valuable objects, reserving the more precious for distribution at São Paulo.

Each filibuster received an almost equal share. Moraes, however, refusing to join the lottery, took as his portion the old men, the women, and children who were unable to march. He wanted none of the ill-gotten gains, and he resolved to free all his prisoners. He proceeded at once to set food before the wretches and to console their sorrows. They received his charity with transports of gratitude, and they were the more thankful as they expected the worst fate from the Mamelucos of São Paulo, whom the Fathers had described to them as a mixture of lust and ferocity, unsoftened by the least trace of piety or religion.

THE NOVICE'S FIRST MISFORTUNE. 43

When the adventurers had taken charge of their spoils, Matheus Chagas prepared to evacuate the village. The Paulista Commando began its homeward march before the red light appeared in the east. The armed men led the van, in the centre and surrounded by guards were bands of pinioned captives, and in the rear came horses and laden beasts under protection of the Mamelucos.

They had not left the village before loud and prolonged sounds were heard, and presently numerous fires broke out in the suburbs of the settlement. The conflagration increased, and a thick cloud of smoke filled the air, which was gradually lit up by the furious flames. It became bright as day, whilst the atmosphere waxed every moment heavier and warmer. The adventurers were startled; none knew whether mere chance or the design of the converts had caused the danger which threatened them. They hastened to quit the village, when Matheus Chagas warned them to beware of ambuscades.

The flames were spread far and wide by a stiff norther. Horribly illuminated were the village, the prairie, and the forest. Frightful noises thundered in the air like a concert of fiends. The roofs and entrances of the houses burst open; huge fragments of masonry, loose tiles, and smoking walls were dashed to earth. The streets were choked with ruins, and the adventurers had immense labour in extricating themselves.

Some of the Mamelucos already spread themselves outside the village, and the rearguard was still struggling to escape the danger and to join those who preceded it.

But whilst the flames lit up the ruins and wrapped the upper horizon in sable clouds, loud shouts and whistlings from afar increased the panic produced by the fire; and the terrified eyes of the Paulistas fell upon armed masses of Guaranís, some hastening in

front, others closing upon the flanks, and others again
hurrying to the rear, till every road was cut off.

Then began a *mêlée* without order, command, or
discipline. The adventurers understood, when too
late, that they had allowed the enemy to enter the
village at night, and thus to co-operate with those
rushing to its relief. Each man fought as best he
could, without being able to guess the number of his
enemies or to divine the result of the combat. Their
ranks were thinned by the bullet, the arrow, and
the sling-stone; their ears were stunned by the fire
and the clamour of the foe; their comrades were
wounded, their friends were killed, afar and near,
before, behind, and on both sides. Felling blows of
heavy clubs, the sharp cutting of the sword-blade, and
stabbings with knife and dagger followed the first
attack, and ended in a system of duels *corps à
corps*, man to man, the most cruel and deadly of all
struggles.

It was a terrible spectacle, lit up at times by the
roaring flames that devoured the village, and which
caused the settlement to shudder as with torture;
groans and cries, shrieks and shouts, re-echoed loudly
the clang and clashing of the sword and the rolling
and reverberation of the musketry. The fugitives
tripped and stumbled over the bodies of the live and
the dead. The ways were choked with loaded horses
and mules. Portuguese and Mamelucos, Carijós and
Guaranís, knifed one another, almost without knowing
their victims. The struggle lasted till Aurora smiled
her rays and lit up with their white light all the
firmament.

Then lay disclosed a terrible scene of destruction.
From the innermost streets of the village to no small
distance in the neighbouring prairie, where the adventurers' vanguard had extended, the ground was spread
with carcases of man and beast, with scattered loads,
arms, and lost booty, all dripping with blood and

blackened by flakes of burning substances, which, whirling through the air, fell upon those whom the combat had disabled.

Few of the filibusters succeeded in saving themselves by flight; the greater part lay dead upon the field of battle; rare were the prisoners, and these were all more or less severely wounded: the Guaranís had conquered, and had revenged the affront put upon them. Their authorities took measures to end the struggle, and to save what they could of the village by quenching the fire; they collected the objects snatched from the grasp of the enemy; they restored order to the people, and they superintended the burial of those who had fallen. Many on both sides were found stark dead. Matheus Chagas, Antonio da Costa, and several notable adventurers lost their lives; and, lastly, four or five wounded Paulistas were taken from amongst the slain and lodged in jail. Manuel de Moares was one of these unfortunates. He had received an arrow-wound in the arm, and his leg was pierced by a ball; the danger was not great, but his sufferings were long and acute.

The captives were committed to those in charge of the Hospitals for treatment and surveillance till they could be tried for their crime. When Moraes was restored to health, he learned with grief and a sinking heart that his companions in misfortune had all died of their wounds.

CHAPTER V

THE NOVICE'S SECOND MISFORTUNE.

THE trial of Manuel de Moraes soon ended. Sundry Caciques and women gave evidence in his favour, and recounted his humane conduct during the days when the Paulistas occupied the village. Such testimony, together with the dress which attached him to the Company of Jesus, had its due effect; the tribunal before which he appeared sentenced him to banishment from the Reduction, and to be placed in the hands of the Provincial at Santa-Fé. The latter was charged with the duty of imposing the penance proper for one who in his noviciate had abandoned the holy Institute of St. Ignatius, and had enlisted under the filibustering flag of the Paulistas.

Accompanied by armed Guaranís, Moraes was transported by land to Villa Rica, distant not less than seventy leagues from Loreto. Here the Fathers of the College kept him confined for more than two months, awaiting the rafts which were being made ready to transport the articles most in demand at Villa Real. This done, he embarked under the charge of Cialdini, a lay Brother of the Company, with a crew of thirty Guaranís, who acted as guards and boatmen.

The little flotilla, laden with the exports of the Reductions, descended the river Ivahy between its avenues of forest giants, entered the Paraná, and, presently reaching the Great Island, was towed up the mouth of the Piquirí. At last it safely made Villa Real, which reposed softly upon the margin of the

THE NOVICE'S SECOND MISFORTUNE. 47

waters, and which represented the most important and populous Reduction built by the Jesuits of La Guayra. The rafts could descend the Paraná no farther; the gigantic rapids known as the Sete Quedos, or Seven Falls, began immediately below.

No sight in nature, however grand or graceful, more delighted the traveller's eyes than this mighty scene. The Paraná here forks to embrace a spacious island, whose dense and sombre forests contrast admirably with the transparent green of the waters and the white flashing of the foam. After their fall the powerful masses of the liquid element reunited, and presented a breadth of more than two thousand fathoms. Thence the bed contracted and the gorge deepened, while the roar and the reverberation became terribly sublime. The least breadth of the cañon did not exceed forty cubits, and a fall of four hundred palms precipitated the torrent into a stupendous kieve or basin, which formed a lake almost two miles in diameter.

The noise of the rapids extended to eight leagues; a cloud of water-dust hung high poised above the fall, forming, under the sunshine, rainbows whose peculiar and fragile beauty tempered and softened the rugged power and sublimity of the scene.

The vast basin, crowned with phosphorescent and opaline fragments of mist, was dotted over with many an islet, whose gigantic trees animated the view of strife and tumult with the charms of life and fertility.

From that spot the waters poured anew over seven consecutive steps, hurrying along the puma and the ounce, the ant-eater, the dreadful boa, and all manner of animals that had taken refuge in the upper islands during the dries, and which had neither time nor strength to escape by swimming. The waters with hollow thunder, repeated by the groaning echoes, were engulfed in a second crater, whose barriers of rocky peaks seemed, like the Titans of old, to threaten the skies: the reflection of the sun athwart the glancing water-smoke fell upon the polished sides of the gorge in sudden showers of light, which by day seemed the playing of sheet-lightning, whilst in the obscurity of night they appeared to be vast walls built of the whitest stone.

It was vain for man's voice to speak there: the puny accents were drowned in the monstrous but majestic music of the cataract, the word of command given by eternal Nature herself.

For more than three months Moraes sojourned at Villa Real, employed by his Father Directors in the service of the church and of things sacred. Not the less persistently, however, did he refuse to rejoin the Institute of St. Ignatius, though his heart was laden with the most grateful and regretful memories of the welcome which he had received, of the instruction which he had obtained, and of the friendships which he had won.

He then set out by land, with a large caravan of Indians and loaded beasts, to the village of Santa Maria Maior, built almost at the embouchure where the São Francisco is absorbed by the Paraná below the "Seven Falls." Here, as the navigation had lost its perils, all embarked in new rafts for Santa-Fé. Moraes, though permitted the society of Father Cialdini, whose edifying discourses soon gained his sympathy, was as strictly guarded as he had been at Loreto.

About a month was spent in descending the Paraná to the Tres Barras, the "Three Mouths," where it receives the waters of the Paraguay and its influents the Pilcomayo and the Bermejo.

Manuel de Moraes was thrown into ecstasies by these varied and sublime scenes, and especially by the dazzle and the glamour of the magnificent stream. On either side were virgin forests, loftiest domes of green, which proved the infinite fertility of the soil;

mighty rivers which added themselves to the Paraná, already itself a sea; birds of every size and shape and hue, the ibis, the toucan, the spoonbill, and giant cranes, that bellowed as they fled from the plashing of the oar into the black recesses of the splendid woodlands; and huge caymans, basking upon the sunny sands, and plunging when disturbed into the vasty deeps, their homes and their castles.

Yet more delicious than the clear and limpid days were the nights spent on the bosom of these solitary Edens. What pictures of soft and tender beauty were disclosed when the pale rays of the moon, piercing with shafts of light the thick foliage of the avenued trees overhanging the waters, glittered upon the phosphorescent surface, forming a mosaic work of silver and gold, and lit up the reflection of a horizon, whose voluptuous and undulating contours were drawn with a master's touch upon the liquid ground!

They passed many a site then desert and unexplored, but presently to be occupied by new Jesuit Missions, when the old should be no longer tenable. Still on both sides are to be seen the ruins of Corpus Christi, Candellaria, Itaqui, Santa Clara, Trinidad, San Cosmo, and others, which owed their existence to the Paulista ravagers of Northern La Guayra. But when our hero looked upon them, they were but the lairs and the asylums of wild beasts.

The voyagers soon made Santa-Fé, where Moraes was received with paternal kindness by the Provincial of the Institute. This good Father enjoined upon him such penances and serious meditations as might decide a return to his vocation, when the Company, forgetting all his shortcomings, would receive him with open arms. But despite exhortations, advice, and three years' compulsory residence in the convent, Manuel persisted in keeping firm to his purpose. The Fathers then resolved upon sending him through Spain to Rome, hoping that the General of the Company would be more successful, and that the Institute would not lose a youth whose varied talents and solid learning were evident to all who conversed with him.

Manuel left Santa-Fé for Buenos Ayres in a launch which plied regularly between the two ports of the Paraná and the Plata. He lived in the house of the Company whilst a convoy was being prepared for a fleet of merchantmen sailing to Cadiz: they were escorted by two Spanish brigantines of war, especially charged to defend them against the squadrons and privateers of the Netherlands, who then infested these seas.

A violent Pampero aided the voyagers by driving them out of the dangerous waters of the Rio de la Plata into the bosom of the Atlantic. Here Moraes again found himself in front of another portent of Nature, the ocean; immense, profound, tranquil, or agitated according to the crises of the currents and the will of the winds. The virgin forest, the wild unnavigable river, the savage beast, the stupendous cataract, the picturesque homestead, the vast prairie, and the lofty mountain—such were the features of the American desert, a wonder of nature, in which the beautiful, the sublime, the varied, and the infinite were all harmoniously blended without the aid of art. Now he contrasted with these majestic scenes the ocean, which could groan like the wind-wrung woods, which could foam like the basin of the cataract, which could roar and rage like the jaguar and the Surucucú serpent, and which could change place and colour, form and physiognomy, rapidly as the varying atmosphere which we things of earth inhale.

Before the first breath of the south-east trade the ships rapidly made northing, although the swiftest were obliged to await from time to time those that lagged behind, number and union being their chief defence against pirates and enemies. Sailing together like a fleet, and constantly exchanging signals with the two escorting brigantines, they had reached the latitude of Fernando de Noronha, when strange sails were seen at a distance dotting the horizon. This unexpected accident disturbed not a little the spirits of the voyagers. Could they be enemies? Would not reconnoitring them lead to greater danger? And yet to fly them, would it not show fear and act as an inducement for foes to follow?

The brigantines hailed one another, and a Council of War was held on board. As usual, the Chiefs resolved not to fight, but to clap all sail upon their convoy, and to hurry away from the danger as fast as possible. Unfortunately the suspected craft wore to windward; they perceived the manœuvre, and they hastened to give chase. The fastest sailers amongst the merchantmen escaped, hidden by the bosom of the ocean and by the immensity of the firmament. The less fortunate fell victims; amongst the latter was the galleon *Santo Ambrosio*, which carried Manuel de Moraes.

As the unknown ships approached they hoisted the colours of the High and Mighty Lords the States-General, and displayed broadsides which completed the discomfiture of the Spaniards. The latter were easily persuaded by a few warning shots to bring-to and to prepare for being boarded. The captain of the *Santo Ambrosio* thought to escape by slinking away, after firing upon the assailant with his two grape-loaded guns. At this signal others of the convoy followed his example. But the Hollanders, though only eight of their ships were right well manned and armed, did not keep silence with their cannon. Puffs of white smoke, cloven by tongues of fire, and the roar of artillery, took the place of air. The *Santo Ambrosio* was pooped between wind and water, and her captain, in order to prevent sinking, was obliged to haul down his flag.

The Netherlanders, sighting the signal, came up in their launches to take possession of the prize. But before they could reach it a fire broke out in the fore magazine, and the wretched crew had the fatal and horrible choice of being burnt, or drowned by the waters which rushed like a torrent through the leak. The air resounded with shrieks of despair, with heart-rending groans, and with piercing cries for pity and assistance. An infernal anarchy reigned on board; no one commanded, none obeyed. Some cast themselves recklessly into the waves, trusting more to them than to the inside of the ship; others leapt into the gigs that were slung to the davits alongside, cut the lashings, and committed themselves to fate. Not a few, seizing benches and planks, dropped overboard, careless where wind and tide might bear them.

The Dutch launches succeeded in saving several of these unfortunates, though many more, engulfed by the waters, perished in the agonies of despair. Amongst those who escaped was Manuel de Moraes. But the *Santo Ambrosio* was not destined to reward the victors; in an incredibly short time she became the prize of the flames and the billows.

The audacious Batavians made up for the loss by seizing others of the convoy, which found no means of escape; and they noisily applauded their own feats and triumph.

Henry Lonq[1] was the captain of the squadron which had fallen in with this good fortune. He was a gallant mariner, who, succeeding in 1630 Willekens, Pieter Heyn, and Pater, swept the sea of Spanish and Portuguese cruisers and traders, caused unheard-of losses, seized a vast number of hostile galleons, and spread the terror of his name far and wide over the ocean. He at once ordered the useless craft to be burned, and the

---

[1] In Dutch the name is written "Hendrick Loncq." The Portuguese simplified the unpronounceable Batavian names, as Piet, Adrian, Vanderburg, and Scóp for Pieterszoon, Adriensz, Wardenborch or Weerdenburgh, and Schköppe.—*Translator's Note.*

THE NOVICE'S SECOND MISFORTUNE. 53

valuable prizes to be carried into Recife, and to be placed in the hands of the authorities who administered the Netherlander Government of the Brazil. Of the ten captured, only four remained seaworthy, and to them were transferred, with a guard of Dutchmen, the cargoes and the prisoners taken out of the others. Then was seen a melancholy spectacle, heartrending for those unaccustomed to such reverses: the six condemned craft were fired, and they sank in the midst of roaring, crackling flames and the loud hurrahs of the Hollanders, who delighted to witness the work of destruction.

When the captain's orders were carried out, the four galleons made sail for Pernambuco, and soon entering the port of Recife (the Reef), they reported themselves to the Court of Directors of the Dutch West Indian Company. All the prisoners having been plundered of their property, were cast loose to make a livelihood as they best could.

It was the year of grace 1632 when Manuel de Moraes thus found himself thrown upon a hostile strand.

The free world to which he had aspired opened itself to him under the most inauspicious conditions.

The morn of life broke with a sickly light through clouds of bitterness, pain, and grief; and thus sorely and sorrowfully began his pilgrimage since the day when caprice or the undefined longings of the soul had torn him from the peace and innocence of the cloister to endure the endless vicissitudes and the misfortunes which his unhappy destiny had prepared for him.

CHAPTER VI.

BEATRIX BRODECHEVIUS.

In 1580, Portugal, overwhelmed by the hosts of the Duke of Alva, and betrayed by her national degeneracy, had become, at the Cortes of Thomar, a mere province of Spain: from that time the Philips of Castile had taken pride in trampling her under their feet, and in overwhelming amidst misery and degradation her memories of past glories and of heroic deeds.

The Hollanders, who had won their independence from Spain, thought only of snatching away the Transatlantic possessions, of seizing the colonies, and of annihilating the maritime commerce of their ancient mistress.

They held as Spanish all the regions in Asia, Africa, and America, which had belonged to independent Portugal and, excited by the hope of plunder, they did not spare those wealthy lands. In 1651 the various cities of the Low Countries raised a strong and well-monied company, afterwards entitled "of the West Indies," with the view of extending their conquests into the New World. Their High Mightinesses, the States General of the United Provinces, approved of the statutes passed by the body, and gave it full right of invading, occupying, and enjoying whatever conquests it might make, for the space of thirty years dating from 1624. After that time it was bound to transfer all its possessions to Government, and to receive as an indemnity the value of its munitions of war, of its fleets, and of the various establishments which it might have founded.

An issue of shares in Holland soon produced the required capital.

The State contributed as subvention a million of florins [1] and a fleet of twenty ships of war, on condition of receiving half the clear profits of the enterprize. The Board or Court of Directors, composed of the Stadtholder of Holland as president, and with eighteen members chosen by the municipalities and the shareholders of Amsterdam, Rotterdam, Groningen, Zealand, and Friesland, resided alternately in the first-named city and at Middleberg.

This high body had charge of the political and internal administration of the Company, thus making it a peculiar and independent state within a state; from which came orders for the levying of troops and the annexation of territory.

The Dutch West Indian Company attempted to inaugurate its rule in Portuguese America by seizing the Bahia de Todos os Santos, and on May 8, 1624, it had carried the City and captured the Governor, Diogo de Mendonça Furtado. But the conquest was lost next year. The invader was compelled to decamp by the armed masses that had mustered in the Reconcave, or Bay of the Captaincy: he was besieged within the limits of his capital, and presently a Spanish armada, commanded by Don Fradique de Toledo, closely blockaded him by sea. Yet the stout-hearted Northmen did not despair. Reinforcements were sent to the Brazil in 1630, and Colonel Weerdenburgh, with 3000 men and two guns, effected a landing at Páo Amarello, three or four leagues to the north; crossed the Rio Doce, fell upon Olinda, the fair capital of Pernambuco and, having seized it by a *coup de main*, duly sacked it. The gallant Ma-

---

[1] Then worth one shilling and eightpence, or two francs ten sous.—*Translator's Note.*

thias de Albuquerque, Governor of the Captaincy, who had only twenty-seven men of reinforcements from Portugal, was driven from the Porto do Recife—the latter being attacked by land and cannonaded by sea—to take refuge in the interior. After burning his magazines and the ships in port, he fell back upon the mainland, and established his head-quarters at the Arraial, or fortified village, do Bom Jesus, on the other side of the Capibaríbe river.

Little by little the Hollanders spread themselves over Pernambuco. They were heroically opposed by those born in the land, and by the Portuguese colonists under the valiant commandant, Mathias de Albuquerque, and by the friendly Redskins, whom the Indian Phelipe Camarão, or Poty (the Shrimp), boldly led to the field. The glorious fort of São Jorge was burned down; the heroic village do Bom Jesus was razed to the ground; and fair Olinda was reduced to ashes. The Company continued its career of conquest, and both Brazilians and Portuguese retired northward and southward, abandoning to the Dutch those territories which they had invaded. The States General also did not neglect to send out ample supplies of soldiers and warlike gear, and to appoint brave and active officers to the several commands. And perhaps the liberality of this proceeding, so rare and so exceptional amongst conquerors and colonists in those times, contributed not a little to reconcile the Brazilian Creoles to the rule of heretics and infidels.

The "irreconcilables" of the land, who could not or who did not succeed in escaping, perforce bent the neck to the Hollander's yoke. The Court of Directors had forbidden public worship in the Catholic churches, which were converted into Protestant chapels, and with difficulty they permitted mass to be celebrated in the open spaces and fields, under the sun of heaven and in the air of liberty. But afterwards commerce was monopolised by the intruder, "heretic on enemy and privateer on heretic;" and the Portuguese had no occupation left to them but to till the ground and to sell fruit and vegetables.

Such was the condition of the Recife when Manuel de Moraes landed there and sought some means of subsistence for himself. The settlement was divided into three distinct quarters. The stores, arsenals, business houses, and principal habitations, official and private, occupied the land-tongue, where the Capibaríbe, joined by the Biberíbe river, flows into the Atlantic. The second quarter overspread the Ilha de Antonio Vaz, formerly a desert and swampy islet, or rather a peninsula formed by the many arms of the former stream. Beyond the Capibaríbe and the Biberíbe the suburbs extended inland, without bridges[1] to connect them with the island, or even with the port. The streams were crossed in canoes and rafts; thus also were transported the sugars and brandies made in the interior, and sent to the Company's agents, who bought them at a tariff fixed by themselves.

Moraes saw at once that of scanty use to him would be the education which he had received in the Jesuit Institute of São Paolo, or the precious gifts of intelligence which Providence had bestowed upon him. Evidently nothing but manual labour would here furnish the means of life. He resolved to begin without delay, and he hired himself as a field-hand to a Portuguese who held land on the left bank of the Biberíbe.

Days, months, and years lagged on without his finding the means to better his destitute condition. In 1636 the Company had substituted for the various Chiefs and Generals of the Court of Directors, Johann

---

[1] The Dutch built two bridges, one from the Recife to the Antonio Vaz, and the other from the latter to the mainland, then called Schoonzigt, now Boa Vista.—*Translator's Note.*

Moritz von Nassau Siegens, popularly known as Count Maurice of Nassau; and no sooner had the latter taken the reins of government than the whole Dutch colony seemed to borrow new life. Southwards the frontiers were extended even beyond the great Rio de São Francisco,[1] and northwards almost to the Maranhão. Nassau was a beneficent monarch. To promote the study of the country, he brought with him naturalists like Piso of Leyden and the famous German Marcgrave, historians like Gaspar Barlé, literati like Plante, architects like the brothers Post, and artists of the Flemish school who had gained a name in Europe. By his persuasion the Company opened free trade to Netherlanders generally, keeping up monopoly only in certain hands, so as to enrich the colony of Recife. He prosecuted corrupt functionaries. He restored order to the finances. He improved the public administration. He reorganised the military. He put an end to the arbitrary abuses of the subaltern authorities. He permitted the Jews to build synagogues, and the Portuguese to attend their churches and solemn processions. He founded schools for the heathen. He restored fugitive slaves to their proprietors, on condition that the latter should swear fealty to his Government. He built forts at Penedo in the São Francisco river, at Porto Calvo, in the Isle of Antonio Vaz; and at many other strategical points. In the head-quarter island he traced the streets of a new City, and laid out for himself a palace named Vrigburg ("the place of repose"), with towers at the wings, and with an observatory by its side. It was connected with Recife by a bridge that spanned the united waters of the Capibaríbe and the Biberíbe. He called the new city Mauritia, and it soon became rich in buildings and grounds. His liberal rule presently

[1] For a full description of this river see my "Highlands of the Brazil." Tinsleys, London, 1869.—*Translator's Note.*

attracted a host of Brazilians, who no longer feared the invader's hostility. Not a few of them accepted the yoke of Holland, including João Fernandez Vieira, who had been one of the bravest defenders of Fort São Jorge, and who had accompanied Albuquerque to the Arraial of Bom Jesus. This Guerilla-Chief preferred a quiet industrious life, and became a financial agent to the Company.

One evening Manuel de Moraes was working on the river-bank, when loud cries drew his attention to the island of Antonio Vaz. The outcry came from two horsemen following at full gallop a lady, who rapidly distanced them in her wild flight. Still they were afar, and the cause of their outcries was not evident. Presently Manuel perceived with terror that the foremost horse was running away with its rider, who kept her seat with difficulty, and that she was in imminent danger unless some strong arm arrest its headlong career.

To witness the scene and to rush to the rescue were with Moraes the work of an instant. It would have been mere loss of time to have canoed across the stream, nor was any canoe at hand. Though the tide ran strong, the Novice did not hesitate, habited as he was, to plunge into the depths. In a few moments he had swum from terra-firma to the island. He awaited the passing of the horse, threw himself upon the animal's bridle, and with a grasp of iron, reined it back upon its haunches. The beast snorted and reared violently, but its spirit was soon broken, and it became helpless and trembling with fear. Moraes drew the rider from the saddle, and placed her fainting upon the ground. Whilst he was restoring her to her senses with encouraging words, the two cavaliers came up. One of them was an aged Hollander, Wilhelm Brodechevius, a member of Council, a friend of Count Maurice, and an important personage in the Company. He warmly clasped the hand that had saved his daughter, asked Moraes his name, his profession and his abode, and promised never to forget his heavy debt of gratitude. By degrees the girl recovered life, and, asking to see the man who had saved her from destruction, expressed her admiration of and gratitude for his courage and kindness.

Assistance was now at hand, and the people brought a litter in which Beatrix was carried home, whilst Manuel proceeded to his pauper quarters. Either the excitement of the moment or the wet clothing which he had worn so long banished sleep from his eyelids, and during the night he suffered all the tortures of a violent burning fever. Gloomy and wretched hours, without a friendly hand or voice to nurse or cheer the sick man, were those that passed till day broke and the warm rays of the sun lit up the windows of his hovel.

He attempted to rise, but felt an inexpressible weakness. He waited resigned till the increasing warmth should restore his strength, when he heard a knock at the door and the greetings of a kindly but unknown voice. With difficulty he arose and withdrew the rusty bolt, at once returning to the pauper cot which acted as bed.

His visitor was the old Netherlander, whose daughter the invalid had saved. Manuel could hardly answer his questions; and Brodechevius, leaving a slave to wait upon him, with money and many instructions to take care of him, hurried away to call a physician. Returning home, he was questioned by his daughter, who would not hear of her preserver being nursed by any one but herself; and who determined to repay her life by restoring him to health under her father's roof. Brodichevius could refuse her nothing. Beatrix was the only pledge of love bequeathed to him by the best of wives, and she had full power over his heart. Broken in spirit by his bereavement, he had quitted Amsterdam as a member of Council to the West

Indian Company; he had then established himself at Recife, and there he existed only for the girl, surrounding her happy, fresh, young life with all the pleasure and luxury which the fondness of a father can suggest.

The result was that Manuel was borne away in a litter, and presently found himself comfortably installed in the house of Brodechevius, where a physician took his case in hand. The fever assumed a malignant type and dangerous proportions. Beatrix often visited the invalid; at times insisting, when Moraes was deaf to the nurse, upon his taking the remedies prescribed; and, encouraging him with soft words, sweet voice, and sympathetic looks, she appeared an angel who stood by his pillow and guided his will.

Beatrix, then aged twenty, was tall and graceful as the girls of her country; her long blonde hair rippling over a broad pure brow, announced her North European origin. Large blue eyes and regular features set in a perfect oval, lips and chin somewhat full, a complexion of clearest white and rose, and a calm retired expression, made the character of her beauty rather more stately than is consistent with feminine softness and delicacy. Like the Sea-queens of old whom the Church converted to saints, gracious in their dignity as commanding of presence, the seriousness of her demeanour imposed more respect than inspired love. She had little of the Southern sweetness which characterises the women of Raphael and Murillo; her face and figure suggested rather the idea of the majestic priestesses as fancy paints them amongst the ancient Gauls. Her blue eyes never wore the humid expression of love, much less were they lit up by the light of passion; but there was something in their look which said, that if ever Beatrix yielded her heart to the keeping of a lover, her attachment would rise to the dignity of perfect devotion, of life-long constancy. Moraes soon yielded himself to the directions of his hostess, and learned for the first time in his life the might and power of a woman who can bend the will, and who can convert the admirer into the submissive slave. He felt restored to health when he fixed his eyes upon the fair presence; in her absence he lost heart and strength, as though she carried away with her the light of his life. Already his heart whispered that Beatrix was necessary to his existence, and by slow degrees a violent passion, mastering every faculty, ruled his heart and head, his body and soul.

Nor less did the girl admire the graceful ways of her young patient; his manners, which were those of Nature's Nobility; the interesting and picturesque language, showing an education far above his present calling; the generous thoughts, which little suited the lowness of his present condition, and the purity of morals and religion that proclaimed the innocence of his soul and the virginity of an uncorrupted heart. But what in him from the beginning was the headlong passion of love commenced in Beatrix with the sympathy restrained by reason. Manuel's bosom boiled over with fiery maddening thoughts, which brought with them as much pain as pleasure. The girl was attached by a sentiment of affection, which only did justice to the admirable qualities, the many intellectual and moral gifts of her preserver. Her gentle virginal fondness passed from her brain to her bosom, where it grew in warmth, and lastly it worked its way into her heart, like the drops which hollow out the hardest stone. Thus with slow steps, and, we might almost say, with a reasonable and philosophic progress, her appreciation took the form of friendship, and friendship the guise of love; each phase being accompanied by a corresponding change of the natural and physical sentiments, till the latter asserted their full and complete ascendancy.

During three months, the illness which prostrated Moraes endured, with alternate gain and loss of strength, till he found himself completely convalescent. The time was enough to arouse and to fix in both the young hearts that mutual feeling which bound them together once and for eternity.

Moraes had shown himself a man of rare merits, condemned only by blind fate to labours unworthy of his education and intelligence, and Brodechevius lost no time in obtaining for him a suitable employment with the Dutch West Indian Company. He was thus enabled to leave his hovel and to establish himself decently at Recife. The old man, without suspecting the secrets of his protégé's heart, opened to him his house, and continued to lavish upon him all the marks of the truest esteem. His daily intercourse with Beatrix only served to increase the love which he delighted to nourish, and softened towards him more and more the girl's heart, till both learned to drain with long draughts the delightful idea of possession. Meanwhile, Moraes found himself brought into close relations with important personages of the Company, and he accustomed himself to the strict and puritanical ways of the many distinguished Netherlanders. All were devotedly and by conviction attached to their Calvinistic worship, and beyond it they dedicated themselves only to the domestic virtues and to the pure and lovely pleasures of home.

But his lofty and independent spirit strove against the forced and heavy discipline of the Reformed Faith. His studies of Catholic dogmas had not silenced his reason, although he himself had desired it in order that all his scruples might give way before the belief in Romish orthodoxy. But now he adhered to his creed less from conviction than by instinct and habit; and his soul was beset with doubts till he could no longer distinguish in religion anything but the systematic theory and practice of virtue and morality.

Finally, comparing the Hollanders of Recife with the Portuguese of São Paulo, he held the Protestants to be more earnest men, and more deeply imbued with the spirit of their cult than the Catholics.

These fatal thoughts led by degrees to a spiritual indifference, a cruel and destroying scepticism, which weakened and relaxed every fibre of his soul. Might not also mundane love have served to produce this unhappy state, and to detach him from the pure and holy religion of Rome, which of all Christian creeds speaks most to man concerning Eternal Life, and shows him most carefully the nothingness of the creature in presence of the Creator, the Supreme Author of the world?

CHAPTER VII.

BEATRIX AND THE NOVICE LEAVE SOUTH AMERICA.

SWIFTLY and happily the days of Manuel de Moraes ran by. He applied himself to the duties of his calling. He studied the arts and the letters of a new land. His liveliest pleasures were in the contemplation of his love, when heart and soul were whelmed in a tide of ineffable delight.

The lovers had not opened to each other the secrets of their breasts, nor had words betrayed their passionate longings. Yet each perfectly understood the other's thoughts, for eye flamed back its answer to eye, and the most trivial conversation bore the burden of intimate sentiment.

We have already observed that Manuel's love was of a far more Southern and physical type, which commanded him through the material senses, subjugated him by its very nature, and belonged to earth and to the region of reality; it was therefore frail and inconstant as man. But the affection of Beatrix seemed to be the longing of soul for soul, however clogged by mortal clay. The girl's feeling was the deeper, because it was the fruit of reason and conviction, ripened by the instincts of her nature, whilst its pure and holy inspiration crowned her soul with a heavenly aureole. Yet not one, but both loved truly and fondly as their several natures permitted, and the strength of mutual sentiment drew them together without one thought of the obstacles which beset their path.

Meanwhile, Count Maurice had raised a strong

force, intending to spread Batavian rule over the southern continent. In May 1637, he embarked three thousand and two hundred Dutchmen, accompanied by a thousand Redskins, upon a fleet of thirty-two warships; and the armada sailed with orders to attack that most important position, the Bahia de São Salvador.

The fleet, entering the great and picturesque bay, landed a strong force and made a violent assault, whilst the citizens defended themselves with the utmost gallantry. The invader stormed the works known as the Alberto, Filippe, Bartholomeu, and Rosario; but attempting to carry the carefully fortified convent of the barefooted Carmelites, he was so doughtily met that perforce he fell back. After losing at least eleven hundred men, he saw that the siege must be raised unless all would perish. Thus foiled, the famous flotilla returned to Recife. Its disastrous failure caused the deepest disappointment to the Prince-Count, yet, with the tenacity of his Northern spirit, he thought only of collecting a still stronger force. Throughout his career, indeed, he never lost the hope of annexing the Captaincy of Bahia to those possessions on the South American continent which were then entitled Netherlander, in contradistinction to what was still Portuguese, Brazil.

In the States, however, the Prince-Count was opposed by his inveterate enemy Artichfsky,[1] a Polish general who had been military governor of Pernambuco before the Company had placed it under Maurice of Nassau. A valiant soldier, highly distinguished during the first occupation of the country, he had retired from Recife upon the arrival of his successor; he retained the best of reputations in Holland, and he lost no opportunity of revenging himself for the slight thus offered to his services, and

---

[1] This is the orthography of the original.—*Translator's Note.*

for the injustice which had ousted him in favour of a rival.

The last terrible disaster enabled this plotting soldier to appear as the Prince's opponent before the Court of Directors at Amsterdam. He easily persuaded them to make him Commander-in-Chief of the army, with the rank of Master-General of artillery, whilst his superior retained only the civil and the administrative authority. And having taken charge of his appointment, he kept up regular intercourse with Holland, openly blaming the conduct of Count Maurice, whilst at Pernambuco he pretended to act independently of, and, as it were, above the higher authority of the civil power.

Maurice of Nassau, exasperated by the conduct of Artichfsky, assembled his private and political council, pointed out to it the impossibility of a colony being governed by two independent and dissident chiefs, and announced his intention of yielding up the Command and of returning home. Those high officials, however, fully appreciating the Prince's administrative capacity, then and there unanimously agreed to exert their extraordinary privileges by deporting to Holland the wily Pole, with due explanation of the motives which had induced them to take this abnormal and extreme step.

Artichfsky being compelled to depart, the Prince remained master of the situation. But our prudent and far-seeing Brodechevius was convinced that the intrigues of the Pole would end in his rival's recall, and, in such case, he was convinced that the concentrated hate of the country people would presently burst out in a struggle for life and death which would expel the arms of Holland from the American continent. Dutch Brazil had, indeed, remained tranquil under the moderation, the experience, and the justice of Prince Maurice's rule: any deviation from this path would evidently lead it to perdition.

M

Brodechevius having resolved to return to Amsterdam with all his household, and that, too, by the first fleet, confided the plan to his daughter and bade her make all preparations. Beatrix received the tidings with grief and bitterness, yet she did not oppose her father's project. She became more reserved with Manuel de Moraes, and at the same time she concealed from him her motive. But this new phase could not escape the lover's eye, and he tormented himself with doubts and questions. Was she wearying of the affection which she must have perceived, although words had not declared it? What could have caused the change? And even supposing the calculated but melancholy and pensive coldness to arise from secret suffering, whence could it have originated?

Vainly did Moraes attempt to tear the veil which concealed the girl's sorrow, whilst her ever-increasing reserve weighed heavily upon his heart. The days became dark and sombre after so many of light and sunshine, perfumed by love and beautified with blissful reveries and delicious dreams.

Manuel resolved to take a daring step; his past happiness, indeed, rendered the present change insupportable. He felt that an explanation was now necessary, whatever might be its results.

A something unknown had silenced the mute language which expressed their mutual feelings; evidently it was best to bare his heart before Beatrix, and loyally to declare his love, to trust the lips with that which the eyes had more eloquently told. He was often alone with the girl, and thus the chance was not wanting. Steeling himself to the task, he asked her boldly and openly what was the meaning of her sadness, what misfortune had happened, what calamity was expected? Beatrix would at first have kept her secret. But Moraes pressed his questions with the firm resolve of being satisfied, and accents of grief came from his heart as he cried—

"Tell me, for pity's sake, tell me all! Thou little knowest how I love thee, how I adore thee!"

The burning words did not startle the girl. She reflected that, after hearing such a confession, she was bound to answer him as openly and as loyally. Though she strove to appear calm, her saddened brow betrayed her; and at times her accents faltered and the voice expired upon her trembling lips. She told him in broken words that her father had announced his return to Holland by the first fleet; that she was to leave Pernambuco for ever; that both must now part.

"Part! part!" he ejaculated as one stunned. "And I remain here when thou goest? And what are then my hopes in life?"

All the force of passion now nerved his soul: he forgot prudence, respect, and gratitude—everything but the inner voice of love which urged him on.

"Why did fate ever throw me in thy way?" he continued with the recklessness of one who has cast the die. "Why hast thou taught me to love thee, I whose heart, tranquil and indifferent, had never learnt what love was?"

Long had Beatrix been accustomed to read his looks and gestures, to see his secret in his coldness and his warmth, in his sorrows and his joys. The mysteries of passion, however carefully hidden, cannot escape a woman's eye. Yet not less was she startled by the warmth and vehemence of his words. At first she feigned not to understand him. She then attempted to change the subject. But as Moraes only insisted the more, she was driven to the last resource, and she replied in sad and measured tones—

"Reasons all the stronger for our parting! I will not deceive thee. I also love thee, and perhaps not less deeply than thou dost, as thy words declare thou dost. I also shall be unhappy when the broad seas roll between us. But I will try to forget thee;

do thou the same. Banish all thoughts of me; doubtless in time we shall live down the folly which common sense condemns."

"I do not understand thee," impetuously exclaimed Moraes. "Why call Love folly? How doth reason condemn it?"

"Thou dost not reflect, nor did I," said a voice of ineffable tenderness, while Beatrix gently took his hand and raised her tearful eyes to heaven. "We imprudently allowed our hearts to meet, our souls to commune together, without looking to the future, without foreseeing how impossible it is that we should become one. I am a Protestant, thou a Catholic; a mighty gulf yawneth between thee and me. My People cannot forget the persecutions and the horrors of which yours were guilty. Bleeding wounds gape between the two Faiths."

"Impossible! impossible!" interrupted Moraes. "I might have borne with this parting had I not known myself beloved. My grief would have killed me, still I should have endured it. But now, now that all is happiness, now that nature smileth upon me, now that the Angels of Heaven speak to me, it is impossible. So thou and I may not part. Whatever place conceal thee I will find thee out. I will follow thee to the world's end. Everywhere shalt thou meet me—me who breathe with thy breath, live with thy life, and am ready to die with thee or to die for thee."

"But what serveth all this," asked Beatrix, who, though as much agitated as he was, retained the power of appearing calm, "if we can never be united, if we are to be parted by Religion and Mankind, by Tradition and Society? I cannot become a Catholic. Thy mayest not deny thy faith. Even if love, in a moment of weakness, should triumph over thy convictions, should make thee a renegade, wouldst thou expect long to escape the pains of perjury, the penalties of remorse? Would not these suffice to wither a love which demanded as its sacrifice an Immortal Soul, an Eternity of Happiness? Would it not seem the merest senseless caprice, when repentance shall have placed the past in its true light? Let thy thoughts be more worthy of thyself. Let me strive to heal these wounds which we have heedlessly, recklessly inflicted each on other. Fancy only that we are two travellers who have met on the desert path, who have rested their limbs under the shade of the same palm, who have cooled their lips with the waters of the same fountain. What then? Let both arise and bid adieu, and each wend the appointed way. In this vale of tears we wander not for ever; we can hardly be said to tread it. In the far future we shall meet to part no more. Like the son of Abraham, thou hast crossed Mesopotamia, but the daughter of Laban may not follow thee."

"Wouldst thou see me die?" asked Manuel, pained and surprised by the strange Scriptural language and by the scornful tones in which the girl spoke. "Better far to have let the fever consume me, than by thy care and thy charity to snatch from it a life which thou hast saved only to destroy."

"The Lord," continued Beatrix, "gave us hearts to love, but the heart must be governed by the Spirit, the Maker's own emanation. Above all, hear we the voice of reason and reflection. We two cannot hope lawfully to become one: remain thou in Pernambuco whilst I go with my father. Thus indeed *must* it be, now that our sentiments are known to each other."

"No, never," cried Manuel. "I would rather slay myself. What is life? What is its worth to the solitary wretch wandering through the weary world? What is Religion, what is Creed, where a man feels that Faith is impossible to him, that he was not born, not created to believe; when he knows that he belongeth to the World, to the Society of his kind?"

These words contained that which made the girl

tremble. She saw clearly that Manuel was blinded by his passion and hurried on to a fatal end. But his love, his devotion, showed a depth and a heat which necessarily flattered her self-love, which exalted high in her eyes a lover capable of such sacrifice. Still she was not so hoodwinked by the instincts of her sex that she could not foreshadow from afar the fatal consequences of such enthusiasm.

"Change of Belief," she said, "demandeth firm conviction, not sudden hallucination. It must be the work of the head, not of the heart. The soul must confirm and support it. Love is transient: when its spell is past, when the bloom wears off, then will Repentance thunder at the door. How I should condemn myself were I to cause thy eternal misery!"

"Fear not," responded Manuel; "only allow me to go with thee to thy home in Holland, so that thou mayest judge the truth of my words by my deeds."

Beatrix promised to give his prayer due reflection, and begged to be left alone. They parted in the greatest agitation.

And now that Manuel de Moraes had told his love, it spurned all the bonds of reason. It subjugated his whole man, intellectual as well as moral. He bent to it as one yielding himself prisoner, or rather as a slave who hugs his manacles and his fetters, holding them to be his highest happiness, believing in them as his manifest inevitable destiny, and loving them as the bestower of especial delights and reveries and rosy dreams.

Beatrix went far deeper in thought. Her heart was won by her lover's heart; but her reason also spoke, and it spoke only of danger to come. The struggle of smiling love and trembling fear filled her mind and wearied her spirit.

She intrusted her secret to her father, confessing that her heart and soul belonged to Moraes, that she could neither leave him nor he forget her, and that no other man should ever be her husband. Nor did she neglect to confide her suspicions that his love was about to change his Catholic faith for Calvinism, with the sole object of accompanying her and of living for her.

Brodechevius highly esteemed the saviour of his only daughter. He appreciated his remarkable intelligence, his rarely endowed mind, and his spirit capable of the most memorable actions. He had no objection to him as a son-in-law; neither riches nor rank were anything in the good old father's eyes, but artificial distinctions—the garb of the man, not the man. The only obstacle to the union appeared to be the difference of faith, and this would be smoothed over only by Manuel's abjuring the Catholic religion and adopting Holland as his home. But he also held it necessary to prove the sincerity and the conviction with which Moraes would face the difficulties of the position. He advised Beatrix to hope from time the proofs of her lover's truth, and to allow him to accompany her, when it would be easier to observe and to judge him.

Early in 1639 the Hollanders' fleet sailed from the coast of Pernambuco. All the personages of our tale embarked upon it, abandoning the Brazilian shores, and Manuel de Moraes took leave of America with the firm intention of never again seeing his native land.

CHAPTER VIII.

MARRIAGE AND REPENTANCE.

THE year had not died out since the return of Brodechevius and his daughter to Amsterdam before Manuel de Moraes abjured the Catholic religion and embraced Protestantism: he married Beatrix with the old Hollander's consent, and finally the adopted country became his home.

Happily at first sped the days in the bosom of this quiet, amiable family. Although there was scant attraction for Moraes in his new faith, he punctually obeyed the orders and he scrupulously fulfilled all the duties enjoined by the Church of Calvin. The change weighed not heavily upon his soul, because the hour of repentance and remorse had not yet struck. Moreover, the charming spouse, who ever showed some precious quality before unknown, and who met his fiery love with a rare abnegation of self and an extreme devotion, still held him by a witchery as delightful as it was novel.

Families of distinction visited at their house; the choicest of society sought their friendship, and the most agreeable intercourse was always open to them. Moraes made the acquaintance, among others, of many Portuguese Jews, who had escaped from the persecution of their Government and of the Holy Office. Condemned by the unjust misconceptions and the stolid prejudices of public opinion, which so rarely means aught but public ignorance, many had found shelter and liberty to worship their own God amongst the judicious Hollanders, whose greatness and glory grew by the industry and by the wealth of the refugees.

Amongst the Hebrews were men of notable merit. Many of them had apparently exchanged their religion for the Catholic faith in order to remain in Portugal, where the worship of the Israelite was not permitted. But the most trifling suspicion, a single word of accusation, was ever enough to seize and imprison, to try and condemn them to the Inquisitional rack and stake. Some entered the monastic orders, assumed the sacerdotal garb, and even took service as familiars of the abominable Tribunal. Still the change of faith and of manners availed them little. None believed in the sincerity of the "New Christian." The few were those who, unwilling to deny their religion, were compelled to expatriate themselves. The many, either from conviction or for worldly motives, adopted Catholicism as the surest pledge of devotion to her dogmas and discipline that they could offer to the Church.

It was enough to be a Jew, to have been one, even to be descended from a Jew: neither insult nor misery, neither prison nor torture, nor barbarous judicial murder was spared to them. Neither sex nor age excepted them from such horrors. By their emigration Portugal lost a rich, industrious, active, and intelligent people, capable of the highest enterprise that the age required. And her sin, her crime, soon brought with it its own and proper retribution.

Amongst the Hebrews then established in Amsterdam figured three Portuguese who have left a name in letters and science. Isaac Orobio de Castro, a celebrated physician in Lisbon and a professor in Seville, escaped disguised from the dungeons of the Holy Office, and was named Chief amongst the Israelite communities of Holland.[1] The second was Manasseh ben Israel, a distinguished naturalist descended from

[1] See René Saint Taillandier, "Les Juifs Portugais en Hollande."

the Jews of Arabia,[1] and Uriel da Costa the third,[2] who had borne civil office in Lisbon, and had conformed to the religion of Rome. This, however, would not have preserved him from the bloody tribunal ever panting to purify religious faith by the baptism of fire—a baptism which burned alive the victims of their atrocious superstition.

The Jewish families carefully preserved in their Netherland home the Portuguese tongue and the customs of their Sephardime ancestors; they formed a free community, building their synagogues, performing their ceremonies, and keeping holy their Sabbath-days, their Pasch and their other traditional festivals.

All that Manuel saw amongst the Protestants of Holland, together with the history and the actual state of the exiled Jews, contributed to strengthen his new faith and to fend off the inevitable day of remorse.

About this time broke out the Portuguese revolution of 1640. The banished Hebrews applauded the glorious rising of the Lusitanians, eager to assert their independence, and to shake off the hated yoke of Spain. Manuel de Moraes, inspired by the happy event, and excited by patriotic memories, published in the same year a memoir defending the rights of Portugal and of the Duke of Braganza, who was called to the throne under the historic name of Dom João IV. He presented a copy to Diogo de Mendonça Furtado, the diplomatist accredited to Holland. Printed at Leyden and in the Castilian tongue, it bore for title, "Prognostico[3] y Respuesta à una pergunta de un Cabalero muy ilustre sobre la Cosas de Portugal."

These events began to remind him of what he was and of whence he came. His own writings filled him with yearning for his own country, and doubts, at first

[1] See Barlæus, "De Rebus Variis."
[2] See Taillandier, quoted above.
[3] Forecast and Reply to the question of an Illustrious Personage upon the Affairs of Portugal.

timid, concerning the honesty and the dignity of his change of Faith crept into his soul. Gathering strength by slow degrees, the harassing uncertainty became a self-accusation in the court of his own conscience. It ended in a self-condemnation which was repentance.

Meanwhile, he was to all appearance happy in his home—none more so. A father-in-law full of goodness and affection; a beautiful, gentle, and devoted wife; a fortune all-sufficient for his station; a reputation for gravity and intelligence; friends who sought and received his company with pleasure—what wanted he more for happiness in this world?

So thought he himself at first, finding nothing in his path but repose and pleasure, flowers and perfumes. But, past the first days of happiness, the small still voice that came from his spirit gradually awoke an agitation of mind which incessantly grew; it presently filled him with a nameless grief, with mourning sadder and deeper than man mourning for the loss of what is dearest to him. At last it stole away with his happiness all the vivacity which had distinguished him, and it left him to wither like a branch lopped from the parent tree.

Manuel would fain have hidden his wound from the world, more especially from the wife whom he still adored, who was the only being on earth for whom he would have sacrificed his life; but the spiritual and moral change that affected her husband could not escape the eyes of Beatrix. Nor was it long before she instinctively divined the cause, and without a hint or a word from Manuel, although she questioned him in every manner about the true motive of the melancholy which weighed him down in spirit.

She trembled; her worst presentiments were now realised. The light of life was about to set in the outer gloom of lifelong expiation. Remorse would soon quench his fiery love, his enthusiastic passion, which at first had been the joys of the senses rather than the mysterious affinity of mind and soul. All her domestic happiness vanished like a happy dream, which with waking ends for ever. Yet she could not complain of ingratitude on his part: he had no other love; he preferred to her no other woman; he still adored her with all his heart; he still lavished upon her the same marks of fond and delicate attachment. But the phantom was not to be laid. He was struggling in the stern grasp of Repentance, of Remorse against the union to which he had offered up what his now opening eyes well saw should not, and could not, be sacrificed by man. He was helpless in the conviction that he had cast away that which is better than reason, than love, than life itself.

She turned angrily, fiercely upon herself, whose weakness had accepted the impossible sacrifice without appreciating its immensity. Beatrix was presently infected by the sadness and the moral dejection that preyed upon Manuel; and both mourned apart over what no communication could either soften or console. Each took a different path; both became solitary isolated beings, connected by society and the world, separated by an immensity of sorrow, which withdrew them each from other as though they had been accomplices in a deed of shame.

They ever avoided sweet mutual confidence. But the intimacy of domestic life was still there, and though both feared explanations, such remarks as these could not at times be avoided:—

"I am the cause," said Beatrix to her husband one day, "of the anguish of spirit which thou art now enduring."

"Thou!" replied Moraes; "believe me, thou art mistaken; rather say thou art my only Guardian Angel. Only last night I dreamt that a frightful monster was rushing at me; I knew my danger as if I had been awake, but I could not move hand or foot. Thou camest to my aid; the monster fled; thy hand saved me."

"Thou hast sacrificed thy life to me," she pursued.

"I know thou dost not regret it; but thou hast also sacrificed to me thy Faith, and I accepted what I never ought to have accepted. And now thou art the prey of torturing repentance. Alas! I see it only too well."

"Love me still," rejoined Moraes, "and all this is nothing. I live only for thee; thy love is the sole cure for these dark hours which have come upon me so suddenly, so unexpectedly, so mysteriously, and which at times gain complete mastery over my mind. Thy presence is my Guardian Angel, the one arm strong enough to defend me from them."

"Moraes," she continued sadly, "I know thee, I love thee, I adore thee. I recognise the enormous sacrifice thou madest for my love; it was my fault for permitting it, not thine. But now there is no escape for us; the terrible consequences rise up like phantoms of the past, and the Lord abandons me. See how everything in this world shows the tie between the Creator and His creature. The forest that rustles, the lake that slumbers, the torrent that dashes itself against the rocks, the wind that whispers, the City that dreams, the bird that warbles, and the dawn that gleams—all these have their several voices in the hymn of general harmony. I alone look upon myself as a useless discord in the immense concert of nature. In the midst of the immortal poem, I am as a line struck out; I am a stone rejected, deemed unworthy of that palace which the Eternal Architect hath built. I hold myself like the colourless face of the waters, which hardly reflect the beauty and the majesty of the flowers, of the trees, of the firmament."

These highly coloured sentiments, the majestic expressions of the Northern mind, made the deepest effect upon Manuel de Moraes. In fact, they probed for him more severely the extent of the wound which grief and bitterness had dealt to the bosom of his wife.

"O my Patron Saint!" he exclaimed, embracing her with the fondest affection, "banish from thy mind these images of sorrow and terror. If I am no longer what I was; if I am but the shadow of my former self, if my intellect be paralysed, thou also canst console me, canst save me; for thou alone canst bind me to this life. Restore to me thy soul; give me back thy faith, which is life—the faith in thy love!"

"I had dreamed," she broke in, "that we should both have found happiness in the same path. The peace and quiet of a home-life have charms for me; thy spirit revolteth against them. Say, what sacrifice wouldst thou have me make to exceed those that thou madest for me?"

"None! none!" cried Moraes; "it is for me to repeat it and prove to thee my devotion. If thou wouldst see me live, cease to suffer, O my soul! Pardon me and pass over these involuntary outbreaks. Thou art not to be blamed, nor am I: here no fault attaches to either of us."

But the lives of Moraes and Beatrix were still more saddened by the want of children, the real tie to existence, the bond which exceeds in lasting strength all other human sentiment, which compels the parents to self-preservation and to a fellowship of labour for the future of what they hold dearest.

Thus the unhappy couple pined away in secret, still loving and still beloved, yet both the prey of endless grief. The prostration of spirit into which Beatrix had fallen was yet greater than the melancholy which had mastered Manuel. The latter bore the blow in his mind and soul; it was dealt by repentance, by remorse, but the strong will of Manhood was able physically to stand up before it. The sorrow that dwelt in the heart of Beatrix fell upon the more fragile frame of Womankind, and her health declined palpably enough to alarm all around her. Her colour, before fresh as the breezes of the north, lost its brilliancy. Her eyes, in happier days so full of life and love, were now faded and lifeless. Her strength departed from her. That form, tall and slight as the palm-tree of the desert, bending and graceful as the cygnet that glides over the bosom of the lake, showed the saddest signs of decay, a general look of physical suffering which afflicted the many who esteemed and loved her.

The change was not lost upon old Brodechevius. He saw his only, his dearly beloved daughter dying out of his sight without knowing what was undermining her health, and without being able to divine the cure. Manuel wept like a child, forgetting, in his love and in this new sorrow, all the melancholy which had oppressed his own spirits. He attempted to console her by every fond deceit, swearing to her that he no longer felt the sad impressions which erst had come upon him; that he was wholly reconciled to the state of life which he had chosen, as one rich in promises of moral utility; and that, without her, existence would be impossible. He conjured her to happiness and length of days by the love which she had bestowed upon him, and by her pity for one who had dedicated himself to her with all the strength of his heart and with all the powers of his soul.

"Moraes," she said to him about nightfall, approaching a lattice that looked out upon the sea-arm bathing Amsterdam, and gazing upon a pale star that shimmered over the short and misty Northern horizon, "seest thou that melancholy orb? That is my existence. Shortly it will drop from the firmament, and its place shall know it no more: it will be engulfed in the glooms of the unseen world. I was happy as long as I saw thee happy by my side. But I caused thy misery, and I must pay to Heaven the penalty of my selfishness. Thy brain is still haunted by thoughts of noble and patriotic duties. Thy mind dwelleth upon the senseless sacrifice which was made in the hour of passion. The cruel tortures ever awaiting him who abandoneth his Faith and that of his forefathers have not ceased to be thy portion. And the moment thou shalt be free, thou wilt return to the bosom of thy Church, a straggler but not lost; thou wilt recover thy serenity by a penitent and holy life; thou wilt make atonement for thy sin, and ever look down upon all earthly things which bar the soul of man from communne with his Maker."

"For pity's sake, for thy sake, for my sake!" he interrupted. "What care I for the Faith of Rome? Is not that of Calvin equally Christian, and far more suited to the dignity and the free-will of Human Nature? No, I have never repented; I acknowledge no remorse. I have told thee so often—how often! Why wilt thou not believe me?"

"Because I read the secret of thy heart better than thou canst," continued Beatrix; "because I am a woman, and I love thee better than thou canst love thyself. God so made me that I must either have passed heart-whole through the world, or once having given away my heart, that I could not but expect from him who accepted the gift, an affection too entire and exclusive to know an idea which did not centre in me. On the day when I first saw how thoughts and yearnings for the past affected thee involuntarily (I know it was against thy will, nor needst thou assure me of it); when I saw thy mind and spirit fail in the struggle with sentiment and penitence, although thy heart was still full of love for me, on that day I felt that my hours in the world were numbered, and that I had no one to look to but to my God."

Manuel was too deeply affected to venture upon a reply, and the dying wife retired to the privacy of her chamber.

Her sufferings were not long. The decay of her strength was completed by a nervous fever. Useless cares were lavished upon her; no physician would minister to a disease which he did not understand. And thus she passed into eternity. Her last moments were grief-full but resigned; she could not but mourn over her early death and her lost old age. Sad and sorrowful was the farewell which she bade to a husband and a parent whom she loved with all her heart; whilst, with the natural piety of her soul, she commended herself to the care of her Eternal Father.

CHAPTER IX.

THE NOVICE'S THIRD TRIAL.

ONCE more Manuel de Moraes found himself alone upon earth. When he tore himself from the cloister, from his family, and from his country, the happy ignorance, the audacious hopes and the wild dreams of youth enabled him to stand up single-handed against the world. But at the death of the only being for whose sake he looked forward to life, his years were verging upon forty, and now the bright career which lay before him was overcast by the shadows and sorrows of experience.

His childish years had not left upon him any deep impression; but the accidents of his early manhood, his wanderings in the backwoods of São Vicente, his adventures amongst the savage Redskins, and more especially the majestic dreams of La Guayra, the splendid nature of the American interior, and the sublime wrath and fury of the ocean, had exalted his mind, and, instead of bowing it down, had given to it a new strength.

And now, at an age no longer so elastic and self-sufficient, everything around him wore another and a far less pleasing aspect. Within himself, where different ideas, struggling for mastery, tortured every fibre of his soul, his prospect was indeed blank. He was prostrated by the yearning memories of a lost wife. By her side how many happy days he had passed in tranquil pleasures and in the dreams of life-long affection! He could not bear to think of the wholehearted, exclusive attachment of that adored being, who had allowed herself to die when she found that every part of his soul was not her own.

He was far distant from his native land, whose image would at times rise before him; he knew nothing of the parents and sisters whom he had abandoned, a step which now led to the deepest grief; he had separated himself from the Holy Roman Catholic faith, the only one which consoles man in sorrow, and which speaks to the heart with persuasive eloquence; his lot was cast in the society of strangers, who could never be to him what his own should have been. Such were his present miseries, and what hope of the future was he entitled to hold?

As he left the house that had so long been his home, his heart was broken to see the change in it. He tore himself away from the unfortunate Brodechevius, leaving with him all the riches of which he might have claimed a part. He took lodgings in a retired part of Amsterdam, that he might be alone with his sorrow.

The City had already risen to importance by its industry and commerce. It was cut by an hundred canals, upon whose banks stood noble buildings and whose waters bore a jostling array of ships. Its prosperity was increased by traffic with the colonies of which Holland had despoiled Portugal during the sixty years' vassalage of the latter under the three Philips of Castile. Rich and rare cargoes were incessantly shipped off to the Brazil, to Africa and to Asia by the Cape of Good Hope. In its streets and within its walls gathered an active, industrious, and enterprising people, who had learned to tame an ingrate nature and an inclement clime, and to create artificial beauties and immense wealth, which gave it an aspect at once comfortable, prosperous, and imposing.

All that Manuel most admired in the works of man began to lose novelty and charm in proportion as memory recalled to him the scenes of the past. Was not the tropical nature more sublime? was not there more delight to the eye in the virgin forests of São Vicente; in the majestic rivers Paraná, Tiété, and La Plata; in the splendid aspect of the heavens, and in the pure delicious atmosphere of Central America? What human art was worthy to loose the shoe-tie of Nature? What comparison was there between an artificial city compelled to fortify herself with dykes against the overwhelming sea and the riant plain upon which reposed the Recife of Pernambuco or the beautiful heights that bore his native village of São Paulo?

In the contrast upon which his mind now dwelt, the race of man followed the climate. The taciturn gravity of the Hollander, however industrious and enterprising he be; the avarice of the Hebrew, though active and energetic, did not gain when compared with the jovial and lively character of the Portuguese, or with the innocence and the virtues of the native American. The moral and religious qualities of the Protestant ministers, fathers of families, men of the world, immersed in domestic cares and business, could have little attraction for one who had appreciated the mystical and holy self-sacrifice of the Jesuits, those mortal denizens of heaven rather than of earth, spending life wholly in the practice of what might await them in the future, in the exercise of loving charity and of perfect philanthropy; men who exposed themselves to the greatest perils, even unto Martyrdom, that they may bring within the fold of the Church a herd of the vilest nomads.

After the worldly he reviewed the spiritual side; he looked with the eye of a philosopher rather than of a divine upon the two creeds, Calvinistic and Catholic. In the former he saw revealed the pride and self-sufficiency of man which, under pretext of liberty of conscience and free judgment, would communicate direct with his Creator, disdaining all mediation, and would interpret by the lights of ignorant or half-learned caprice the difficulties of the Divine Law and the mysteries of the Holy Evangel. Whereas Catholicism, far wiser, had organised a gradually progressive Church, ever adapting itself to the wants of each generation; she had raised Mankind according to its deserts, whilst at the same time she bowed the human spirit in the presence of the Supreme. Finally, she explained to her votaries the sacred text and dogmas in the simplest of forms, and, the better to preserve the individuality of the Bride of Christ, she inculcated obedience to a Single Head.

Again, what temerity in the direct address of the creature to the Creator! How much arrogance in banishing all pomp from the temple! What contumacy in rejecting those admirable men, whose dedication to ascetic life and to the joys of eternity, had raised them to the rank of saints! How much of crime in that revolt against the successor of St. Peter, to whom Protestants preferred the rule of some being raised from the dust, devoid of prestige, some self-constituted prophet and heresiarch, like Luther and Calvin! His imagination dwelt with delight upon the character of the Catholic Church, at once grave, serene, and attractive; upon the many-sided nature of that ancient and venerable creed, which rejoiced society with the pomp of its solemnities; which by the soft sadness of its chants and hymns reminded Man of his nothingness; which lightened the dark places of his soul by Confession and Communion, and which by the Last Sacraments at the dread hour of Death prepared him for Eternal Life, contrite and resigned, expecting the Divine pardon and the infinite mercy which never abandon the hapless children of Adam.

The consequence of his reflections was a deluge of remorse overwhelming his spirit. This existence without Faith, without Love, was it not that of the degraded savage? To barter Catholicism, which nourishes, which supports, which elevates the soul, for the cold, calculating, interested dogmas of Calvinism, was it not a crime darker far than any sin against human morality?

The wife who could have turned the current of these gloomy thoughts, who would, perhaps, have blunted the stings of conscience which tortured him as with the poison of scorpions, was now, alas! no more. He had not a single friend to modify the direction of his ideas, which were running into extremes, or to lead him once more into the busy haunts and paths of men. His painful bitter days dragged their slow length along. His nights were sleepless, spent between cruel memories and pungent remorse. Remained not one tie that bound him to life. He loathed society, and yet he found no remedy in solitude. Days without rest, nights without repose, affected his mind through his body; these mingled sufferings soon wasted away his health and destroyed the little of youth and elasticity that remained to him.

At times he would force himself from the town to breathe the free country air. But the change brought no relief. He looked upon fields artfully cultivated, watered by dull canals, fenced with exemplary regularity; he found them nude of forest trees and spontaneous vegetation, and deserted by the birds that sing their hymns of love, canticles that rise to the throne of God, a harmonious orchestra which proclaims and salutes His omnipotence. His heart sank deeper still as he remembered his New World plains and pampas, whose immensity, whose majestic charms, and whose ineffable sublimity appear to be the image and the symbol of the Divine Providence. Where were the young waters whose headlong course sprang over the precipice to sport with the white rocks in the basin below? Where the swelling streams of mature age which, reposing upon beds of flowers and blossoms, delighted the eyes and taught the gazer to look up to Nature's primal source, and to contemplate the omnipotence of the Universal Architect? Alone, and deep in these thoughts, he paced along a canal in the neighbourhood of Amsterdam. Already night had spread her black mantle over the firmament, and had wrapped him in her gloom before he perceived that it was time for him to end his walk.

Suddenly the silence of the air was interrupted by the soft accents of a woman's song, accompanied by an instrument which he had known in his youth, and which he had not heard since leaving the dear Brazilian shore. It was the Portuguese guitar, which murmured a melancholy sound like the distant harmony of the harp. Attracted by a sympathy he could not resist, Manuel approached the cottage whence the music came. He listened to the words of the melody, and involuntarily he trembled, hearing that they were Portuguese, pronounced by Portuguese lips. Who was the angel that whispered in his ears the song which his childhood had loved, and what might they express? Affection, passion, or the madness of love?

Little by little he distinguished the words; he lost the strength to stand, and he sank, supporting himself upon a stone.

To him it was a sermon rather than a song; a reproof, not a rhyme; a penitential psalm, not a hymn; a curse rather than a blessing. The following were the verses which fell from the minstrel's lips in rapt and heartfelt tones:—

I.

O sweetest faith! O blessed creed!
Drained with our milk in infancy,
Blent with our souls when children trained
To pray around a mother's knee!

THE NOVICE'S THIRD TRIAL.   89

2.

What power of life, what power of love
From out our hearts thy thoughts can tear?
What charm of change, what might of time
To touch the heavenly gift shall dare?

3.

Place me where every woe is mine,
Thirst, hunger, jail, and stranger land;
Yet shall my soul hold fast the boon
Till Death extend his icy hand.

4.

Thou legacy of priceless worth
By Heaven bequeathed to erring man,
Thou pledge to man that God is God,
Thou secret of th' immortal plan!

5.

Lives there on earth a thing so vile
That on the ashes of his sires
Can heap reproach, and make their creed
The victim of his low desires?

6.

His be it o'er the earth to roam
Like one accurst with endless curse,
Without a wife, a child, a friend,
To dull the pang of dire remorse!

In the spirit of man the Creator has placed a mysterious fibre for the purpose of impressing him through the superstitious, the fantastic, the supernatural, of beating down his vanity, and of proving the difference of the two substances which compose him—the one a frail vile frame, born of depravity; the other an immaterial, eternal essence, a spark of the Divine fire, to which it will fly upwards when freed from its tenement of dust.

However robust and stubborn be the spirit, it trembles before the sudden sight of a corpse, it bends contrite in the presence of a tomb, and it is filled with sombre thought by a Cross descried in the forest or on the river-bank, deserted, as was by the people Israel the God-Man who sacrificed Himself for the Salvation of the World. The unexpected music of the Church-bell, a melancholy Canticle heard at unlooked-for midnight hours, a solemn Miserere chanted under the Temple-dome—who can resist these influences, nor feel the sudden painful emotion that shakes the limbs, that freezes the blood, that commands the mind, that prostrates the spirit, and that compels the most sceptical soul to religious thought and to melancholy musings?

Manuel de Moraes felt one and all of these impressions as he heard the Portuguese guitar and the song, doubtless repeated by some banished daughter of Israel, who, with her faith, had preserved the picturesque language of her sires upon the shores of the Northern Sea and under the frigid Batavian air.

"Renegade! renegade!" cried a voice from his bosom, plunging his whole being in a flood of painful cruel remorse. "Renegade! renegade!" were the terrible accents which thundered in his ear. "Without a wife, a child, a friend!" was not such his solitary exile upon earth? Had the verses been expressly directed and applied to his own case? Was not this accident the forerunner of the wrath of Heaven?

He had not bodily strength enough to bear the violence of his emotions. Losing his senses, he fell upon the turf which clothed the humid soil. Hours and hours rolled by before he returned to life, nor was any good Samaritan accidentally led there to put forth the hand of charity and to save him from his danger.

Already the horizon was becoming visible under the pale brassy light that foreruns the Northern morn, putting to flight the shade, melting the glooms with its tepid breath of life, and presently pouring the flood of day over the immensities of earth and air and sea. The dampness of the ground aroused him from his long swoon, and lent him strength to arise and to recover himself from the death-like lethargy.

Slowly, and with frequent pauses, he walked towards the City, trembling as the fatal lines which had read his sentence still rang in his ears.

"I have abandoned my country! I have denied my Faith, without conviction, without conscience," he repeated to himself, "and those faithful ones who have endured for it every woe—thirst, hunger, prison, and strangerhood, misery, torture, and death! O Father Eusebio de Monserrate! art thou not the writer of these lines which place upon my forehead the brand of shame? Didst thou not warn me of the wretched fate awaiting him who dared to prefer the stormy ocean of the outer world to the peaceful waters within the Church of God?"

He wanted air to breathe, light to stimulate, and faith to tranquillise a soul agitated by the most violent and desperate inner struggle.

Physical weakness called for repose, but rest fled from the torments of his spirit; the couch was a bed of thorns, which tore his skin, which wounded his bones, which penetrated into his very vitals.

A deadly sickness came over him, and bore him to the verge of the grave. But his constitution was still strong enough to throw off the taint, and he was reserved for worldly trials even more calamitous than those which he had yet endured.

His first step, on rising from his sick-bed, was to seek some Catholic place of worship. His object was to ascertain what would be, upon a mind diseased, the effect of the pomp and ceremonies of the Faith which he had so lightly deserted, and whose heavy retribution had now come upon him.

Man in his earlier years easily disdains religious ideas. From a so-called philosophic indifference he readily lapses into that scepticism, and perhaps into that active form of irreligion, which mocks and scoffs at all things sacred. He is surrounded by so many sensual delights, by so many novel pleasures, and by so many charms of the intellect and the imagination, whilst the fire and fervour of youth assist them to absorb him, and to lead him astray from the road to heaven. The world tempts him with her siren-smiles and scenes; Nature speaks to him with all her witchery, gilding the wide horizon with so many pictures of ecstasy; the warbling of the bird is so sweet, the perfume of the flower is so intoxicating; society offers to him nothing but friendship and love, and Fancy paints existence with the rainbow hues of a poet's dream. But let him double the Stormy Cape which forms the half-way stage of his Earthly journey, of the years which he may expect to live. Then, indeed, as he looks out into the future, the view sadly changes; the horizon narrows to a span, and the short vista before his eyes ends in a shrouded corpse, a coffin, and a hollowed grave, with Death and the glooms of Chaos brooding around. O unhappy! It is now that Religion must lighten these terrors; it is Faith that must sow the seed of Hope, of firm trust in the Divine pity, which alone can pardon the waste of years, the abuse of life, the neglect of opportunities offered only to be thrown away.

Such were the thoughts which led Manuel to seek the Church of his forefathers. "Here, haply," he soliloquised, "I may find some rest from a disease which knoweth no cure."

He was shocked at the aspect of the Holy House where the rites of Rome were celebrated by the faithful few who had not conformed to the Calvinism or the Lutheranism of Holland. It had none of the splendour of the Temple, and it hardly showed the decency which we expect in the place where men assemble to address their Maker. The external appearance was almost secular; it was a meeting-house, not a fane, and the curse of the fanatic Calvin seemed to be set upon its brow.

Trembling with excitement, he pushed open the Church-door almost convulsively. Within he found himself fronting three altars adorned with statuary and tapestried with symbolical flowers, typifying eternal Light and Life. On one side was the vase of holy water which washes away the sins of man. The priests were intoning the solemn Mass, and the fumes of incense mingled with the voice of praise, the choir, and the melody of the organ; whilst winged Angels and prostrate Saints seemed to intercede for the repenting sinner; the sacred vestments of the Religious and their acolytes met his eyes, and the venerable accents of the Latin tongue struck upon his ear. These were the details of a spectacle which, even within that pauper house, breathed all the Majesty of the one true Church.

Does not the traveller, weary and footsore with treading the burning sands under a fiery sun, rejoice with all his heart at the sight of an oasis in the Arabian desert? Is there aught more delicious to one, whose tongue is parched and whose limbs are relaxed by devouring thirst, than the melody of the crystal spring bubbling from the hillside? Such upon the tortured soul of Manuel was the effect of the wellknown, never-forgotten scene. A sweet sense of relief stole on his spirit, as though the goal of Salvation were in view; a ray of light pierced the dark secrets of his inner being, and the dew from on high shed balm over his wounded and broken heart.

Humbly the penitent bowed himself down to earth. Hope returned with the voices of the celebrants and the presence of the altars; with the aspects of the Saints, the mute language of the symbolical flowers and ornaments, and the harmonious pealings of the organ. He raised to the throne of the Eternal the cry of his repentance, and from the depths of his soul he implored the immensity of Divine compassion. During several hours he knelt motionless, until, firm in his resolution to repent, he felt that Heaven was vouchsafing a something of its infinite mercy to his vows of a new life, of a better future. Nor did he leave the holy precincts till those, whose duty it was to clear them, had announced that the doors were about to be closed.

At length he had found the theriac which could counteract the poison of his spirit. "What," now whispered the inner voice, "what penance will it enjoin in order to complete the cure, to restore eternal health?"

CHAPTER X.

PADRE ANTONIO VIEIRA, THE JESUIT.

AT dawn on the next day Manuel de Moaesr left Amsterdam for the Hague. Reaching the capital of the States-General, he at once inquired for the residence of the Envoy and Diplomatic Agent accredited by Portugal to the Government of the Stadtholder. This was no other than the celebrated Jesuit Father Antonio Vieira, a preacher of marvellous eloquence, a master of Lusitanian style, and a personal friend of his monarch, Dom João II., who, the better to carry on against Spain the war of independence, had charged him with the important mission of negotiating peace with Holland.

Manuel, begging to be admitted into the presence of this illustrious personage, was led to a room simply furnished, and more distinguished by the modesty of its appointments than for the luxurious ornaments by which diplomatists, who rely so much upon outward appearance, attempt to exalt their own credit and the dignity of their nation. Presently he descried in a distant corner a man wearing the long black soutane of St. Ignatius, with a dark skull-cap, from which iron-grey locks escaped. The Jesuit sat in an arm-chair before a rough table strewed with papers, and he was so absorbed in writing that he did not perceive that any one had entered the room.

The Novice gazed at him with curiosity and wonder. His stature was little above the average, and without the least sign of corpulence. A tall broad forehead, with salient protuberances and deeply wrinkled across; lively and sparkling eyes; cheeks and chin furnished with a thick, short-cut beard which was beginning to whiten; an aspect of austerity which commanded respect, and which could be imposing as it was dignified.

That soutane, that scull-cap, which he had not seen since he left the Rio de la Plata, revived the reminiscences of São Paulo, and overclouded his thoughts with painful images of the past. He fell under the delusion that he was still in the Company of St. Ignatius, and standing once more in the venerable presence of those virtuous and holy men, whom he yet venerated from the bottom of his heart.

Not daring to approach the Jesuit or to disturb his occupations, he awaited the moment when the priest would perceive his presence and address to him a word. This soon came to pass. Antonio Vieira, turning by chance, saw a figure standing behind him in submissive attitude and, without a gesture or moving from the arm-chair, he asked the business of his visitor.

"I am a Portuguese," responded the intruder humbly, "and I would speak with your Reverence."

"What may be thy name?" inquired the priest, in the same manner as before.

"Manuel de Moraes," answered the unfortunate, with diffidence.

Antonio Vieira at once arose from his arm-chair, advanced a few paces towards his visitor, scanned him nearly and observantly, and presently thus addressed him—

"I know it well. Be seated, and say what thou wouldst say."

"I was born at São Paulo," continued Manuel, still standing, for he did not dare to sit down in the priest's presence.

"I know! I know!" interrupted the Jesuit. "I

wish not to turn over pages which will increase thy sorrow. All thy life is familiar to me."

"Since your Reverence knoweth all," continued Manuel, "it were useless for me to trouble you, to waste your time."

And an expression of disappointment appeared upon his countenance. Antonio Vieira at once saw it, and proceeded to remove the unpleasant impression with a kindly look, and a half smile which died upon his lips as soon as they had formed it.

"Thou art in the wrong," resumed the Jesuit; "sit down and let us speak together. I belong to the Society of St. Ignatius. It seems as though your memory has not been treacherous to the servants of God who educated you at São Paulo. Have you any complaint to make against them?"

"Oh, no!" exclaimed Manuel; "they have implanted for ever in my heart and soul a most fond and yearning affection. But I, reverend Sir, deceived myself into the belief that my vocation was not for the holy mysteries of the Company. The Enemy of Mankind seduced me from her peaceful and glorious asylum. Those ascetic virtues, that exemplary career of constant self-sacrifice, appeared to be beyond my strength. I wanted a call, faith, constancy of soul. I preferred a home life, to assist my family in worldly labours, to belong to society. My father drave me from home; I gave myself up to adventure. I wandered about the desert. I was taken prisoner."

"That is nothing," interrupted the Jesuit, whose darkened brow and firmly closed lips restored his usual appearance of severity.; "here there is no crime, hardly even shortcoming."

"Pardon me, reverend Sir," cried Manuel with sobs and casting himself upon the ground. "You are right, you are wholly right. But will not God pardon a true and sincere repentance? Yes, I repent— I repent! The hour of madness is past. I am ready to make any sacrifice for the remission of my sins. I long to confess, to perform any penance imposed upon me, to suffer any pain and punishment that can restore me to my sacred religion, the only one which I know to be the true Church of God; to my country, to the bosom of my parents, and to the Holy Company. I would fain end my days in the service of the Lord, hoping for His pardon in the world to come."

The priest fixed upon him a long and penetrating gaze, as though he would read his conscience, probe the depths of his soul, and ascertain the truth and spontaneity of his retractation. Here was no wild Gentile, pure and innocent, barbarous and untaught, ignoring social and religious ideas, converts of whom Vieira had found so many in the depths of the Brazilian forests, and whom he knew so well to recruit into the Catholic host, to animate with the holy faith of Christ, and to transform simply and suddenly by baptism and belief which left the heart without one adverse or malicious thought. Vieira was a master as well as a missionary: he had accustomed himself to look upon the denizen of the wilds in Bahia, Maranhão, and Pará as a child who, with the sincerity and conviction of its age, accepts the counsels of religious tuition, and who obeys them with all the force and fervour of soul and spirit. But very different was the penitence of a Portuguese who had forgotten his creed, who had been false to his duties, and who had exchanged his religion for the schismatic doctrines which were then agitating the world. Much more difficult and serious also was his own position in the presence of a man whom he knew to be learned and intelligent, and whom he saw tossed and torn by the storm within.

"Manuel de Moraes," said the Father, now assuming the tone of the Priest; that which becomes one who speaks not like a man, but as the representative of the Almighty and of His Church, "how shall I believe thy words, which are contradicted by a long course of persistent sin, when a list of infamous crimes accuseth you?"

"Not only accuseth, reverend Sir," returned Manuel, "say rather denounceth, condemneth me. I know it better than can any other. Doth this step savour of self-interest? Is ought wanting to me in life, if I desired to continue my present course?"

"Thou art subtle," replied the Jesuit. "I knew thee well by thy writings, and by thy fame for the talents which God hath bestowed upon thee. I doubt not thy patriotism: thy work upon our movement of independence proveth that well. But that is not enough. No! religion is superior even to love of country. What is our Native Land or our home, what is family or society, without the faith of Christ, of His Apostles, of His canonised Saints, of His one and eternal Church, of His Vicar upon earth, the Supreme Pontiff of Rome? Without these, I say, what is man? A frail being of flesh and blood, colourless and void of gifts, inert nature, miserable savagery, *animal brutum*. All mundane interests must bow before things Divine and the holy aspirations of the spirit; to man his family, to the family society, to society his country: whilst even this must be as naught compared with the one true and everlasting religion of God, the Holy Roman Catholic Apostolic Church, whose most humble slaves are the Disciples and followers of St. Ignatius. These are the men whom thou didst deny and whose creed thou didst cast off."

"It is sincere, O my Father," interrupted Manuel, "it is sincere, my penitence! I am tortured by remorse. Let me not die before retracting and expiating my errors, my crimes. Suffer me not to end in the pains of hell, which already claim me as their portion. Take pity upon me; guide me. Teach me the way of hope, which may console, even if it cannot save."

These words, accompanied by a flood of tears which

bathed the speaker's face, were uttered with accents of such heartfelt woe and utter conviction, that the Jesuit could not but feel impressed in favour of his penitent. He took from his bosom the heavy crucifix suspended from its rosary, and presented it to Manuel, who hastened to kiss the holy symbol with fervent affection, and to give evident signs of conscientious repentance.

"Arise, sinner!" said the Father, opening a door and pointing to an oratory within. "There is the place of prayer. There is the image of God. Bend thee before it; address to it thy prayers; implore of it thy pardon."

Manuel hastily arose, glided into the chapel, closed the door, and fell upon his knees before an altar whose silver lamp and four waxen tapers diffused around a dim religious light. Over it was a life-size picture of the Crucifixion. Blood dropped from the Divine hands, the feet, and the many wounds which had torn the body. A majestic and heavenly serenity sat upon the countenance, which was pale with the pallor of death. From the darkening eyes came the last look of purity and of ineffable innocence: it seemed still to proclaim before the world the eternal truths of Religion, of Morality, and of the brotherhood of Mankind. The artist had placed at the foot of the Cross, which she embraced, the weeping Mother; yet, through the grief which tare her breast and the woe that charged her countenance, appeared the sublime expression of Love and Hope. On one side of the picture St. Ignatius de Loyola preached discipline and enthusiasm to the Church Militant arrayed against Protestantism and other damnable heresies. St. Peter on the other, wearing the august tiara of the Roman Pontiff, the head of the Catholic Faith, showed to a world the Keys of Heaven.

At the sight of the holy memorials, Manuel felt as though healing flowed through his veins. His soul, warmed by the mysterious flame of pitying and saving love, no longer shuddered in the cold dry breath of Calvinism. Implorings for compassion, the fervent prayer of youth, and sincere evidences of faith and conviction were not forgotten. Hope, Life, and Eternity smiled with a novel aspect. Before him lay a vague and misty future, it is true ; but no longer black, as before, with the despair which had filled his soul.

For a time, during which he was left by Antonio Vieira in this position of the penitent sinner, Manuel seized the opportunity to savour with long draughts the joys of repentance, and to plunge into his lost faith till it penetrated through and permeated his whole spiritual being. He became another man, changed, restored to belief, and eager to re-enter the service of the Eternal and of His Universal Church. Thus by every manner of sacrifice, which had now no terrors, he hoped to redeem his sins and crimes, and to merit ultimate salvation.

Walking with noiseless footsteps, the far-famed Jesuit stood by his side and perceived that he was absorbed in celestial contemplation, fervently adoring and filled with pure and holy thoughts, whilst his countenance shone out its supernatural joy. He savoured the penitent's contrition; he felt convinced that the act of conscience was spontaneous and sincere, and that both Catholicism and the Company would gain much by this abjuration of apostasy.

The Father was accustomed to witness similar scenes of heartfelt repentance and of the deepest devotion suddenly inspired and following close upon horrible careers of crime. He regarded them as the spiritual work of that Divine Providence which loves to draw out of evil good, infinite and invaluable, which desires not the death of the sinner, but would rather show that the broken and contrite heart can find forgetfulness, and even forgiveness of its offences, and which thus can save the wretches who, after the mad course leading to destruction, arrest themselves in time, and have recourse to its ineffable mercy.

Had not St. Ignatius himself commenced his life in the tumults and turmoil of scandalous misdeeds? Had not many an offender, suddenly converted by the glorious works of the Fathers of the Company, enrolled themselves as disciples and become examples of the choicest virtues? Had not the Institute at times recruited to itself and obtained fresh splendour from wretches who had deemed themselves lost, and whom a new life of self-sacrifice had enabled to seek their own salvation and to do heroic and humanitarian service for the Company? After a life of vice, which had sunk her into the lowest misery, had not Mary Magdalen succeeded in becoming a canonised saint of the Church?

The Jesuit had too much experience to fear any delusion in signs so expressive, and he was overprudent to neglect so propitious an opportunity of recovering for the Institute an intelligence of the first order, and a mind distinguished by great and goodly gifts.

He aimed at something higher than triumphing over whole tribes of naked savages wandering in the backwoods of the Brazil, and called by his voice into the fold of the Church. He did not hold the Institute to be especially intended for catechising and civilising the hordes of the American deserts, although even there the disciples of St. Ignatius had excelled all others by exposing themselves, with the courage of enthusiasm, to hunger and thirst, to persecution and torture, to the poisoned arrow and to the deadly tomahawk. Nor was it enough for him that they should, like São Francisco Xavier, the Apostle of India, win the abjurations of Rajahs and of idolatrous Asiatic peoples. A far loftier and nobler ambition exalted and directed his efforts. He burned to see the Company rise in prestige throughout Europe, boldly combating the schisms which split the Catholic Church, counselling the Civil Authorities, directing Emperors, and taking charge of the Temporal Power and the march of Governments.

A true revolutionist, in politics as in religion, he never allowed his pen to rest from the task of propagating his plans, whilst from the pulpit he addressed the Kings and Nobles, the Priests and laymen who crowded to hear him preach, and to admire his portentous eloquence, his deep wisdom, and his varied knowledge. Convinced that the Company of Jesus was the chosen instrument of the heavenly Church and its earthly Head, he allowed himself no repose. He had made the temples of Bahia, of Lisbon, and of Rome re-echo to the harmonious sounds of his voice, and the Press groan under the uninterrupted task of reproducing the periods which fell from his pen. Ere now he had been intrusted by Royalty with secret missions to Rome, France, and Holland; and, as a Statesman, he was engaged in negotiating alliances with other foreign powers in favour of his own country, still threatened by the Spaniard.

The fire of genius was in his words—they burned like a consuming flame, they pierced like the sharpest poniard. They attracted, subdued, captivated the hearers' hearts, and at the same time filled them with enchantment. His style displayed all the closeness of logic, every nicety of grammar, every flower of rhetoric; it was at once individual and characteristic, correct and sublime, weighted with a prodigious fund of erudition and lightened by imagery the most appropriate, varied, and interesting.

Padre Antonio Vieira, born [1] at Lisbon, brought up

---

[1] Born February 6, 1608; died July 18, 1697. Almost a Brazilian by career. No great friend to other Jesuits, and rather of a secular and political than of religious turn. A man of immense vanity, indiscreet of speech, violent in resentment, overbearing in manner. Great and patriotic withal. He brought

and educated at Bahia, with his mighty soul, sublime spirit, and extraordinary eloquence, with a frame broken to labour and fatigue, and with a courage which never feared the face of man, was justly deemed one of the most singular combinations that the world ever saw. Half Portuguese and half Brazilian, half Religious and half Civilian, half a Patriot and half a "Roman," he enjoyed throughout life the universal fame which he merited, and he bequeathed to posterity a name rendered illustrious by virtue, genius, and true greatness.

himself into trouble with the Inquisition because he said it was better in Portugal to be Inquisitor than King. He was suspected of having to do with the murder of Francisco Tolles de Menezes, Alcaide Mór of Bahia. His portrait is in Varnhagen's "Historia Geral do Brazil," ii. 50.—*Translator's Note.*

CHAPTER XI.

THE NOVICE BIDS ADIEU TO HIS WIFE'S GRAVE.

WE left Padre Antonio Vieira standing by the side of Manuel de Moraes and unwilling to disturb his rapt devotion. But when the opportune time came, he placed himself before the penitent, gave him with awful solemnity the priestly benediction, and, kneeling by his side, he implored Divine mercy to receive back the sheep that had so long strayed from it into the fold of the Church. Then rising, he said to Manuel in accents the most impressive, "Enter the Confessional, kneel before the Priest of thy God, and reveal all thy heart to him."

Manuel obeyed. Long was the Confession, though only a summary of the errors, the sins, and the crimes of thought, word, deed or pen, mortal or venial, of action and intention, of commission and omission, which had stained the renegade's career. It was often interrupted by abundant tokens of sorrow, by heart-broken sobs, and by floods of tears. His task ended, the Jesuit arose, fixed his eyes upon the altar, as one who asks advice or aid, and muttered prayer after prayer. He then absolved his penitent; imposed upon him the penance which was to usher in a change of life. Presently, leaving Manuel in the oratory, he retired to a private room, deeply affected, but at the same time satisfied with what had happened, and conscious of having won another triumph for the Church.

Manuel was once more a changed man. His

countenance wore an expression of settled sadness; but he had recovered health of body by complete repose of heart and brain. The act of publishing his recantation, as Padre Antonio Vieira ordered, was to him a new source of joy. Constant to his religious duties, he lightened his inner man of the insupportable weight which before crushed him; he broke with the world around him; he cut off all connection with former acquaintances, and from that moment the Confession, the Church, and the closet occupied all his time. The Jesuit, who esteemed and already loved him, recommended writing a history of Portuguese America, whose annals the penitent knew perfectly, with especial reference to its invasion and occupation by the Dutch, whose tongue was familiar to him, and whose books he read with ease. He waited till the abjuration appeared complete, and then announced to him the necessity of visiting Lisbon, there to obtain the pardon of his Sovereign, leave to re-enter the Company, and, with permission of the Provincial, to make the object of his life the catechisation of the native Brazilians.

"Thou must," said he, "reinstate thyself both with the Society and with the Government. In the Brazil thou wilt be exposed to excessive toil, to exceeding fatigue, to incessant danger, perhaps to a cruel death, bound to the stake or by the piercing of the savage arrow. But thy sacrifices and thy good deeds shall pay the heavy debt of all thy sins; a merciful Deity will receive thee into His Divine arms. And not only will the Redskin Brazilians prove thy steadfastness by calamity and bitter life, thou wilt suffer even more at the hands of the Europeans and their Creole descendants who, without one thought of religion or morality, live only to amass riches by capturing, plundering, and destroying the hapless Gentiles. At their head again are the colonial Governors and authorities, insatiable persecutors, tyrants, despots, for whom there is no law, human or divine; these thou wilt have to confront in the service of the Company and in the practice of Christian virtue and of the dogmas and discipline of the Church. With heroic deeds of spirit and body thou must efface the black pages with which thy giddy and ill-chosen career hath filled the volume of thy days. In one who returneth to the path of truth from errors and crimes, Faith and conscientious convictions will not satisfy God; many serious sacrifices and the lifelong practice of virtue are indispensable before thou canst purify thyself in presence of the Eternal and of thy neighbour. I also have crossed the desert and the virgin forest; I have climbed the rugged mountain, swum the roaring stream, and conquered space immense. I, alone, unarmed, trusting to the cross of Christ which hung around my neck, fortified by faith and onwards driven by the desire of doing my best services to the Church, have found myself face to face with savage tribes whose names are unknown. I have seen the bow drawn, the arrow shot, and the tomahawk with its horrible and frightful sough grazing my hair. I have found myself bound to a tree, stripped of my clothing, and made ready for death by torture. I have witnessed the dreadful old women, thirsting for my blood, approach me with their calabashes, smear my body with the red and black colours which show the sacrifice, and dance like furies around me, writhing like serpents in hell, and howling like the souls of the damned. By a miracle from Heaven, I survived to catechise many of these miserables, who were touched by my words; at my prayers they abandoned their wild ways and nomad life, and by my advice and exhortations they received baptism and exchanged perdition, now and hereafter, for social life and the Faith of Christ. I founded many villages of these converts, who became as good Catholics and vassals as, nay, better than, the conquerors

of their country, the higher race of Europe. All this
I did without feeling that the burden was heavy, the
sacrifice severe. But the Portuguese adventurers,
especially the Governors, Captains-general, authorities,
and public employés of the metropolis, these were—
yes, I own it—the very touchstone of my patience and
humility. Such is the life of the Jesuit missionary.
As a man, he belongeth to Humanity only by the spiritual tie, and to Society by his life of sacrifice. As a
priest, he may not live in the repose of a cloister or in
the communion of his fellow-countrymen. He is the
property of the wilds, of distant missions, of perils, of
the lost Pagan souls, of an inglorious death in the
bush or the swamp. His goods and his joys are not
of this world. Remember José de Anchietta[1] and
Manuel da Nobrega. So pass thou through life from
earth to heaven amid the reefs and shoals which ever
oppose thy way, so as to prove thy devotion and to
purify thy soul. Advance without bending the neck,
without losing evangelic resignation, without renounc-
ing piety, without forgetting Christian charity, without
discouragement, without looking behind thee. Assume a new garb and, returning to the Company of
Jesus, ennoble and exalt thyself in the service of the
Church and in propagating her Faith by holy and
glorious deeds. Such be the penance enjoined upon
thy sins—such the balsam which shall heal thy remorse!"

Manuel took delight in hearing these narratives and
counsels of the distinguished and venerable speaker.
The proposal also met his desires. His love and his
social duties had ended with the passing away of the
one human being who had so mightily enchanted and
bewitched him. At times he visited the grave which
held her mortal spoils, and with yearning heart and
flowing eyes he strewed it with fresh flowers. But it
did not open to receive him; his heart now told him

[1] The "Thaumaturgus of the Brazil."—*Translator's Note.*

how fatal had been the hallucination which once mastered all his senses, and which caused the deadly falling off from religion that had so terribly tormented his soul.

Moreover, it presently so happened that Brodechevius, whose virtues and whose benefits had endeared him as a father, could not survive the death of Beatrix: a few months after the last adieu, he followed his daughter on the way of death. What now remained to detain the penitent sinner in Holland?

The advice and the exhortations of Padre Antonio Vieira sounded in his ears as another hope of conciliating himself with God and with His Church. When the Company once more should have opened her arms to him, would he not be able, by returning to her bosom, by dedicating himself to her service, and by going back to his country, to see once more his beloved mother and family, to receive the parental pardon, and to spend his latter days in a useful, beneficent, and holy life?

He had no terror of the toils and the sacrifices which might be reserved for him. He did not fear the missionary's hard task, because it would exalt him in the love of God and fortify him in the belief of the Catholic creed. And might it not be his lot to win by his actions the remission of his sins, and to obtain mercy from on high?

He prepared to leave the Netherlands for ever. Unable to travel by land, or to embark at any French port on account of Spanish dominion in Belgium, he took passage on a Dutch ship sailing for Rotterdam. Padre Antonio Vieira provided him with introductory letters to the Provincial of the Jesuits in Portugal, to some high functionaries and powerful nobles in Lisbon, and especially to Dom Francisco Manuel de Mello. The Novice then took leave of his protector, who was obliged, in the service of his sovereign, to visit Münster.

He would not, however, shirk the sad duty of bidding the last farewell to her who in life had ruled his heart and spirit, who had bewitched him to the point of losing his reason and of perilling his immortal soul. He set out for Amsterdam, which recalled to his mind the many events that began with seeming happiness, presently to become pain and sorrow. He walked straight to the cemetery where stood the tomb which he sought. It was adorned with a marble column, surrounded by iron posts and chains ; and it bore, in large gilt letters, the name of BEATRIX DE MORAES, with the dates of her birth and of her death. Pale roses blew around it ; a sombre cypress overshaded it with its thick and untrimmed growth, and small shrubs scattered about bore their melancholy blossoms.

He was profoundly affected by the aspect of the tomb, by the silence which reigned around, and by the memories that started up from his soul. He drew near it with respect, whilst the bitter tears burst in showers from his eyes. He threw himself upon his knees, directed his prayers to God and, scattering upon the grave the torn flowers and broken shrubs which betokened his bereavement, he cried in the agony of his heart—

"Wife, loved and lost! an unexpected fate brought us together, a mad passion ensnared us, a crime sprang from our love! we were the mutual cause of our calamities, of thy death, of my misery. So may God pardon us in the world of Eternity, whither thou hast already passed, and where I shall not be slow to follow thee! God alone is great!"

He cast one last long look behind. He had done all his duty. He had braved the cruel proof, and he had found strength to withstand it.

He then took ship at Rotterdam for Lisbon.

When running down the dangerous channel which separates France from England, where the winds rage with frightful and continuous violence, the waves threatened more than once to cast the wretched craft ashore. Before doubling Cape Finisterre, Manuel was not spared by the Bay of Biscay, so celebrated for its eternal gales; the rushing billows, the dashing currents, and the furious blasts seemed bent upon destroying the frail galley and its imprudent inmates. The crew overcame every danger. But as the ship entered upon the ocean and was driven afar by the impetuous east winds, the shores of Portugal seemed to retire. More than forty days had sped before the peaks of Cintra hove in sight. They crossed the Tagus bar with sprung masts and tattered sails, whilst rations and water were completely wanting. Right happy were all when, running round the headland, they found themselves afloat upon the smooth surface of Father Tagus, off the fortresses that guarded the watery way.

Manuel de Moraes had to endure, when landing, as was the custom of the age, endless inquiries and the most rigorous search. He then presented himself to the Provincial of the Company who, after consulting the recommendatory letters of Antonio Vieira, received him with kindness and softness of manner, curiously dashed with surprise and even fear. Hardly, however, had two hours sped, when Familiars bearing the insignia of the Holy Office and armed soldiers appeared at the gate of the Institute of St. Ignatius, and demanding admittance to the Provincial, filled the cloisters and all the neighbourhood with alarm. When in presence of the venerable priest, they laid before him an order of the Tribunal demanding the person of one Manuel de Moraes, who, lately arrived from Holland, had taken sanctuary with the Company, a man charged with the crimes of abjuration and apostasy, and thus subject to the Inquisition.

The Provincial held hasty conference with the most respectable ecclesiastics whom he could summon, touching the defence of his rights and the honour of the Institute. All agreed upon one point, that the unheard-of order of the Inquisitional Tribunal was an insult to the powers and privileges of the Company, but that the Provincial was not justified in resisting by force. They advised him to give up the prisoner, and at once to protest before the Sovereign and his Government; to claim his penitent as a member of the Institute, and to judge him according to its rule. The order of the Holy Office was obeyed. Manuel de Moraes left the house of the Company, and passed into the power of the Inquisition.

CHAPTER XII.

THE INQUISITION OF LISBON IN THE SEVENTEENTH CENTURY.

In 1645, the date of our tale, the Inquisition sat in the Largo do Rocio of Lisbon; the edifice was a shapeless but massive construction, without architectural beauty, but imposing by the strength of its fortifications; and it commanded the square with its sad dead walls of stone and its ponderous iron gates.

Detached at the bottom of the Rocio, surrounded by soldiers and guards, who watched day and night, containing the halls of the Tribunal, the penitentiary dungeons and the chambers of question and torture, the palace drove far from itself and from its neighbourhood the peaceful masses of the people, who never sighted it without devout crossings, benedictions, and respectful pulling off of hats, lest suspicion of orthodoxy lead to inquiry and to punishment.

To-day not a stone of the barbarous edifice remains. One by one they were torn down and cast away by the exasperated populace of Lisbon, when the Cortes, constituted in 1821, abolished the Holy Office, and extinguished for ever that most execrable Tribunal. Upon its site now rises the Theatre of Maria II., substituting pleasure, mirth, and rational amusement for the scenes of pain and anguish, of blood and horror which, staining the pages of Portuguese history, took place within those grim walls. Time has as usual brought forth his Nemesis.

Entering the principal gate between files of armed

guards, and casting his eye upon the gigantic statue of Faith which stood threatening at the summit of the main staircase, Manuel de Moraes felt a deadly cold run through his veins, and his brain turn dizzy with frightful thoughts inspired by the Genius of the place. He crossed sundry courts, all gloomy, even in the bright sheen of a Lisbon sun. He descended and ascended several flights of steps, whose darkness was only half dispelled by the pale gleam of oil-lamps hanging from the walls. He heard the hoarse and melancholy sounds of heavy hinges that creaked and groaned as their doors were opened and shut. Within, he breathed a foul atmosphere which seemed the exhalation of corpses; the stones appeared to drip human blood, and the moans of pain and woe echoed and resounded through the long vaulted passages. The Familiars all wore the same attire; a large cross of yellow cloth stood out from each breast, and every face was hidden in the folds of the hood. They flitted here and there like spectres or avenging demons bound on their eternal errands of wrath and destruction.

A lugubrious silence, an extraordinary horror, characterised this pandemonium; all the precincts of the edifice were made to inspire terror, and the senses of the wretches who entered there for the first time failed them for unutterable fear.

After many turnings and whispers exchanged by the Guard and the Familiars, Manuel found himself in a bleak gallery where the way was barely shown by a lamp glimmering in the centre. An iron door opened as if by magic in one of the sides, and he was introduced into a low-ceilinged cell, from which goodly light and air were barred; it appeared less like a room than a sepulchre hewn in the live and dripping rock. The door was bolted upon him as he entered the solitary dungeon, which could hardly have admitted two men together. Bed there was none, nor a single article of furniture. The only thing which he remarked was an earthen crock, apparently full of water, placed in a corner of the cell. The brick flooring supported the straw bundle representing a sleeping-place. The heavy gloom which oppressed the site was broken by a sickly ray shot through a narrow crevice in the upper wall by a lamp that stood in the nearest corridor; this hole also served to keep the prisoner under the eyes of his guards, who watched every gesture and movement, whilst their ears caught the moanings and sighs of the victims, however prudent and careful to moderate them.

Alone in this terrible position, Moraes applied himself to a minute examination of the cell. His eyes ran over the floor, the ceiling, the walls. Here and there he imagined rather than descried purple stains, marks, as it were, of blood, daubed and sprinkled upon the frail ground-work of dust and smoke, and melancholy inscriptions traced by victimed hands.

Sad and bitter thoughts rushed into his mind. Was this gore that reddened the walls shed by those whom the Holy Office had found guilty? Were these writings upon the stone, which time had rendered undecipherable, the eternal adieux of those who had left the dungeon? Might there not be some name, some date, some sign which would betray the secret thus bequeathed to a posterity of prisoners?

Some of these mysteries were to be divulged to him. The frightful aspect caused his body to shiver, and his spirit quailed before the dark history of the Tribunal. At that period the Inquisition was in fullest vigour; it spread terror throughout the subject World, and it was generally execrated with profound secrecy for its monstrous crimes, and for the violence which rendered all opposition to it impossible.

Fatigue soon induced sleep, and the Novice's conscience, at least, was tranquil, as it had been since the day when he abandoned Calvinism and returned to the bosom of the true Church. How long he slept was uncertain, to him; night was confounded with day in the continuous glimmer of the central lamp, nor was there even a greater or a less amount of illumination in the persistent monotonous twilight which gloomed the rest of his solitary cell.

He taught himself to expect the morning when, without the prison door being opened, a fresh crock of water and a hard dry loaf were thrust into his cell through an aperture contrived for such purpose in the wall. At these times a hollow voice as from a cavern would ask him to receive them, and to pass out the empty water-pot—the latter disappearing with the same mysterious precautions. It was vain to speak: no question was ever fated to obtain an answer.

He resolved to count the times when his supplies were renewed, and thus to ascertain the number of his prison days. Already some forty had passed, when he heard the shuffling sound of steps and low whisperings exchanged outside the door—these noises were louder than those to which his ear had become accustomed.

"Now it is my turn," he said to himself, "or that of some neighbour victim going to question and torture."

A few minutes afterwards his door grated open. He rose and descried a figure covered in a long black cloak.

The entrance was again closed, and the twain found themselves so near together in the narrow space, that they were hardly able to raise hand or to make a gesture.

"Thou art Manuel de Moraes?" asked a mild and composed voice.

The prisoner determined that he stood in presence of one of the judges charged with examining and interrogating him. The questioner's serene and almost kindly accents were decided to be a holy device, the Inquisitors being well known to deceive their victims by a show of pity; to induce by soft and deceitful words a mad confidence and confession of the most secret thoughts or false revelations and tales of imaginary crimes invented merely to escape punishment.

Resolving, however, to speak the truth and the whole truth, be the result what it might, and not to be cozened by fallacies and fascinations, the Novice replied to the cloaked figure in a resolute tone—

"Without doubt I am Manuel de Moraes."

"And thy native country is the village of São Paulo, in the captaincy of São Vicente of the Brazil?" continued the interrogator.

"It is true," repeated Moraes.

"Thou wast a Novice in the Company of Jesus? Thou didst desert the Institute and cast off the cassock?" rejoined the other.

"I may not, I ought not, and I would not deny it," ejaculated the prisoner.

"And thou dost not recognise me?" said the figure, placing himself in the glimmering ray shot athwart the gloom by the corridor lamp; casting aside his cowl, and showing a face worn by years and clothed with the whitest of beards, a head denuded of hair and the soutane of the followers of St. Ignatius.

Manuel examined him in vain. His eyes would not distinguish the man who stood before him. He searched his mind for memories of the past. Not a single idea would come to his aid.

"No, I cannot," he replied bitterly. After a few moments of silence and of visible anxiety, Manuel resumed, "Doubtless the holy Fathers would punish me for having fled their House, and thou art sent to make these inquiries of me?"

"Banish from thy mind," answered the Jesuit, "these fancies, which are mere foolishness. Our Company counselleth, influenceth, convinceth by persuasion, and by appeals to man's conscience. She doth not bind his will by physical force. She doth not chastise the rebel and the criminal by the corporal punishments of confinement and torture. Almighty God is the only Judge to whom she committeth the sins of mortals. Thou art not imprisoned by order of the Institute of St. Ignatius de Loyola. Thou art accused by the Tribunal of the Holy Office. I come to visit thee as thy friend and thy companion of bygone days, after obtaining with much difficulty permission to enter these dungeons."

The words, slowly spoken and uttered with a certain unction and even affection, profoundly impressed the unhappy Manuel, and inspired him with a conviction of their truth and candour. But who was the man who addressed him? The idea of not being able to recognise and to thank him worked trouble in his brain.

"What, then, wouldst thou have of me?" gently returned the prisoner.

"I have lately arrived from Holland, bringing letters and recommendations from the venerable Antonio Vieira, who saved thy soul from the precipice of eternal perdition."

"If thou be, as thou dost suggest, a Jesuit, thou wilt find in the House of the Company the letters and documents which I left behind when the Familiars of the Inquisition hurried me away from the sacred walls."

"Our Provincial hath taken charge of all," continued the visitor sadly; "he hath forwarded to each one the letter directed to him, the better to enlist sympathies in thy favour. Unhappily, and I must not conceal it from thee, all his efforts appear fruitless."

"I see death before me!" murmured the captive. "I regret it cometh so soon, because I have not yet purged myself of my great sins and crimes. I would live long enough to perform the necessary penances

THE INQUISITION OF LISBON.

and sacrifices. But the Lord hath heard my sincere repentance, and He will assuredly take pity upon my weakness."

"Thou knowest not that thou art already condemned?" asked the voice.

"Condemned without being heard?" ejaculated Manuel.

"Thou wast denounced as a heretic and apostate to the Holy Office in Lisbon; the proceedings were entered upon and the sentence was passed. Whilst still a refugee in Holland thou wast relaxed in effigy by the Act of Faith of April 6, 1643, and thy name was inscribed amongst those condemned to death."

"Doth naught then remain to me in this world?" exclaimed Moraes. "Then leave me during the short remaining moments of life to pray in peace, that the Lord may grant to me His endless mercy."

"Thus thou wast already a criminal, and, as such, subject to the Inquisition," continued the old man. "When thou daredst come to Lisbon, relying upon a new abjuration, and upon the protection of the venerable Antonio Vieira, the Holy Office knew thee to be an inmate of our House and claimed thee for its justice."

"Whilst the Institute of St. Ignatius gave me up and left me?" exclaimed Manuel, with visible signs of resentment.

"What can the Company of Jesus do against the Inquisition?" returned the priest. "They are wholly different from, nay, they are antagonistic to each other. This is a temporal power, a civil tribunal; with its Judges, Guards, and Familiars, its trials, its instruments of torture, and its condemnations, to purify the faith and to keep inviolate the orthodoxy of Rome. That confineth itself to things spiritual and holy, charged only with spreading its lights and its doctrines over the world. With what difficulty it hath saved the Brazilians from the Inquisition, which would have extended its power amongst them as in Portugal. The two Orders are separated by a great gulf; they live in constant opposition. One would cut down and cast into the fire the tree which beareth bad fruit. The sons of St. Ignatius would heal the affected part, and hasten to save the trunk and the sound branches which may still flow with sap and bear kindly food for the use of man."

"At least send me," interrupted Manuel, "a Priest, a friend who may hear me confess, and may be with me during my last short pangs."

"And what came *I* to do here?" asked the Jesuit in a tone of hurt feelings, "wherefore have *I* made my way amongst these gloomy vaults, had I not been especially charged by our Provincial and permitted by the Holy Office to see thee, to speak with thee, and to treat thee as a member of the Company which, like Jesus, never abandoneth its disciples?"

"O thanks! O thanks!" cried Moraes, falling at the Father's feet and fervently kissing them.

"Rise, my son," continued the figure, assisting the penitent to stand up, and clasping him in his arms; "it is not yet time for confession or for the last preparations. At present I am but a friend who would console thee; so give me all thy confidence; it will be enough for thee to remember who I am to call to mind the past."

Manuel perceived by the ear rather than the eye that these words were pronounced amidst repressed sobs, and that a flood of bitter tears coursed down the cheeks of his unknown friend.

But despite every effort, his memory failed to find any clue by which he might recall to himself that time-worn figure, that venerable head, those soft attractive accents, and those kindly gestures, which, nevertheless, left him in no doubt of his visitor's sincerity.

For a few instants there was a painful silence, which

neither of the men chose to break; it was ended by the unknown, who, impressing a paternal kiss upon the brow of the younger man, asked him in a clear sonorous voice—

"And still canst thou not remember me?"

But Manuel's thoughts were entangled in the meshed skein of his wandering and erring life; he could hit upon no recollection which could tear the veil hanging dark before his eyes.

"Behold," continued the voice, speaking slowly, the better to arouse his companion's memory, "behold on the summit of yon myrtle-dotted hill-slope the Holy House of the Company of Jesus, with its hollow square, its adjoining chapel, and its strong low tower. By its side clusters a village of whitewashed and red-tiled houses and huts thatched with yellow grass, forming crooked streets and alleys, which, like the steps of a staircase, run up and down the ridge of red clay. See on the other side the enclosure of fruit-bearing trees, the orange, the guava, and the cashew apple, from whose boughs the Sabiá-thrush and the painted parroquet salute the newly-born dawn, the departing day, and the power and majesty of Him who made them. Remark below the enclosure, which extends to the hill-foot, the rivulet, here flowing limpid and serene, there bubbling over its pebbly bed, and bedewing the wild-flowers which spring from its fair green marge. Cast thy sight still farther upon those immense forests glooming the plain, where the great river Tiété rolls his waters, and where the uplands of the Penha, bluer than the atmosphere, bound the splendid amphitheatre. Breathe the air perfumed by the leaves and flowers which kindly Zephyr gently waves to and fro; by the blossoms which the parent tree never casts to lie in the sad decay of a European autumn. Mark the copper-coloured crowds that fill the temples, that pray so devoutly, that form religious processions, and that respect and obey the Fathers of the Company. What village is this which thy memory paints, if thine eyes behold it no more? And now canst thou not recollect me?"

"O God, my Lord!" cried Moraes, "what wounds this priest teareth open, and yet I cannot for my life remember him!"

"There, on a hill-top, lay quiet and retired the small white house with its red-tiled roof," continued the figure. "In it lived one José de Moraes and his family. God called him away before he could pardon himself for the imprudent haste with which he drove a son from his door."

"Then my father is dead! O unhappy again! Enough!" interrupted Moraes. "Take pity upon me, and, for mercy's sake, tell me who thou art!"

"Still thou hast not discovered me?" asked the Father. "How beset is thy spirit by the terrible delusions of thy misspent, erring life! Remember, my son, one who said to thee, 'Thou wilt be wretched! The Catholic Church is the Divine reason, the sole Salvation of Mankind; there can be no rest for him who abandoneth her, and who plungeth into the depths of this world of woe.'"

"Eusebio de Monserrate!" exclaimed Manuel with a fresh burst of grief. He caught the old man in his arms and, suddenly losing his senses, he fell upon the cold floor of his dungeon.

CHAPTER XIII.

THE "QUESTION" OF THE INQUISITION.

FATHER Eusebio de Monserrate walked straight from the palace of the Inquisition to the House of the Company, where he sought the presence of his Provincial.

He related, word for word, what had passed between him and Manuel de Moraes, expressing the firmest conviction of the penitent's sincerity, and hoping that the stray sheep, once more received into the fold of St. Ignatius, would be no small gain both to Religion and to the State.

As regards the purpose of the dread Tribunal, he persistently asserted his belief that the sentence passed during the criminal's absence would be carried out, and that the wretch would not be spared at the first Act of Faith performed by the Inquisition. He dwelt upon the necessity of employing all means to save the Novice, by claiming him as subject to the Company's jurisdiction and a fugitive from her cloisters. And, in order to tear him from the grasp of the Holy Office, he suggested that interest be made with all manner of men, Ministers, public functionaries, and Nobles, Jesuits, Bishops, and the high officers of the Church. It was necessary to secure the co-operation of the many in order to invoke with success the authority of the King and the Queen.

The two Fathers determined to visit all their friends and those for whom Manuel had brought letters from Father Antonio Vieira. To the latter the Provincial wrote a summary of what had happened, and impressed him, in urgent terms, with the necessity of leaving no measure untried, especially by a missive directed to the Sovereign, and imploring a personal favour.

Within a few days many men in power were induced to undertake the cause of Manuel de Moraes. Amongst the most influential were the Confessor of the King and Queen, Duarte Nunes de Leão, and the Chief Justice of the Tribunal of Supplication, João Pinto Ribeiro, private secretary of the Monarch.

Unhappily, Dom Francesco Manuel de Mello could lend no aid, having himself lost his liberty. None would have been of more avail when he first arrived at Lisbon: he was equally distinguished by the power of his pen and by the services which his sword had rendered in the Brazil, in Flanders, and in Catalonia, and by his patriotic sentiments in favour of Portuguese liberty and nationality. He had sacrificed wealth and honours in Spain, exposing himself to the persecution of the Governors of Castile, from whose dungeons he had escaped by buying off his jailers. But, on his return, to Portugal, he was drawn into an unhappy quarrel at Belem with one Francesco Cardoso, whom he killed in a moment of anger. For this offence he had been imprisoned, and expecting his trial, he was compelled to think more of his own safety than of saving another.

The King and the Queen found themselves surrounded by prayers and petitions to save Manuel de Moraes. Dom João IV., whose authority was not yet solidly established in Portugal, hesitated to interpose his prerogative in a case completely within the jurisdiction of the Holy Office. He had risen to a throne during the storm of a revolution. He had won a crown by a patriotic movement, unanimous amongst the people, but he counted a bare majority amongst the Clergy and the Nobility. At every moment he was compelled to put down reactionary movements, and the risings of those who preferred obeying Spain to ranging themselves on the side of Portugal and freedom. He was often obliged severely to chastise the titled classes, and even the Bishops, who plotted against him. The power of Castile would have still been too great for Lusitania, had not the former happily been occupied with crushing other insurgents in various parts of her wide dominions; and thus her numerous hosts, divided and dispersed, could not strike the one decisive blow.

Not the less, however, was Dom João compelled to administer his Kingdom with the greatest moderation, and to avoid increasing the difficulties and dangers which from all sides rose up around him. What then mattered the life of a Jesuit Novice compared with the anger and resentment of the Holy Office, which at that time influenced so powerfully the popular mind, and which lent its aid to his national government? He knew that his own Hidalgos and highest Ecclesiastics took a pride in belonging to the Inquisition, and even in serving it as Familiars. He was well aware also that the people trembled before all its actions and judgments, deeming them Divine rather than human.

With more policy than sentiment or justice, the King avoided answering the applications of his most devoted friends and his chosen councillors. Although sincerely attached to and thoroughly confiding in his Queen, Dona Luiza de Guzmão, who had taken part with the Jesuits, he would not in this case lend an ear to her words.

Eusebio de Monserrate had guessed rightly that, without the direct intervention of the sovereign, all efforts would be of no avail. The dread authority of the Holy Office at that time overshadowed the heart of Portuguese society.

None would dare, none had the power to brave it with impunity save the King in person, by virtue of his individual prestige, and by the acknowledged necessity of supporting his efforts to free the country against the forces of Castile.

Scattered in every direction were the spies of the Inquisition, who hastened to pervert every thought, word, and deed into something which might be reported to the execrable Tribunal. It seemed as though the walls had ears, the furniture had eyes, and the very air could read the deepest secrets of the soul. The best-hidden plans found their way to the Holy Office, and the latter never hesitated or delayed to send warrants for persons, to institute proceedings, to pronounce rigorous sentences, to administer punishment, and to raise the gibbet and the stake. Thus the Lieges, a superstitious multitude, were terrified by the horrible spectacles of the Acts of Faith, and were taught to look upon them as sacraments of the Church.

No class, no condition of man, could escape this infernal jurisdiction. It was the only judicial tribunal before which disappeared all rights and privileges, which bent before its might old men and young, women and children, householders and proletaires, workmen and merchants, seculars and regulars, nobles and the high officials of the Church, even the ministers and the confidants of the Monarch.

Yet did not Father Eusebio despair of success in his labour of love. As new and greater obstacles rose in his path, as his projects were defeated and brought to nothing, so he applied his spirit the more ardently to seek new measures which should command success. His bosom was fired with the *amour propre* of the Jesuit, who would not tamely put up with the affront which the Inquisition had offered to the Company, by seizing from it a Novice and a member in order to try and to condemn him. Furthermore, he was moved by the love and sympathy which Manuel, when yet a youth, had won from him.

These were two powerful reasons, to which was added another of equal importance for the priest. Had not the Novice's repentance been sincere? Was he not ready to undergo any discipline, or penance, or act of contrition imposed upon him? Could he not contribute important service to Religion, to the Company, to the State, and to the Gentiles of the Brazil? Had not the Lord pardoned him when his spirit spontaneously conceived the idea of abandoning wealth and rank in Holland, to reassume the soutane of the priest, to seek the laborious and miserable life of the missionary, to return to his former faith and religious belief, like the lost sheep which regains the fold, like the prodigal son who seeks his father's home? And when God had shown Himself so merciful, was it for Man to insist upon strict justice, upon harsh condemnation, upon the death of the sinner?

Meanwhile the Tribunal had entered upon the prisoner's case. After revising the proceedings instituted during his absence, and annexing to them a summary, the Holy Office proceeded to the necessary examination of the offender, who during six successive days was taken from his dungeon to the Hall of the Judges. At first, insinuating questions and subtleties, carefully and purposely prepared, were addressed to him, with the object of detecting contradictions, and of extracting the required confession. The captive, however, maintained an unaltered demeanour, serene and composed, as his words were truthful and serious. He frankly related all the facts of his life, all his errors and hallucinations, all his sins and crimes. Nor was he more reticent about his remorse, and the spontaneous repentance which his own soul had conceived, had brought forth, and had held up publicly and frankly before the eyes of men.

The judges, persuaded that they would obtain more information concerning matters which better suited their designs by applying the usual question, passed from voluntary declarations to those torn from the victim by torture. They began with the "little angels" (*anjinhos*), a soft, endearing name, derisively given to ironthumb screws which, with horrible sufferings, crush the fingers and the toes. They determined that the penitent should confess a false and malicious return to Catholicism, in order that he might pass over to the Brazil and aid his former associates, the Hollanders, in invading and conquering America. Manuel nobly endured these barbarities, whilst with tearful eyes he called upon the holy name of Christ, who in bearing the sins of the world had suffered agonies still more terrible than his own.

The judges, thus disappointed, adjourned to a future opportunity the appliance of other instruments. They intimated, however, to Manuel that it would be better for him to confess the truth of his own free will, than to have it torn from him by the most dreadful sufferings.

The Holy Office was not wont to hurry its proceedings or its judgments. Whole years were spent in its dungeons, without the Tribunal moving to do them justice, by the innocent as well as the guilty, by men falsely accused or merely suspected, and often without the slightest proof of criminality. Not contented with facts, and with seeking to divine thoughts and motives, it sought to gain time, whilst the victims were surrounded by the most vigilant espionage which saw and heard everything they did and said. One for refusing to eat a bit of pork on a certain day, another for some chance expression of rage or resentment, this for a gesture or action maliciously interpreted, that for not blessing himself or praying at the canonical hours—all such trifles served as inductive proofs to establish a crime which rested only in the imagination of the Holy Office.

The interrogatories and the first tortures were followed by the evidence of witnesses, who deposed that, according to the general voice, Manuel had become converted to Calvinism, had worshipped in Protestant temples, and had married a schismatic woman. Desirous of obtaining ampler confessions, the Familiars again applied questions to the accused. His neck was enclosed in a "gonilha," or ring made fast to the wall; and thus he was made to stand on tiptoe in a cramping and almost suffocating position, a torment more terrible than any barbarity imagined by the tyrants of the Middle Ages.

They then lashed his sides and chest with scourges of metal wires, which covered him with blood. But the victim, superior to physical pain, was resigned to his fate: he constantly repeated the same declaration, and he supplied no new elements of doubt or of suspicion to his cruel judges. Finally, he was stretched on the bed of Procrustes, a board bristling with spikes: here he fainted as if dead, after losing blood which escaped from every pore.

They then carried him back to his dungeon, placed him upon a mat somewhat softer than usual, and treated him with the greatest care. Their object was to prevent his escaping by death from the public and exemplary chastisement prepared for him by the Holy Office.

His sentence, when passed, confirmed that of the year 1643. The heretic was doomed to appear at the great Act of Faith, covered with the infamous insignia of fire, and to be garotted in the public square as an apostate and an obstinate professor of a false faith.

The report of this resolution soon came to the Jesuits' ears, and the Fathers were filled with despair and with the liveliest resentment.

All redoubled their zeal in urging on their friends, and in devising means to arrest the decree of the dread Tribunal. They applied themselves more urgently than ever to obtain from the King a sign-manual in favour of the wretched Novice.

But all was in vain. The letters of Antonio Vieira, the ghostly counsels of their Majesties' Confessor, the opinions of the Secretaries of State and of the high officer called "Escrivão da Puridade," the supplications and the interest made by the Nobles whom the Sovereign most delighted to honour, nothing would induce the King to shake off the reserve which he had chosen to assume.

Eusebio de Monserrate at length devised a happy plan. Visiting a sister of the Novice, a certain Dona Clara da Incarnação, the widow of a Portuguese, who had transferred her residence from São Paulo to Lisbon, he prepared her to throw herself with her children at the feet of the King and the Queen, and to implore their mercy for her miserable brother. With the Court Confessor he arranged an opportunity at the first time when Dom João and Dona Luiza were proceeding to the Oratory for the purpose of receiving the Sacraments.

When the moment came, Dona Clara and her young family were introduced into the palace by a private door, and she found herself on the very passage of the Sovereigns.

"Mercy! mercy!" cried with one voice the suppliants, falling at the feet of the King and his Consort, seizing the hems of their garments, and bedewing them with copious and bitter tears.

All the suite were melted with pity. Dom João, profoundly moved, could not utter a word.

The weeping Queen hastened to console the unhappy sister, who placed in the royal hand a petition humbly praying for pardon of the penitent. It was a touching, a heart-rending scene.

The royal Confessor reminded his Majesty that God is infinite in His compassion, and that earthly sovereigns have no higher prerogative, and none more grateful to Heaven, than that mercy which compares their functions with those of the Deity. Dona Luiza promised the heart-broken family all her efforts, and begged them to retire and to be comforted.

After this scene the Monarch could no longer turn a deaf ear to the prayers of his Consort, or allow her to fail in keeping her word. He directed his " Escrivão de Puridade" to claim summarily and peremptorily from the Holy Office the person of Manuel de Moraes, who had obtained the royal pardon; and he commanded that the latter be delivered, as a member of the Institute, to the Society of Jesus, in order that he might incur the pains and penalties judged proper by his Superiors.

This order was at once transmitted with the royal sign-manual to the Inquisitor-General; and it was intimated that he was expected to render implicit obedience, with his well-known zeal in the service of his God and his King.

Still Eusebio de Monserrate was not without anxiety. Would the Judges of the Holy Office obey the command? Could they not hold themselves superior to all temporal authority, taking their prerogative upon the briefs and decisions of the High Pontiff of Rome? Might they not reply to the King by reminding him that it was necessary to purge the Catholic faith and to save her creed; and would the Monarch persist in carrying out an order which had been obtained from him rather by sentiment than by conviction, which came from the heart rather than from the head?

CHAPTER XIV.

THE LAST SCENE—THE NOVICE'S DEATH.

MEANWHILE the Tribunal of the Holy Office of Lisbon resolved upon, and publicly announced, an Act of Faith to take place upon the 15th of December 1647.

Eight condemned criminals were to be burnt at the stake; ten were reserved for the punishment of the garotte; thirty-four were sentenced to walk in the Procession bearing the insignia of fire, and three were "relaxed" in effigy, being absent or having been able to escape.

The announcement of this barbarous spectacle filled the Lisbonese with excitement and apparent joy. None would dare to absent himself from a solemnity so sacred and profitable to the soul, from an Act which remitted sins, and which had power with the Almighty to open for believers the gates of Heaven, and to lead them by the Indulgences gained on such occasions to Salvation and Life Eternal. And though some Jews may have had their doubts touching the Divine nature of the sacrifice, who would risk persecution and perhaps torments, dreadful as those allotted to the condemned, in case of not being present or of not appearing full of gladness?

The scaffold and stakes were prepared in the great Square, the Campo de Santa Anna. Those doomed to figure in the ceremony were duly warned. Some were allowed interviews with confessors chosen by themselves, and were privileged to receive one or more members of their families with whom they desired a last melancholy adieu. All the condemned were transferred to especial prisons under the civil authorities, there to pass the remainder of the term to which they had been sentenced in the palace of the Holy Office. Thus they were made over "to be relaxed," as the phrase was, by the secular arm; for the Inquisition only sentenced to death, and was never guilty of shedding Man's life-blood.

To Manuel was announced his punishment, death by the garotte, and he was also indulged with the permission to choose a Ghostly Father, and to be visited by one of his relations. He named Padre Eusebio de Monserrate to accompany him during his last moments, and his sister, Dona Clara, to receive his last farewell.

Both these requests were granted. It is not possible to describe the meeting between the brother and sister. Manuel, physically broken down, cruelly tortured by the wounds of the terrible instruments which had entered into his flesh, with hair and beard turned grey-white long before Time had touched their natural colour, was morally crushed by losing the hope of a long penitential career, pleasing to God and useful to the world of men.

Time and toil, travel and trouble, mental torture and bodily torments had so changed his appearance, that Dona Clara did not recognise her brother till repeatedly assured that Manuel de Moraes was standing before her. They embraced tenderly, and murmured words of affection and endearment, broken by many a sob and by floods of scalding tears. They spoke of their parents, now no more; of their sisters and of their relations still living at São Paulo; of the family, that had changed its abode to Lisbon; of their birthplace; of the old house, their once happy home, and of the scenes and adventures of their youth. They thus revived memories which affected their hearts with intolerable yearnings: the joys of the past made their present misery appear by contrast only more hopeless and profound.

"My excellent father! my adored, my sainted mother!" repeated Manuel. "Ye are both in the bosom of Eternity and in the presence of your God. In a little while shall your unhappy son leave this world to meet you there. Pardon him! O pardon one who added so much to your unhappiness on earth, but who has also himself loved much and suffered much!"

The interview outlasted an hour. Its result was necessarily to prostrate still more the strength of the unhappy Novice. He would not lose sight of his sister till the Familiars of Holy Office compelled her to retire, and removed him from the terrible palace of the Inquisition.

It was now the turn of Padre Eusebio de Monserrate, who presented himself in the character of Ghostly Father and chosen Confessor of the man condemned to die. He related to his penitent the commands of the King, not concealing at the same time his apprehension, which now appeared but too well founded, that the Tribunal would ignore them; and he was the less hopeful inasmuch as to the present moment he could not find that the Judges had even deigned a reply. He warned his young companion of former years that the fatal day appointed for the Act of Faith was fast approaching. He ended by assuring the Novice that it would be better for him to prepare for meeting his God by opening all his soul to his Priest, and by receiving full Absolution, so as to pass into Eternity with soul tranquil and prepared by the Holy Sacraments.

Manuel prostrated himself before his Confessor and friend. He frankly revealed all the worldly hopes and the ambition which had deluded his spirit, the sins and crimes which he had committed during his wanderings from the fold, and the thoughts which possessed his soul at that solemn moment. Both knelt, rigid in prayer, before the sacred Cross which symbolised the martyrdom of the Son of God. Finally, the priest accorded to his penitent the consolation of absolution, and recommended him to the mercy of the Most High.

It was already the morning before the Act of Faith was to take place. The Holy Office had taken no step to answer the order forwarded to it in favour of Manuel by the royal "Escrivão de Puridade." The Provincial of the Jesuits still exerted all his influence to secure obedience for the command. At length, however, as all the preparations for the horrid ceremony had been duly made, it was bruited abroad that the Inquisition would not dare to despise the pardon granted by the King, however exceptional and irregular. The Judges determined to obey the royal commands after sending forth Manuel de Moraes to the Act of Faith as a heretic, bearing the insignia of fire, and making him take part in the procession preparatory to the execution of their sentences.

The fatal day at length dawned. With the first rays of light the citizens hung the houses along the streets and squares, through which the victims were to pass, with damask counterpanes, crosses, crucifixes, and images of saints, candles burning before them. The ground, which at that time was not paved, bore strews of leafy branches. The Oratories, scattered about the thoroughfares, glittered with cierges and lamps, with bouquets and strings of flowers. The bells of all the Temples incessantly rang forth their joy, saluting the triumph of the Catholic Church, which, by chastising the bad and by terrifying the turbulent and the hard of belief, was saving the true Faith of Christ. The soldiery defiled to their various posts about the Largo de Santa Anna, carefully preventing all, except those of the cortège, from penetrating within the circle reserved for the work of the gallows and the stake.

Heaps of dry faggots and loose straw, and scaffolds erected by their side, terrified the eyes of the vulgar. Familiars with cowled heads and masked faces, and wrapped in the cloaks of the Holy Office, upon whose breasts shone the large cross, surrounded in crowds these instruments of the last cruelty.

At the appointed hour the King and Queen, followed by their Secretaries and Councillors of state, and by the whole throng of Courtiers, took their places, as was the superstitious practice of the age, in a balcony fronting the scene. Everywhere fluttered and ran from place to place, each one praying and blessing himself with no little noise and excitement, an immense crowd of the populace. The mob is never wanting at any spectacle of public mourning or rejoicing.

And now the artillery of the Arsenals, the Fortresses, and the Fleet roared their salutes. Again the bells of the Churches rang a merry chime, and picturesque bouquets of fireworks rose high in air, splitting into a thousand lines and points of light, and bursting with the noise of bombs. It was the signal that the Auto da Fé had set out from the Palace in the Largo do Rocio, and was proceeding to its destination, according to the rigid etiquette prescribed in such matters. The van was formed by the Familiars of the Holy Office, mounted, weaponed, and carrying black banners spangled with red flames, the emblems of the blood-stained Tribunal. Followed them Priests and Friars of different orders, with heads uncovered and reciting lugubrious prayers. Footguards, carrying harquebusses, swords, and long daggers, masked and in the habit of the Inquisition, surrounded the numerous victims. These were bound to one another; all walked barefoot, and their heads and faces were hidden in black hoods powdered with bright flames, whilst two eyeholes completed the disfigurement.

Next walked the members of the Holy Office, preceding and surrounding the Inquisitor-General, who was shaded by a canopy; they were escorted by more than two hundred Familiars, amongst whom, according to tradition, were Hidalgos and Nobles of the first houses in the realm, Magistrates and high functionaries, Capitalists and Merchants, Traders and men of all classes and conditions of society.

The rear of the procession was brought up by a Corps of Cavalry, with band and timbrels which never ceased playing.

The Procession to the Act of Faith halted in front of all the Oratories and the images of Saints which stood upon its passage, and thus a considerable time elapsed before it arrived at the Largo de Santa Anna.

The banners were flown and the drums ruffled. Each member of the cortège took the place allotted to him. A crier read aloud the list of those condemned to the stake and to the garotte, and of the penitents sentenced to be present at the execution. Amongst the latter was the name of the unhappy Manuel de Moraes, spared capital punishment by the especial grace of Dom João. An ecclesiastic then offered up a prayer to Heaven; all around him reverently kneeling and interceding for the souls which were about to leave this world.

The last orders were given. The victims condemned to the flames mounted the pyres by ladders, and were bound to wooden stakes planted in the midst of the faggots. Fire applied to the straw at once spread to the whole pyre. Arose a pitchy cloud of smoke licked by tongues of flame, and every ear shrank from the screams and shrieks and moans of unutterable anguish, which ceased only when the wretches disappeared in a sheet of consuming fire.

To this succeeded the more merciful penalty of the garotte. The hangman, by one turn of the winch, instantly strangled and dislocated the necks of the less guilty. Their mortal remains, however, were cast upon the still burning piles, that the condemned might all be confounded in one common doom.

Lastly, a Procession of the pardoned penitents walked round the stakes and the gallows. Most of them were supported by the Familiars and the servants of the Holy Office—they had no longer strength to drag their limbs along.

At the end of the ceremony the Court returned to the Palace of the Inquisition.

Immediately on passing through the principal portals of the edifice, the Inquisitor-General gave orders that Manuel de Moraes should be taken from amongst the penitents and be restored to the Jesuits: the latter had gathered there in numbers to receive him and to escort him to the house of St. Ignatius.

The transfer was ceremoniously made; a document was drawn up, and duly signed by all the authorities concerned in the matter. The penitent, being unable to stand, was placed upon a bench of stone till the formalities were ended.

When Padre Eusebio de Monserrate drew near to take his friend's arm, to raise him and to lead him forth from the palace of the Holy Office, Manuel, after attempting to rise, slipped from the kindly grasp, sunk upon the bench, and then fell to the ground.

The Jesuit hastened to tear open his mask and clothes. He found that they contained a corpse. Manuel de Moraes no longer lived the life of this world.

Eusebio de Monserrate then knelt by the body and cried in anguish, "O Lord! O Lord! receive into Thy bosom this repentant sinner, and pardon with Thine infinite mercy one who, if he has greatly offended Thee, hath suffered so much at the hands of Man."

FINIS.

PRINTED BY BALLANTYNE, HANSON AND CO.
EDINBURGH AND LONDON.

www.ingramcontent.com/pod-product-compliance
Lightning Source LLC
Chambersburg PA
CBHW021359230426
43666CB00006B/577